Amiya K. Samanta
Prof. Somnath Ghosh

A 3D Hypoelastic Model of RC Structure using lower order EAS elements

D1799907

Amiya K. Samanta
Prof. Somnath Ghosh

A 3D Hypoelastic Model of RC Structure using lower order EAS elements

Lower order solid elements, Finite element approach, Three-dimensional, Enhanced assumed strain

LAP LAMBERT Academic Publishing

Impressum/Imprint (nur für Deutschland/only for Germany)
Bibliografische Information der Deutschen Nationalbibliothek: Die Deutsche Nationalbibliothek verzeichnet diese Publikation in der Deutschen Nationalbibliografie; detaillierte bibliografische Daten sind im Internet über http://dnb.d-nb.de abrufbar.
Alle in diesem Buch genannten Marken und Produktnamen unterliegen warenzeichen-, marken- oder patentrechtlichem Schutz bzw. sind Warenzeichen oder eingetragene Warenzeichen der jeweiligen Inhaber. Die Wiedergabe von Marken, Produktnamen, Gebrauchsnamen, Handelsnamen, Warenbezeichnungen u.s.w. in diesem Werk berechtigt auch ohne besondere Kennzeichnung nicht zu der Annahme, dass solche Namen im Sinne der Warenzeichen- und Markenschutzgesetzgebung als frei zu betrachten wären und daher von jedermann benutzt werden dürften.

Coverbild: www.ingimage.com

Verlag: LAP LAMBERT Academic Publishing GmbH & Co. KG
Dudweiler Landstr. 99, 66123 Saarbrücken, Deutschland
Telefon +49 681 3720-310, Telefax +49 681 3720-3109
Email: info@lap-publishing.com

Zugl.: Jadavpur University, Kolkata, India 2009

Herstellung in Deutschland:
Schaltungsdienst Lange o.H.G., Berlin
Books on Demand GmbH, Norderstedt
Reha GmbH, Saarbrücken
Amazon Distribution GmbH, Leipzig
ISBN: 978-3-8443-3186-8

Imprint (only for USA, GB)
Bibliographic information published by the Deutsche Nationalbibliothek: The Deutsche Nationalbibliothek lists this publication in the Deutsche Nationalbibliografie; detailed bibliographic data are available in the Internet at http://dnb.d-nb.de.
Any brand names and product names mentioned in this book are subject to trademark, brand or patent protection and are trademarks or registered trademarks of their respective holders. The use of brand names, product names, common names, trade names, product descriptions etc. even without a particular marking in this works is in no way to be construed to mean that such names may be regarded as unrestricted in respect of trademark and brand protection legislation and could thus be used by anyone.

Cover image: www.ingimage.com

Publisher: LAP LAMBERT Academic Publishing GmbH & Co. KG
Dudweiler Landstr. 99, 66123 Saarbrücken, Germany
Phone +49 681 3720-310, Fax +49 681 3720-3109
Email: info@lap-publishing.com

Printed in the U.S.A.
Printed in the U.K. by (see last page)
ISBN: 978-3-8443-3186-8

TABLE OF CONTENTS

NOTATION

x, y, z Coordinate of a point.

ξ, η, ζ Intrinsic coordinate system

V_P Volume of parent element

V_R Volume of reinforcement element

D 3D Linear elasticity matrix

D_P Incremental concrete constitutive matrix.

D_R Incremental constitutive matrix of reinforcement (uniaxial tension /compression).

B_P 3D Strain displacement matrix for parent /concrete element.

B_R 3D Strain displacement matrix for reinforcement element.

B_J Strain displacement matrix for interface /joint element.

B_α 3D Strain displacement matrix for EAS modes only.

B_α^{18} 3D Strain displacement matrix for 18 nos. EAS modes.

B_R ID Strain displacement matrix for reinforcement.

B_0 3D linear Strain displacement matrix

B_L 3D Strain displacement matrix for large deformation.

$T_{\sigma,gl}$ 3D Transformation matrix for stress from global to local.

$T_{\varepsilon,gl}$ 3D Transformation matrix for strain from global to local.

l_i, m_i, n_i Direction cosines corresponding to i-th direction.

σ 3D Stress matrix.

$d\sigma$ Stress increment vector.

i, j Subscript /superscript representing Axes of orthotropy.

ε Green's strain.

$d\varepsilon$ Strain increment vector.

ε_P 3D Strain matrix for parent element.

ε_α 3D Strain matrix for EAS modes only.

ε_0 3D linear Strain matrix

ε_L 3D Strain matrix for large deformation

ε_{ui} Equivalent uniaxial strain increment in i-th direction.

ε_{ci} Ultimate /Peak Equivalent uniaxial strain increment in i-th direction.

ε_{fi} Breaking point Equivalent uniaxial strain increment in i-th direction.

ε_t Ultimate uniaxial tensile (cracking) strain of concrete.

ε_m Ultimate uniaxial tensile strain of concrete at failure.

ε_{cu} Ultimate uniaxial compressive (cracking) strain of concrete.

ε_{cm} Ultimate uniaxial compressive (failure) strain of concrete.

ε_{cb} Ultimate biaxial compressive strain of concrete.

R_{ci} Concrete strength in i-th direction at current principal stress ratio.

R_{fi} Concrete breaking point strength in i-th direction at current principal stress ratio.

A_i, B_i, C_i Constants in Popovic's equation.

γ_{ij} Shearing strain in plane i-j

$d\gamma_{ij}$ Shearing strain increment in plane i-j

E_S Elastic modulus of reinforcement in tension.

E_{Sh} Strain hardening modulus of reinforcement in tension.

f_y Yield strength of reinforcement.

ε_{yp} Ultimate uniaxial tensile strain at yielding of reinforcement.

ε_{yf} Ultimate uniaxial tensile strain at failure of reinforcement.

w_p Standard Nodal displacement vector for parent element

w_α EAS Nodal displacement vector for parent element

K_P^e Element Stiffness matrix for parent material.

K_R^e Element Stiffness matrix for reinforcement.

N Shape /Interpolation function.

N_α Bubble function.

J Jacobian Matrix evaluated at the integration point of element.

J_0 Jacobian matrix evaluated at the center of element.

l_R Length of reinforcement element.

k Stiffness of joint /interface element

u_S Displacement vector at support.

u_f Displacement vector at free node.

s Slip.

s_1, s_2, s_3 Limiting slip values as per Modelcode-90

α Degrees of freedom against EAS modes.

τ Shear Stresses

τ_{max} Maximum /peak bond stress

τ_f Bond stress at failure (considering only friction).

E_0 Initial Young's modulus of concrete.

E_i Total secant modulus in i-th direction of orthotropy.

E_{crack} Softening modulus of concrete in tension.

E_{soft} Softening modulus of concrete in compression.

E_t Softening modulus of concrete in tension.

μ_0 Initial Poisson's ratio of concrete.

μ_{ij} Poisson's ratio (Lateral strain in i-th direction due to stress in j-th direction)

G_{ij} Total secant shear modulus in plane i-j.

Ω Parameter in incremental elasticity matrix

σ_i Principal stress in i-th direction.

σ_0 Octahedral normal stress /mean stress.

θ Angle of similarity /Lode angle.

J_2, J_3 Second, third deviator stress invariant

J_3 Third deviator stress invariant

F Yield Function of principal stress state.

S Failure surface expressed in terms of principal stresses.

f_t Ultimate uniaxial tensile stress.

f_{cu} Ultimate uniaxial compressive stress.

f_{cb} Ultimate biaxial compressive stress.

f_1 Ultimate compressive stress on biaxial compression meridian.

f_2 Ultimate compressive stress on biaxial tensile meridian.

α_t Non-dimensional tensile strength.

α_c Non-dimensional compressive strength.

C_{cr} Cracking modulus of concrete.

G_f Fracture energy of concrete to produce unit area of continuous crack.

w_f Crack band width.

A_r Cross-sectional area of a reinforcement.

R_P Residual forces for a parent element.

Subscript /Superscript

P Parent element.

R Reinforcement.

c Concrete.

b Bond.

e element.

g global.

l local.

j Joint.

α No of D.O.F. against bubble function.

List of Figures

List of tables

Synopsis

A procedure has been developed to carry out three-dimensional (3D) analysis of reinforced concrete structures employing finite element technique, which uses lower order elements, in particular, HCiS18. Low order elements have advantages for 3D analysis since they allow reasonable easy mesh-generation and data interpretation. But, the use of low order finite elements in two or three dimensions, when applied to incompressible or quasi incompressible situations, causes the well known volumetric locking phenomenon, detected in many situations such as linear elasticity, applications with plastic deformations, viscous incompressible flow etc. Attempts were made to improve performance of lower order 2D isoparametric element based formulation using reduced and selective integration schemes, B-bar method, additional incompatible modes, but to a few specific problems and also under certain conditions of mixed formulation. All these attempts were made aiming at removing inherent difficulties (locking etc.) particularly in thin structures. Even these methods can only analyze certain specific problems, where it is possible to study the behavior of the structure with necessary simplification by adopting the assumptions of 2D analysis.

On the other hand, one may opt for 3D modeling to avoid the shortcomings of 2D modeling in order to achieve most realistic analysis and to arrive at an optimal solution. The proposed procedure utilizes 8-noded isometric solid /hexahedral elements HCiS18 with enhanced assumed strain (EAS) formulation, recently developed in the literature, to predict load-deformation and internal stresses produced in case of a simply supported RC beams in linear as well as nonlinear regime. One of the objectives of this work is to demonstrate the general applicability and to explore the potentiality of using lower order solid elements in the 3D finite element analysis with an aim of developing a general analytical method for the study of reinforced concrete beams for the entire load history.

It is well known that the RC structures are highly non-homogeneous due to discrete presence of the reinforcements. A lot of research works have been done, where due attention has been paid to model concrete and the reinforcing steel with different physical and mechanical properties, which needs to be combined together through an interaction model to represent its composite behaviour. Attentions have been paid to model concrete in numerous ways, viz. linear elastic, damage mechanics and fracture mechanics based formulation to simulate the experimentally found behaviour of RC structures. Also attempt was made to model reinforcement along with its interaction with concrete in different loading conditions.

This study formulates the composite behaviour of concrete and reinforcements in rigid /perfect bond situation and their mutual interaction in bond-slip condition considering continuous interface elements at the material level taking care of non-linearity of bond-slip relation even at the initial stage of the loading. Details of the constitutive model and analysis method used are discussed. Three-dimensional analysis of a simply supported RC beams and frames have been carried out employing proposed finite element technique. The enhanced assumed strain (EAS) formulation has been utilized to predict load-deformation and internal stresses both in the elastic as well as nonlinear regime.

Nowadays there are many powerful finite element programs available commercially, which can deal with a very large number of variables and formulations. With the rapid growth in infrastructure throughout the world, it's very difficult to use and update the same to cope up with new developments in technologies. Also they are not directly suitable to solve a problem in hand. Therefore, a substantial effort has been made to write simple finite element programs in the form of FORTRAN subroutines. The main emphasis has been given to understand the mechanics of concrete structures by considering both material as well as geometric non-linearity with appropriate failure criteria in an elegant way so as to minimize the gap between numerical solutions and experimental results. The proposed material model is based on orthotropic hypoelastic model developed by Balan et al.(1997). The hypoelastic model is dissipative by nature and it doesn't consider any flow rule as such. Instead it is based on a fictitious equivalent uniaxial strain to take care of the entire deformation path during loading. Predictions from the proposed FEM model are found to be reasonably close to the experimental observations found in the literature.

Chapter 2

Literature Survey

In this chapter, a brief survey of the literature in connection with material as well as finite element modeling of concrete and reinforcement together with concrete-reinforcement bond has been presented. Literature survey has been done in the following area; i)Material modeling of concrete, ii)Reinforcement modeling, iii) Bond-Slip modeling, iv)Failure criterion of concrete and v)Finite element modeling.

2.1 Material Modeling of Concrete

The application of finite element technique for the purpose of modeling composite action for discontinuous systems particularly for RC structures have received a considerable interest by various authors. The earliest publication on such an application was done by *Ngo /Scordelis (1967)*, where simple two dimensional(2D) beam model were developed with constant strain triangles and in particular, bond link elements were used to describe the bond-slip effect. It was a case of 2D linear analysis with predefined cracks to evaluate principal stresses both in concrete and reinforcement along with bond stresses. In 1968, Nilson introduced nonlinear material properties for concrete and steel as well as nonlinear bond-slip relationship into the analysis to perform nonlinear analysis with the help of incremental load method. Attention was also given to introduce new crack direction in subsequent iterations. These two pioneering works contributed a lot for the growing interest today on application of finite element tool for the analysis of RC structures both in linear as well as non-linear regime. In 1970, Franklin developed a nonlinear analysis technique to account for cracking within finite elements and the redistribution stresses in the structure in two dimensions for the RC frames as well coupled with shear wall. In line with the above, plane stress elements were mainly used by numerous investigators for the same with an emphasis on constitutive relationships of the materials, cracking and elasto-plastic behavior.

For the analysis RC beams, *Rajagopal (1976)* developed a layered rectangular plate element in which concrete was considered as an orthotropic material. Similar methods were also followed by many other investigators to analyze RC beams and slabs to include the effect of temperature, creep and shrinkage, tension stiffening.

Hillerborg et al. (1976) introduced fracture mechanics concept into finite element analysis by means of the energy absorption G_c in the energy balance approach, and applied it to the bending of an unreinforced beam with an explanation to differentiate between bending strength and tensile strength, and the variation in bending strength with beam depth. A study for nonlinear finite element analysis of reinforced concrete framed structures with a brief description of material properties used and the nonlinear finite element formulation to account for the material and other non-linearities due to cracking and yielding was carried out by *Krishnamoorty /Paneerselvam (1978)*. It presented a rigorous analytical tool along with the computer program, for the analysis of reinforced concrete framed structures under various stages of loading up to failure and is useful for the study of various parameters that influence the design of such structures.

Elwi /Murray (1979) developed a nonlinear three dimensional (3D) constitutive relationship based on the concepts advanced by Darwin *et al*, Sanez and William *et al.* incorporating a multi-axial relationship between stress and strain to simulate the nonlinear behavior to be expected in real structure. Attempt was made to incorporate the equivalent uniaxial strain concept of Darwin, Bashur and Pecknold, the nonlinear representation of Saenz, and the Argyris failure surface in such a way that the relationship correlates well with the best experimental results. The formulation of a hypoelastic orthotropic material is discussed in detail. The model is defined in the form of an incremental stress-strain equation in which the material parameters are obtained from stress-'strain equivalent uniaxial strain' relations and the incremental elastic modulli are derived in terms of the strain parameters. The other parameters required for the definition of the incremental properties, i.e. those describing an ultimate stress surface and those describing the corresponding equivalent uniaxial strain surface are also defined.

Gupta /Akbar (1984) pointed out that in most conventional methods of reinforced concrete analysis, cracks are formed in the principal stress direction and are not allowed to change direction with the change in state, which leads to crack directions inconsistent with the limit state. Hence a simple model of forming cracks in reinforced concrete was proposed assuming that the cracks are formed in the direction of the major principal tensile strain and that the direction can change with the change in strains, which are consistent with the limit state. *Channakeshava /Iyenger (1988)* described an elasto-plastic cracking constitutive model for the nonlinear analysis of plain and reinforced concrete structures which includes cracking in tension, plasticity in compression, aggregate interlock, tension softening, plasticity of steel, bond-slip and tension stiffening and also developed associated finite element software with various features.

The concept of smeared crack approach introduced by *Kollegger /Mehlhorn (1990)* to model the cracking phenomena in nonlinear analysis of RC structures. A material model employing the smeared crack (i.e. considering only average stresses at an integration point) concept for the analysis of reinforced concrete surface structures was proposed and focused on the numerical treatment of cracked reinforced concrete in a state of plane stress, of course with due attention to the modeling of tension stiffening, the reorientation of the principal tensile strain direction and the compressive strength of cracked concrete. It has been shown that after cracking, the reorientation of the principal tensile strain direction has to be taken into account. Otherwise experimental failure loads will be considerably overestimated. It also shows that the compressive strength of cracked concrete depends on the transverse stress state and may be reduced to 80% of the uniaxial strength due to transverse tension and tension stiffening is independent of the angle between reinforcement and principal tensile strain direction.

In this context, two different methods emerged viz. the fixed crack and the rotating crack model. In fixed crack model, cracks are supposed to form in a direction perpendicular to the principal stress direction when it exceeds concrete tensile strength and the crack direction remains unchanged in course of subsequent loading. In fact, it was well accepted by the researcher at the very early stages due to its easy formulation. Subsequent studies, however, showed that it causes numerical instability as a result of singularity in stiffness matrix and later on this difficulty was overcome by introducing variable cracked shear modulus. In rotating crack model, crack direction changes with subsequent loading path depending on the current principal strain direction. Also the assumption of no shear strain in the crack plane eliminates the requirement of cracked shear modulus. This model is particularly useful in analytical studies of global behavior of RC structures rather than the local effects in the vicinity of a crack.

Stevens et al. (1991) formulated a constitutive model based on modified compression field theory (MCFT) and strictly in terms of average stresses and strains for both the concrete and reinforcing steel leading to the finite element analysis of two-dimensional(2D) reinforced concrete structural elements. An approximate analytical solution for the progressive failure analysis of reinforced concrete shallow beams using the principles of fracture mechanics was carried out by *Raghuprasad /Iyenger (1992)*. It highlights on the limitations of applying linear elastic fracture mechanics(LEFM) and considered crack initiation and propagation till failure using 1D model based on equilibrium equations and nonlinear fracture mechanics principles.

Vechhio (1992) showed that the lateral expansion of concrete subjected to compression (i.e. the Poisson effect) plays a significant role influencing the behavior of reinforced concrete element in tension-compression states and the resulting confinement effect provided by the reinforcement opposing the expansion can result in significant strength enhancement and improved ductility in post-ultimate stress regimes. A formulation based on modified compression field theory (MCFT) was presented with the use of a secant stiffness based solution procedure involving the concept of material prestrains. It has been shown that the consideration of expansion and confinement effects generally results in a significant improvement in the accuracy of the analysis. *Vechhio /Collins (1993)* performed a number of experimental investigations to determine the degree of compression softening that significantly influences the strength, ductility and load-deformation response of a concrete element. Also a number of analytical models have been proposed to represent the compression softening effect observed in cracked reinforced concrete in tension-compression states. The data collected reveal that compression softening is clearly present and significantly influences the behavior of cracked reinforced concrete under certain conditions.

Sankarasubramanian /Rajasekharan (1996) proposed a nonlinear hypoelastic constitutive relation for the analysis of plane and axisymmetric reinforced concrete structures based on equivalent uniaxial strain concept and a new ultimate strength surface for concrete. The back propagation algorithm of Rumelhart et al. is used to train the artificial neural network for experimental results of concrete and is used to describe the ultimate surface. Thus a new failure criterion of concrete is proposed and a finite element nonlinear analysis of concrete structures to study the nonlinear load deflection behavior, crack pattern and principal; stress contours. *Amara K.B. (1996)* developed a new method based on Griffith energy balance to postulate brittle fracture in the continuum thermodynamics framework to find a beam model for crack growth in plain and reinforced concrete sections. The model is used on a local scale to simulate the mechanisms of crack formation during the crack-growth process with emphasis on aspects of crack-growth stabilization of reinforced sections. Comparison of the energy balance model (EBM) with a fracture mechanics based model shows that energy based models may offer more accurate tools for fracture analysis of reinforced concrete sections.

Yon et al. (1997) determined the fracture properties for linear elastic fracture mechanics(LEFM), singular fracture process zone (S-FPZ) and non-singular fracture process zone (NS-FPZ) models from the experimental results of three-point bend tests and compared. All three fracture models could simulate the measured load and crack mouth opening displacement (CMOD) versus load-point displacement relations. However, for the LEFM model the stress intensity factor needed to increase continuously with crack extension, and for the S-FPZ model the fracture process zone characteristics need to change continuously if the critical stress intensity factor was to remain constant. The LEFM model showed the largest resistance and the slowest crack extension, while the NS-FPZ model showed the smallest resistence and the fastest crack extension. The responses for the S-FPZ model were intermediate between those for the LEFM and NS-FPZ models and the total fracture energy densities for the S-FPZ and NS-FPZ models were equal.

Bouzaiene /Massicotte (1997) proposed a generalized constitutive model based on hypoelastic theory, which characterizes the stress strain relationship of plain concrete under monotonic and cyclic proportional loading. The behavior of concrete is modeled using a normalized scalar damage parameter, the equivalent strength concept, and either the Willam-Warnke five-parameter or the Hsieh-Ting-Chen four-parameter failure surfaces. The important features of volumetric dilatation, the transition state from brittle-softening to ductile-hardening behavior, degradation of the elastic modules under cyclic loading, and the post crushing state are taken care of by the proposed constitutive model along with a finite element program.

Kwak /Filippou (1997) dealt with the finite element analysis of the monotonic behaviour of RC beams and beam-column sub-assemblages considering a plane stress field, where concrete and reinforcement were represented by separate material models which are combined together with a model of interaction through bond-slip to describe the behavior of the composite action. The rotating crack model for the reinforcement, which is embedded inside a concrete element, was used to simulate the structural behavior of reinforcements along with an improved cracking criterion, which is derived from fracture mechanics principles. This representation concludes that (1) the inclusion of tension-stiffening is important for the independence of the analytical results from the size of the finite element mesh and also avoiding numerical problems in connection with crack formation and propagation; 2) tension-stiffening effect and bond-slip cause opposite effects on the response of RC members. While tension stiffening which accounts for the concrete tensile stresses between cracks increases the stiffness of the member, bond-slip leads to a stiffness reduction. In lightly reinforced beams, these effects can cancel each other at certain load. Since bond-slip increases with loading, while tension stiffening does not, consistent results can be obtained when both effects are included in the model. Moreover, the effect of bond-slip clearly outweighs the contribution of tension stiffening in heavily reinforced beams and beam-column joint sub-assemblages. In these cases the exclusion of the bond-slip effect can lead to significant overestimation of the stiffness of the member and 3) the tensile strength of concrete has insignificant effect on the load displacement response of RC beams. Crack formation and propagation is rather influenced by the fracture energy.

Balan et al. (1997) developed a three-dimensional(3D) hypoelastic orthotropic material model for nonlinear finite element analysis of concrete under short-term cyclic loading, which may take into account of tri-axial nonlinear stress behavior, tensile cracking, compression crushing and strain softening. The material model is a hypoelastic orthotropic model that extends the equivalent uniaxial strain concept advanced by Darwin and Pecknold, Bashur and Darwin and the failure surface description of Willam and Warnke. The model is implemented and evaluated in a finite element program. *Bazant (1997)* chose a classical truss model (or strut and tie model) for shear failure of reinforced concrete beams and modified it to describe fracture phenomena during failure. The failure is assumed to be caused by propagation of a compression fracture across the concrete strut during the portion of the loading history in which the maximum load is reached. The compression fracture may consist of a band of splitting cracks that later interconnect to form a shear crack or shear fracture band inclined to the strut. The width of the fracture band is assumed to occupy only a portion of the strut length and to represent a fixed material property independent of the beam depth. It shows that a size effect on the nominal strength of shear failure must exist and that it should approximately follow the size effect law proposed by Bazant(1984).

Selby /Vecchio (1997) described the applicability of the modified (secant stiffness based) compression field theory for general 3D nonlinear analysis of reinforced concrete solids based on stress-strain relationships of an orthotropic nonlinear elastic model under multi-axial stress conditions. The formulation accounts for complex behavior such as concrete strength enhancement due to confinement, concrete strength degradation due to transverse cracking, tension stiffening and crack slip. The models assume short-term, monotonic loading conditions. *Barzegar /Maddipudi (1997)* proposed a 3D constitutive model for FE analysis of plain as well as reinforced concrete based on smeared cracking approach. A simple hypoelastic formulation with modification to approximate the post-peak behavior in compression is used along with five-parameter ultimate strength envelope for the stress space. The post-cracking model is based on the fracture energy concept with particular emphasis on mesh objectivity through automatic generation of crack bandwidth using 20-noded solid isoparametric elements. It includes the effect of bond-slip in the context of embedded representation of reinforcement in 3D. It reported that for the analyzed cases, the effect of bond-slip on the global behaviour was found to be insignificant. Generally a small constant shear retention factor(<0.1) was found appropriate to avoid spurious multiple cracking at sampling points.

Bhatt /Kader (1998) describes the results of a non linear 2D finite element analyses to predict the shear strength of rectangular reinforced concrete beams using a single material model for concrete. In the present study, the best prediction was for beams with shear reinforcement with a small spacing of stirrups. The main result for this is the mode of failure, which is ductile.

Vechhio (1998) reported a three-dimensional static nonlinear finite element analysis for a flanged shear wall. In particular to the test case, it concludes that 2D analyses fail to capture some important 3D effects and ignoring tension-stiffening effects results in substantial increases in post-cracking deflections and a slight lowering of the ultimate load capacity. Also compression softening effects (i.e. the degradation in compressive strength of cracked concrete due to the influence of transverse tensile strains) is not a significant influencing factor for the test specimen. *Vechhio F. J. (2000)* suggests that analysis method based on the smeared rotating crack concept do not adequately model the response of shear-critical concrete beams containing little or no shear reinforcement with the help of MCFT. *Vechhio F. J. (2001)* proposed a conceptual model of disturbed stress field model (DSFM) as an alternative smeared crack model to describe the behavior of cracked reinforced concrete element considering a hybrid formulation between a fully rotating crack model and a fixed crack model. The formulation described builds on the concepts of the modified compression field theory, treating cracked concrete as an orthotropic material with unique stress-strain relationships in compression as well as tension and to consider the local conditions at crack locations because the presence of the cracks create disturbances in the stress field that can influence behavior. Advancement in the formulation, relative to MCFT include a new approach to the reorientation of concrete stress and strain field, removing the restriction that they be coincident and an improved treatment of shear stresses on cracked surfaces.

Hartl et al. (2000) and *Hartl /Elgamal (2000)* proposed a 3D finite element formulation for reinforced and prestressed concrete structures with embedded 1D elements. The concrete was modeled in terms of plasticity employing Ottosen failure criterion and the Rankine tension cut-off. The contribution of the reinforcements or prestress tendons to the stiffness matrix was superimposed on the respective parent elements without any additional degrees of freedom. Bond-slip was modeled by introducing supplementary interface elements, after the displacement field has been computed. Modeling of concrete was done with due attention to cracking, shrinkage, creep and developing anisotropy due to load applied.

Ghandehari et al. (2000) investigated splitting of concrete caused by pullout of deformed rebars. The influence of specimen cross-section size and geometry on the relationship between the components of stress and relative displacement at the interface is evaluated. *Iyengar /Raviraj (2001)* pointed out that LEFM model is not applicable to concrete as it often displays "strain-softening" behavior and presented an analytical study of non-linear fracture of beams using a blunt crack model. Results for both the blunt crack model(BCM) and the fictitious crack model(FCM) are compared for nonlinear softening relations.

Balan et al. (2001) presents a hypoelastic constitutive model for three dimensional finite element analysis of concrete structures under monotonic, cyclic proportional and non-proportional loading based on the concept of equivalent uniaxial strains that allow the assumed orthotropic model to be described via three equivalent uniaxial stress-strains curves as per Popovics and Sanez. The characteristics of these curves are obtained from the ultimate strength surface with a cap model in the principal stress space based on Willam-Warnke curve. The post peak behaviour is adjusted to account for the effects of confinement and to describe the change in response from brittle to ductile as the lateral confinement increases. The model simplicity makes it particularly attractive for the study for the study of reinforced concrete sub-assemblages where numerical efficiency is important to minimize computational costs.

Gomes /Awruch (2001) deals with some aspects related to 3D numerical modeling of reinforced concrete structure using the finite element method. Some subjects such as the solution technique of the nonlinear equilibrium equation and the constitutive model for concrete and reinforcement steel are emphasized and commented. A robust method for the evaluation of the intersecting points of the embedded reinforcement bars into the 3D finite element mesh is also presented. The main advantages of the generalized displacement control method with the generalized displacement parameter to improve the response of the concrete and reinforced concrete analysis are highlighted. The proposed method for reinforcement embedding was successfully implemented overcoming the drawbacks found in the previous methods. Some topics, like the bond-slip between concrete and steel were not included.

Cho /Hotta (2002) proposed a tri-axial constitutive model based on the orthotropic hypoelasticity formulation using so called the strain enhancement factor to account for increasing ductility in high confinement of concrete. It is also developed a 3D finite element model for reinforced concrete structural members based on the proposed constitutive law of concrete with the smeared crack approach. The concrete confinement effects due to the beam-column joint are investigated through numerical examples for simple beams and structural beam member. Concrete at compression fibres in the vicinity of beam-column joint behaves dominant not only by the uniaxial compressive state but also by the biaxial and triaxial compressive states. For the reason of the severe confinement of concrete in the beam-column joint, the flexural critical cross-section is observed at a small distance away from the beam-column joint. These observations should be utilized for the economic design when the concrete structural members are subjected to high confinement due to the influence of beam-column joint. In this paper, concrete confinement and its effects on the flexural strength of reinforced concrete beam member in the vicinity of beam column joint have been studied mainly based on the observation of numerical results, with limiting to the case of no transverse shear reinforcement. Since triaxial stress of concrete in member test does not able to be measured directly through experiment, this study is mainly focused on the numerical observations.

Kwon /Spacone (2002) used a 3D concrete law for the analysis of concrete specimens and reinforced concrete columns subjected to different load patterns. The hypoelastic, orthotropic concrete constitutive model includes coupling between the deviatoric and volumetric stresses, works with both proportional and non-proportional loads and is implemented as a strain driven module. The finite element implementation is based on the smeared crack approach with rotating cracks parallel to the principal strain directions. The original model by Balan et al is modified to include the coupling between the deviatoric and the volumetric stresses following the definition of a coupling modulus proposed by Gerstle.

Cho /Park (2003) investigates the finite element prediction of the compressive strength of concrete near the flexural critical regions of RC beam-column members under a single or a double curvature bending. For this reason an analysis model of the 3D hypoelasticity based finite element predictions of RC structures has been presented. Using the developed program, three RC beam-column members subjected to axial forces combined with bending moments have been analyzed. From finite element predictions it has been predicted that concrete in the vicinity of a beam-column joint reacts not only under a uniaxial compressive stress state but also under a multi-axial compressive stress state and that a flexural critical cross section is observed at a small distance away from beam-column joint. This is because the concrete in that region is confined by the existence of a beam-column joint and that region is commonly the flexural critical cross section of the RC beam-columns in a frame. It is also observed that the confining effect on concrete in that region is larger under double curvature bending than under single curvature bending. Due to severe confinement of concrete at the beam-column joint in a frame, the flexural critical cross section is observed at a small distance away from the beam-column joint, and the actual flexural span length of the ember is shown to become shorter than the real span length of the member. This observation attempts to point out some aspects for the actual economic design practice to be followed for a structural member in a frame.

Bazant /Canel (2005) presented a new microplane model for concrete, which improves the representation of tensile cohesive fracture by eliminating spurious excessive lateral strains and stress locking for far post peak tensile strains. To achieve improvement a kinematically constrained microplane system simulating hardening non-linear behavior is coupled in series with a statically constrained microplane system simulating solely the cohesive tensile fracture. This coupling is made possible by developing a new iterative algorithm and by proving the conditions of its convergence. The special aspect of this algorithm is that the cohesive softening stiffness matrix is used as the predictor and the hardening stiffness matrix as the corrector. The softening cohesive stiffness for fracturing is related to the fracture energy of concrete and the effective crack spacing. The postpeak softening slopes on the microplanes can be adjusted according to the element size in the sense of the crack band model. Finally an incremental thermodynamic potential for the coupling of statically and kinematically constrained microplane system is formulated.

Rabczuk et al. (2005) describes a two-dimensional (2D) approach to model fracture of reinforced concrete structures under (increasing) static loading conditions. The concrete is described in compression by a non-local isotropic damage constitutive law. In tension, a fictitious crack /crack band model is proposed. The influence of biaxial stress states is incorporated in the constitutive relations. The reinforcement was described with beam elements using an elastoplastic constitutive model with isotropic hardening. Except the cracking, the interaction between the reinforcement and the adjacent concrete plays a significant role in the fracture process of reinforced concrete structures. A bond model is described which is able to capture both of the failure mechanisms, a pullout and a splitting failure. This approach is applied to prestressed concrete beams with different failure mechanisms.

Remarks

Even though many studies on the constitutive behaviour of concrete have been done, uncertainties still exist about complexity in modeling parameters. In particular, a very little work has been done on the three dimensional analysis of reinforced concrete structures using solid finite elements, because of higher computational effort and lack of knowledge of the material behaviour under multiaxial stress states. Hence there is a need for simple material model of RC structures in three dimension, which may be applicable for all general engineering purpose.

2.2 Reinforcement Modeling

Another aspect of RC structure is that it is highly non-homogeneous due to discrete presence of the reinforcements. While modeling RC structures as layered structure, many authors have considered steel as a separate layer embedded and distributed evenly. Hardly a few literatures are reported, where due attention has been paid to model the reinforcing steel with different physical /mechanical properties in its exact spatial position in the respect to the element.

Elwi /Hrudey (1989) developed a 2D geometric relations required for an embedded finite element representation of generally curved reinforcing bars or prestressing tendons. This approach has the important advantage that the geometry of the reinforcement has virtually no impact on the choice of grid-work for the parent elements as for practical reasons, the reinforcing layers are described in global coordinates independently of the finite element mesh. An inverse mapping procedure is developed to transform global coordinates of points on the reinforcement layer including a bond-slip model. The procedure is successfully tested using both regular and irregular meshes on three test problems, a uniform strain field and two version of a quarter ring under external pressure.

El-Maine /Citipitioglu (1991) presented a practical and powerful technique for the discrete representation of arbitrarily oriented reinforcement in FE analysis of prestressed and reinforced concrete structures. Isoparametric quadratic and cubic finite elements with movable nodes are developed utilizing a correction technique for mapping distortion. Reinforcing bars and / or prestressing tendons are modeled independently of the concrete mesh. Perfect or no bond as well as any bond-slip model can easily be represented. The procedure is successfully tested for bonded and unbonded reinforcements. The present technique has the following advantages; (1) reinforcement of arbitrary type and location can be represented independent of finite element mesh., (2)different bond conditions at different nodes can be represented at the same time and it allows the use of any material model. Although the method is presented for the 2D analysis, it is also applicable to 3D analysis with the help of the shape functions and derivatives in a straightforward way.

Cheng /Fan (1993) suggested an effective method for modeling reinforcement arbitrarily oriented in concrete as reinforcement plays a significant role in the stress-strain behaviour of RC structures, especially when the failure stage of the structures is approached. The concept of constrained and non-constrained zones of concrete due to the presence of reinforcement is developed and a reinforcement confinement coefficient is proposed. Furthermore, a flexible method for the modeling of reinforcement with arbitrary orientation and not passing the nodes of the concrete element is also proposed. The authors offer an attractive way in modeling reinforcement confinement action in finite element analysis.

Barzegar /Maddipudi (1994) described an automatic procedure for spatial modeling and inclusion of straight segments of embedded reinforcement in a mesh of solid isoparametric elements representing concrete is presented. This procedure alleviates the laboratory task of generating the input data for the embedded bar elements in 3d finite element analysis of RC structures, particularly when modifications /refinements to the concrete element mesh are made and /or reinforcement arrangement are changed. Each straight segment of reinforcement is identified by the coordinates of its two end points and its intersections with the faces of the solid elements are determined. The stiffness of each composite RC element can then be computed using an inverse mapping procedure to obtain the coordinates of the integration points along the reinforcement elements in the concrete parent element axes. The presented formulation has been used in 3D FE analyses of RC structures assuming perfect bond as well as bond-slip between concrete and reinforcement. It has been found that the introduction of bond-slip nodes significantly increases the bandwidth of the generated stiffness matrix. A possible remedy using the isoparametric elements with movable nodes has been proposed by El-Mezaini and Citipitioglu(1991). However it is not applicable in cases where a concrete element is crossed by more than one reinforcement segment and /or where reinforcement-concrete-intersection points are on the faces rather than the edges of concrete solid elements. Although the formulation has been presented in the context of reinforced concrete with straight bar segments, it may also be used in FE analysis of prestressed concrete structures having profiled tendons; each tendon may be represented with straight segments, hence enabling the tendon to be mapped in the concrete element mesh automatically using the global coordinates of various points on the tendon.

Remarks :

In conclusion, when RC structures are modeled based on continuum mechanics, contribution and distribution of stiffness of reinforcements should be considered appropriately. In general there are three methods available for modeling of reinforcement, e.g. the discrete, the smeared and the embedded approach. The first one represents reinforcements by truss elements those are connected to the mesh at the concrete/parent element nodes and hence finite element mesh generation becomes dependent on reinforcement layout. The second one (smeared) is more suitable for homogeneous or uniformly distributed reinforcements, such as wall panels. So they can't be generally applied to 3D structures. Within embedded approach, proposed by *Elwi and Hrudey (1989), Barzegar and Madipuddi (1994)*, these restrictions were removed and even the reinforcements are superimposed as one dimensional uniaxial element with the same displacement field as parent/concrete element without any additional node /DOF.

2.3 Bond-Slip Modeling :

Accounting for interaction between parent material/concrete and the reinforcements are done to make RCC structure to behave in a more realistic way because concrete is a strong, relatively durable in compression and reinforcements are strong, ductile in tension. This composite action requires transfer of load between concrete and steel. This load transfer mechanism is referred as bond-slip, which is depicted as continuous stress field in the vicinity of steel-concrete interface. As the loading on RCC structures are gradually increased, this bond-slip increases, as result relaxation of steel stress takes place more and more and an equilibrium is set up in the domain. In bond behaviour, slip takes place due to damage in concrete adjacent to the bars exhibited by cracking /crushing. Lundgren (1999) developed an interface model based on plasticity theory with fully three-dimensional features. For all practical analysis of engineering problem, this approach is not very appealing, as it requires extremely large computational time.

Beer (1985) introduced a generally applicable and simple joint /interface element for three- and two-dimensional finite element analysis involving non-linear slip and separation. The proposed element can model joints /interfaces for shell-to-shell, shell-to-solid and solid-to-solid interfaces in either 2D or 3D situations finite elements. The element is more sophisticated than joint element developed previously and because of the assumption that it has zero thickness is particularly suited for modeling rock joints and fractures The performance of the element is also tested on typical problems involving shell-to-shell and shell-to-solid interfaces.

Polak /Blackwell (1998) presented a constitutive model for tension in cracked reinforced concrete members subjected to monotonic loads is presented. Special emphasis is placed on the bond between concrete and reinforcement as the main factor influencing tension stiffening in cracked reinforced concrete. The model was developed for the members subjected to bending and axial loads. The constitutive formulation was implemented into a cross-sectional analysis program and was used to analyze 14 specimens, which are tested in bending and in-plane loading. The approach taken in the development of the model was to assume that the bond between concrete and reinforcement was the main factor influencing the tensile response of cracked reinforced concrete members.

Desir et al. (1999) presents a new modeling of bond-slip phenomena at steel-concrete interface concerning both constitutive and numerical modeling. The interface is treated as a surface to which standard thermodynamic concept have been extended along with plastic hardening law to develop the constitutive modeling. The relative displacement at the interface results in the jump of a function and can be incorporated in finite element analysis as slip DOF. This formulation has been held to be general and capable of covering the entire range of successive interface deterioration, which is of great value when serviceability and ultimate limit state are considered and deformations are to be analyzed. Furthermore, the prediction of higher value of bond stress at the interface, closed to the loaded point, denotes less contribution of the interface in the force transfer and therefore over estimate the steel force. One can say that in the cracked zone the concrete does not contribute any more, while in the rest we observed a shifting zone before that one where plastic relative displacements occur at the interface. These Simulations gave a good agreement between the model discussed above and the real behavior of the materials. The comparison with experimental data advocates the use of a bi-linear local law. Considering the scatter of bond stress-sleep values obtained in the experimental test, the model may capture with reasonable confidence the interface behavior. The parameters for this model can be determined within inverse analysis and access to the intrinsic behavior of the interface can be also done through numerical micro-mechanics.

Goncalves et al. (2000) developed an interface finite element for 3D problems based on the penalty method. The proposed element can model joints /interfaces between solid finite elements and also includes the propagation of damage in pure mode I, II and mixed mode considering a softening relationship between the stresses and relative displacements. Two different contact conditions are considered; point-to-point constraint for closed point (not satisfying the failure criteria and point-to-surface constraints for opened points. The performance of the element is tested under all modes of loading conditions. The damage model considered are based on the indirect use of fracture mechanics considering the area under the stress /relative displacement curve equal to the critical fracture energy. An advantage of this procedure is to model damage propagation as well as initiation, avoiding the definition of initial flaws.

Salari /Spacone (2001) presented two general formulations of one-dimensional structural members with deformable interfaces. The interface accounts for the bond-slip between the element components. The first formulation is the classical displacement based formulation; the second one is a novel force-based approach. The two formulations are derived from the equilibrium and compatibility differential equation of the problem. A special force recovery procedure, based on residual deformations, is presented for the force based formulation. Two applications are used to illustrate the two formulations; the first is a reinforcing bar with bond –slip, the second is a steel-concrete composite beam with partial interaction between the steel beam and the concrete slab. Examples of a bar with bond failure and of a composite beam with weak connection show the precision of the force-based element and its capability to trace the complex response of softening members with a limited number of elements. The proposed force-based formulation applies to the case of any line element where bond-slip plays an important role and needs to be explicitly considered. The development of such elements is fundamental toward the development of rational frame element and their use in nonlinear frame analyses.

Kwak /Kim (2001) proposed analytical model which can simulate the bond-slip behaviour between reinforcing steel and concrete is proposed. Unlike the classical bond-link or bond-zone element using double nodes, the proposed model takes into consideration the bond-slip effects without taking double nodes. After determination of the boundary condition at both ends of a reinforcing steel, the deformation of the steel at each node can be found through the back-substitution technique from the first to the final steel element using a governing equation that was constructed based on the equilibrium at each node of steel and the compatibility condition between steel and concrete. The numerical model results in an effective use in the case of complex steel arrangement where the steel elements cross the sides of the concrete elements and 2) turns the impossibility into a possibility in considering the bond-slip effects in one and three dimensional finite element analysis. In addition the nonlinear solution scheme based on equilibrium at each node of steel and the compatibility condition between steel and concrete is developed in connection with the model.

Wang /Liu (2003) proposed a new analytical model to describe the bond strength between a ribbed reinforcement bar and concrete. The model is based on the partly cracked solution of a thick-walled cylinder exposed to radial internal pressure. Instead of considering the minimum crack number in previous solutions, smeared cracking and average stress-strain of concrete in tension are used in radial direction to describe the softening behavior of concrete. The results are compared with Tepfers' classic solutions and other previous solutions.

Tzamtzis /Asteris (2004) presented an efficient FE analysis technique which shows great versatility in analysis complex discontinuous system subjected to static, dynamic or seismic loadings. The method incorporates discontinuities in the analysis discontinuous structures by the use of interface elements designed to simulate the actual behaviour at the interfaces between the contacting materials. Several case problem studies that exhibit discontinuous behaviour have been performed in order to demonstrate the potential and applicability of the proposed method of analysis. One of these studies is reported in Part-II of this paper, where a nonlinear model for the analysis of unreinforced masonry walls is presented. Response results obtained, demonstrate that the overall response of a discontinuous system to external loading is significantly affected by behavior at the interfaces between contacting materials. Through the inclusion of discontinuities with particular measurable properties, the proposed method of analysis conforms better to actual conditions than do other methods where a continuum is assumed.

Even though many studies of the bond-slip relationship between the mating surfaces have been conducted, a considerable uncertainty about this complex phenomenon still exists because of many parameter involved. Some of the investigators have opinion that this effect may be included in tension stiffening model. Also a very little effort has been done so far on three-dimensional behavior of RC structures because of the computational effort involved and the lack of knowledge of the material behaviour of concrete in multi-axial stress states.

Remarks :

In conclusion, an approach that was initially introduced by G. Beer (1985) using isoparametric joint /interface element and was later on used by Hartl et al (2000), where bond slip situations are being considered introducing supplementary interface elements of zero thickness, is used in this work. Within this approach, global displacement field is calculated at first considering perfect bond between reinforcements and concrete and then the slip is calculated by relaxing the perfect bond at the material level. This method finds it most suitable in representing the bond mechanism between reinforcement and concrete.

2.4 Failure Criterion of Concrete

A considerable amount of analytical and experimental research on strength theory of materials under complex stress state was done in the 20th century. Strength theory is an important foundation for research on the strength of the materials and structures, and is widely used in mechanics. It is of great importance in theoretical research and engineering applications and is also very important for the effective utilization of the materials. In particular, the actual behavior and strength of concrete materials is quite complicated. The behavior of concrete is affected much by the physical and mechanical properties of its components and as a result concrete shows a great variety of responses under different loading conditions. That's why only a single mathematical model is not expected to describe its behavior completely for all practical applications. Hence a proper definition of failure must be postulated specific to the situation and accordingly failure criteria of concrete must be chosen under combined stress states.

Many model /criteria have been described ranging from one-parameter model (criterion) to the multi-parameter model. Most of them are the single strength theory adapted only for one kind of materials. These could be categorized into three series of strength theories. They are series of single-shear strength theory (SSS theory), the series of octahedral shear strength theories (OSS theory) and the series of twin-shear strength theory (TSS theory). The SSS theory forms the lower bound for the entire possible convex limit surfaces on the π-plane. The OSS theory is a nonlinear function; it forms curved limit surfaces mediated between the SSS theory and the TSS theory. The TSS theory is a new series of strength theory. It's a linear function and forms the upper bound for the entire possible convex limit surfaces on the π-plane.

In general, one-parameter criteria are used for those materials having same strength both in tension and compression ($\sigma_c = \sigma_t$). Two-parameter criteria are used for those materials, which have hydrostatic stress effect (tensile strength is lower than its compressive strength, $\sigma_c > \sigma_t$). It is better to use three-parameter criteria for those material having uniaxial compressive strength not equal to uniaxial tensile strength (σ_t) and the equal-bi-axial compressive strength (σ_{bc}) not equal to the uniaxial compressive strength (σ_c) i.e. $\sigma_c \neq \sigma_t \neq \sigma_{bc}$. The multi parameter criterion is used for more complex cases. No single model or criteria has emerged which is fully adequate.

The unified strength theory is a better criterion in the sense that it is able to reflect the fundamental characteristics of the material, viz SD effect (different compressive and tensile effect), hydrostatic pressure effect, the effect of intermediate principal stress and gives good agreement with existing experimental data. It is physically meaningful and can be expressed by a simple mathematical equation, which includes all independent stress components. The unified strength theory is not a single criterion; it is a system, a series of continuously variable criteria covering the entire region from lower to upper bound. Most of the previous yield and failure criteria are special cases or approximation of the unified strength theory.

It is very important to choose a reasonable strength theory in research and design. The results of the research and design depend strongly on the choice of strength theory in most cases. The selection of correct strength theory becomes even more important than the calculations. The bearing capacity of structures, forming limit of FEM simulations, size of plastic zones and orientation of shear band and plastic flow localization will much be affected by the choice of strength theory. More experimental results of strength of materials under complex stress state and more accurate choices of strength theory are demanded for research and engineering application in the future.

The study of failure criteria for the nonlinear analysis of concrete structures has been consistently highlighted for last few decades. As discussed in Chen(1982), there are mainly two types of failure criteria for concrete; (1)theoretical failure criteria and (2) Empirical failure criteria.

2.4.1 *Theoretical failure criteria:*

The maximum tensile stress criterion, developed by Rankine in 1876, is the first theory related to the strength of materials under complex stress states. According to this criterion, tensile failure occurs once the maximum principal stress at a point inside the material reaches the concrete uniaxial tensile strength f_t (the corresponding shear stresses are ignored). The equation for the failure surface defined by this criterion is σ_t $=f_t$, where σ_t is the maximum principal stress or the first principal stress. The corresponding surface is defined as the fracture-cutoff surface or tension-failure surface or simply tension cutoff. This theory is generally acceptable to determine whether a tensile or a compressive type of failure has occurred for concrete.

The Mohr-Coulomb failure criterion(1900) states that failure of a material is governed by the relation $|\tau| = c - \sigma \tan\phi$, where the limit shear stress τ in a plane is dependent only on the normal stress σ in the same plane a point, c is the cohesion and ϕ is the angle of internal friction of the material. The main disadvantage of this criterion lies in that the intermediate principal stress or the second principal stress is not taken into account. In addition, its tensile and compressive medians are straight lines, which is not true for concrete under a large hydrostatic pressure.

Von Mises failure criterion (or octahedral shearing stress criteria) came up in 1913. It states that yielding begins when the octahedral shear stress reaches a critical value k. It may be expressed as $\tau_{oct} = \sqrt{\dfrac{2}{3}J_2} = \sqrt{\dfrac{2}{3}}.k$, where τ_{oct} is the octahedral shear stress, J_2 is the second invariant of the stress deviator tensor and k is the material constant. Similar to the Mohr-Coulomb failure criterion, this failure criterion only takes into account of the influence of first principal shear stress on the material strength. The intermediate principal stress is commonly ignored. As a result, the difference between the tensile and the compressive strength of concrete are not taken into account.

Drucker and Prager (1952, 1956) proposed a failure criterion to rectify the shortcomings of the Mohr-Coulomb criterion. In this failure criterion, a smooth approximation to the Mohr-Coulomb surface is adopted as a simple modification of the von-Mises yield criterion in the form $f(I_1, J_2) = \alpha I_1 + \sqrt{J_2} - k = 0$, where I_1 is the first invariant of stress tensor, α and k are positive constants at each point of the material. It may be noted that this equation reduces to von-Mises yield criteria when α is set to zero. The Drucker-Prager failure criterion is still not suitable for the analysis of concrete structures because of the round shape of its failure surface in the deviatoric plane (where the difference between the tensile and compressive strength of the concrete can't be reflected).

Yu and He(1991) suggested the unified strength theory(UST) based on assumption that the plastic flow of stress is controlled by the combination of the two larger principal shear stresses and their corresponding normal stresses. A class of convex criteria can be obtained by varying the coefficient in the UST to suit different materials like metal concrete etc. The UST may be represented as

$$\tau_{13} + b\tau_{12} + \beta(\sigma_{13} + b\sigma_{12}) = C \text{ when } \tau_{12} + \beta\sigma_{12} \geq \tau_{23} + \beta\sigma_{23}$$

$$\tau_{13} + b\tau_{23} + \beta(\sigma_{13} + b\sigma_{23}) = C \text{ when } \tau_{12} + \beta\sigma_{12} < \tau_{23} + \beta\sigma_{23}$$

Where $\tau_{13}, \tau_{12}, \tau_{23}$ are the principal shear stresses and $\sigma_{13}, \sigma_{12}, \sigma_{23}$ are the corresponding normal stresses. $\sigma_1, \sigma_2, \sigma_3$ are the principal stresses such that $\sigma_1 \geq \sigma_2 \geq \sigma_3$; C is a material strength parameter, b and β are the coefficients that reflects the influence of the intermediate principal shear stress τ_{12} (or τ_{23}) and the corresponding normal stresses on the strength of the material respectively.

The advantage of this failure criterion is that it covers all previously developed theoretical failure criteria. However, it is unable to reflect the difference between the equal biaxial and uniaxial compressive strength of concrete and the effect of hydrostatic pressure on the concrete strength is not appropriately accounted for.

A three-parameter UST was developed by Yu et al.(1992)

$$\tau_{13} + b\tau_{12} + \beta(\sigma_{13} + b\sigma_{12}) + a\sigma_m = C \text{ when } \tau_{12} + \beta\sigma_{12} \geq \tau_{23} + \beta\sigma_{23}$$

$$\tau_{13} + b\tau_{23} + \beta(\sigma_{13} + b\sigma_{23}) + a\sigma_m = C \text{ when } \tau_{12} + \beta\sigma_{12} < \tau_{23} + \beta\sigma_{23}$$

where σ_m is the hydrostatic pressure and 'a' is the coefficient reflecting the effect of the hydrostatic pressure on the concrete strength. Compared with the other failure criteria, this failure criterion can explain the effect of hydrostatic pressure on the concrete strength and also take into consideration the strength increase when concrete is under biaxial compression. However, its tensile and compressive meridians are still linear and hence this model can't be used for the analysis of some concrete structures e.g. dam, prestress concrete, where concrete is usually under high hydrostatic pressure.

Further Yu et al.(1997) developed the five-parameter UST to simulate the concrete strength under various states of stress. This failure criterion can be expressed as

$$F = \tau_{13} + b\tau_{12} + \beta(\sigma_{13} + b\sigma_{12}) + A_1\sigma_m + A_2\sigma_m^2 = C \text{ when } F \geq F'$$

$$F' = \tau_{13} + b\tau_{23} + \beta(\sigma_{13} + b\sigma_{23}) + B_1\sigma_m + B_2\sigma_m^2 = C \text{ when } F < F'$$

where A_1, A_2, B_1, B_2 are the coefficients reflecting the effect of the hydrostatic pressure on the concrete strength. This failure criterion gives good agreement with the experimental results and its failure surface represents concrete strength perfectly well. However it is difficult to determine the coefficients of the criterion due to exhaustive involvement of biaxial or triaxial material tests.

2.4.2 *Empirical failure criteria:*

Bresler and Pister (1958) suggested a failure criterion to resolve the drawbacks of the Drucker and Prager failure criterion, which has linear tensile compressive meridians. According to this failure criterion, the failure of concrete occurs when the octagonal normal σ_{oct} and shear stress τ_{oct} at a point satisfy the following equation.

$$\frac{\tau_{oct}}{f_c'} = a - b\frac{\sigma_{oct}}{f_c'} + c\left(\frac{\sigma_{oct}}{f_c'}\right)^2,$$

where σ_{oct} is considered positive when compressive strength of concrete f_c' is positive. The failure paramets a, b and c can be determined by curve fitting of available experimental test data. This failure criterion still can't describe the difference of concrete tensile and compressive strength in that the shape of its failure surface in the deviatoric plane is round. Moreover its tensile and compressive meridians meet the hydrostatic axis under a low hydrostatic pressure.

Reimann(1965) suggested a four-parameter criterion for concrete that is subjected to compressive stresses only and is given by

$$\frac{\xi}{f_c'} = a\left(\frac{r_c}{f_c'}\right)^2 + b\left(\frac{r_c}{f_c'}\right) + c,$$

where ξ is the hydrostatic coordinate, which reflects the influence of hydrostatic stress on the concrete strength, r_c is the compressive meridian. a, b, c are parameters which can be obtained from concrete triaxial material tests. It is an improvement over the Mohr-Coulomb failure criterion as it considers the curved tensile and compressive meridians. However its application is limited as it is applicable to concrete in compression only.

Kupfer et al.(1967) suggested a failure criterion based on their experimental test results, given by $[\beta(3J_2) + \alpha I_1]^{1/2} = f_c'$, where a and b are the material parameters which are determined by the curve fitting of the experimental works. This failure criterion is only suitable for the analysis of concrete structures in the state of plane stress.

Willam and Warnke(1975) developed a five-parameter failure criterion to reflect the behavior of concrete suffering low and high compressive stresses. Its failure surface can describe curved meridians and the elliptical type of noncircular cross section. The tensile and compressive meridians are given by

$$\frac{\tau_{mt}}{f_c'} = \frac{r_t}{\sqrt{5}f_c'} = a_0 + a_1\left(\frac{\sigma_m}{f_c'}\right) + a_2\left(\frac{\sigma_m}{f_c'}\right)^2 \qquad \text{when } \theta = 0^0$$

$$\frac{\tau_{mc}}{f_c'} = \frac{r_c}{\sqrt{5}f_c'} = b_0 + b_1\left(\frac{\sigma_m}{f_c'}\right) + b_2\left(\frac{\sigma_m}{f_c'}\right)^2 \qquad \text{when } \theta = 60^0$$

where τ_{mt} and τ_{mc} are the octahedral shear stresses corresponding to the tensile and compressive meridians, respectively. r_t and r_c are the radii of tensile and compressive meridians respectively. a_0, a_1, a_2, b_0, b_1 and b_2 are the constants, which can be determined using experimental data, and θ is the Lode angle. This failure criterion agrees closely with the experimental data. Nevertheless it is difficult to determine its parameters, as it requires biaxial material tests of concrete.

Ottosen(1977) suggested a four-parameter criterion involving all the stress invariants

$$(I_1, J_2, \cos 3\theta) \text{ as } a.\frac{J_2}{f_c^{'2}} + \lambda.\frac{\sqrt{J_2}}{f_c^{'}} + b.\frac{I_1}{f_c^{'}} - 1 = 0,$$

where $\lambda = \lambda(\cos 3\theta) > 0$ in which θ is the Lode angle; a and b are the constants which can be determined by the uniaxial compressive and tensile strengths $f_c^{'}$ and f_t respectively together with biaxial and triaxial strengths. The advantage of the failure criterion is that it closely agrees with the experimental results, when concrete is in triaxial compression or biaxial state of stress. However it is difficult to determine the coefficients of the failure criterion and the concrete strength in tensile and compressive meridians is overestimated under the high hydrostatic pressure.

Hseieh et al.(1979) suggested a four-parameter criterion involving the stress invariants I_1, J_2 and the maximum principal stress σ_1, which can be expressed as

$$f(I_1, J_2, \sigma_1) = a\frac{J_2}{f_c^{'2}} + b\frac{\sqrt{J_2}}{f_c^{'}} + c\frac{\sigma_1}{f_c^{'}} + d\frac{I_1}{f_c^{'}} - 1 = 0$$

where constants a, b, c and d are determined as 2.0108, 0.9714, 9.1412 and 0.2312 respectively determined from the experimental results.

Kostovos(1979) suggested a failure criterion for concrete, in which the approximation function for the meridians is derived from a wealth of experimental data. The shape function in the deviatoric plane is an elliptical function similar to that proposed by William and Warnke (1975). It may expressed as

$$\frac{\tau_{octt}}{f_c^{'}} = 0.633 \left(\frac{\sigma_{oct}}{f_c^{'}} + 0.05 \right)^{0.857} \qquad \text{when } \theta = 0^0$$

$$\frac{\tau_{octc}}{f_c'} = 0.944\left(\frac{\sigma_{oct}}{f_c'} + 0.05\right)^{0.724} \qquad \text{when } \theta = 60^0$$

$$\tau_{oct} = \frac{2\tau_{octc}\left(\tau_{octc}^2 - \tau_{octt}^2\right)Cos\theta + \tau_{octc}\left(2\tau_{octt} - \tau_{octc}\right)\left[4\left(\tau_{octc}^2 - \tau_{octt}^2\right)Cos^2\theta\right]^{1/2}}{4\left(\tau_{octc}^2 - \tau_{octt}^2\right)Cos^2\theta + \left(\tau_{octc} - 2\tau_{octt}\right)^2 + 5\tau_{octt}^2 - 4\tau_{octt}\tau_{octc}}$$

where τ_{octt} and τ_{octc} are the octahedral shear stresses in the tensile and compressive meridians respectively. σ_{oct} is the octahedral normal stress (hydrostatic pressure), τ_{oct} is the octahedral shear stress i.e. radius in the deviatoric plane. The advantage of this failure criterion lies in that it has simple expressions. However the concrete strength tends to be overestimated in the high hydrostatic pressure.

Podgorski(1985) suggested a general five-parameter failure criterion applicable to different materials similar to Ottosen(1977), but not suitable for concrete at high hydrostatic pressure. Wang and Fan(1998) suggested a UST based failure criterion similar to Yu and He (1991) and Kostovos(1979).

Generally the main advantage of empirical failure criteria is that they are in good agreement with the experimental results, though not based on clear theoretical background. Moreover these failure criteria either involve triaxial material tests or unable to accurately predict strength of concrete under high hydrostatic pressure.

Fan et al. (2001) proposed a piecewise linear unified yield criterion called the twin –shear (TS) unified. It is based on a kind of orthogonal dodecahedron stress element. The effects of intermediate principal stress are taken into account such that most available loci on the π-plane are embraced in a unified manner. The most prominent characteristics for the criterion are their capability to represent the effects of the intermediate principal; stress σ_2 in the piecewise linear form. Besides, it is capable to represent not only convex limit surfaces but also nonconvex limit surfaces Future research could focus on the pursuit for some criteria that can bridge different criteria both on the π-plane and on the meridian plane.

Wilson (2002) mentioned that P.W. Bridgman's early work on flow and fracture in the presence of hydrostatic pressure showed no systematic effect on strain hardening. The experimental observations led to the conclusions that yielding does not depend on hydrostatic stress and that the yielded material is incompressible. Classical plasticity theory was largely built on these observations. Nonlinear finite element analyses using the von Mises (yielding is independent of hydrostatic stress) and the Drucker-Prager (yielding is linearly dependent on hydrostatic stress) yield functions was performed. The finite element results using a von Mises yield function and a Drucker-Prager yield function are compared to the experimental results. The von Mises yield function consistently overpredicts the actual load-displacement response. For the load at failure, the failure displacements predicted using the Drucker-Prager yield function essentially matched the test data. The failure displacements predicted using the von Mises yield function overestimated the experimental failure displacement by 20 to 65 percent. Hence the Drucker-Prager yield function was consistently more accurate than the von Mises yield function. The differences between the von Mises and the Drucker-Prager yield criteria may be much smaller for plane stress conditions. The good agreement between experimental and numerical results indicates that isotropic hardening, when coupled with the Drucker-Prager yield function, adequately describes the strain hardening. In summery, the yield behavior is more accurately modeled using a yield function that includes a hydrostatic stress term. The Drucker-Prager yield criterion was shown to capture the hydrostatic tensile stress effects on yielding without introducing complications and additional expense. The only additional data requirement for the Drucker-Prager yield function is the yield strength in compression.

Yu M.H. (2002) presented a survey of the advances in strength theory (yield criteria, failure criterion etc.) of materials (including metallic materials, rock, soil, concrete etc) under complex stress states, discusses the relationship among various criteria and gives a method of choosing a reasonable failure criteria for applications in research and engineering. Three series of strength theories, the unified yield criteria, the unified strength theory and others are summarized.

Remarks :

In general, concrete failures are of two types; tensile type and compressive type. Tensile type is characterized by brittleness due to formation of cracks and loss of tensile strength, whereas compressive type is by ductility due to loss of strength arising out of concrete crushing. In fact there is no brittle or ductile material in reality, rather a material exhibits brittle or ductile post-failure response under different conditions of loading due to material degradation for a fractured concrete. Hence a suitable single failure criteria is necessary which can represent the same efficiently either due to tensile or compressive or due to mixed failure. This part of past literature survey has supported the author to choose the most appropriate one for the development of the procedure and computer code of the problem at hand.

2.5   Finite Element Modeling

As far as finite element analysis is concerned, a lot of works mainly based on two-dimensional (2D) modeling of RCC structure without reinforcements and based on various integral methods has been reported in different reputed journals in last few decades. Attempts were made to improve performance of 2D isoparametric element based formulation using reduced and selective integration schemes, B-bar method, additional incompatible modes, but to a few specific problems and also under certain conditions of mixed formulation. All these attempts were made aiming at removing inherent difficulties (locking etc.) particularly in thin structures. Even these methods can only analyze certain specific problems where it is possible to study the behaviour of the structure with necessary simplification by adopting the assumptions of 2D analysis.

In applications of 3D analysis, the standard quadratic 20-noded hexahedral element has been used, though it has high number of nodes involving a large number of degrees of freedom and necessitates large computational time. Since comparatively lower order elements have the advantages for 3D analysis due to easy mesh generation, data interpretation and lower computational time, improvement of such type of element performance has drawn attention of the investigators. Among the lower order elements, the linear isoparametric elements are the simplest constant strain elements. However it has got some well-known deficiencies as far as the finite element analysis is concerned. It cannot represent the state of stress in pure bending accurately due to inherent volumetric and transverse shear locking phenomenon. Several methods were described by Wilson et al (1973), Taylor et al (1976) in this regard to improve the performance of the standard linear quadrilateral and hexahedral elements with the introduction of additional imaginary incompatible degrees of freedom to represent different modes of deformation, of course that are condensed prior to the assembly of elements. This difficulty with the associated locking phenomena has also been overcome using a different concept of Enhanced Assumed Strain Approach (EAS) by Simo /Rifai (1990) in near incompressible and bending situations, where the strain field is enhanced with inclusion of additional variables. Numerous growth in this line have been reported in the literature

Simo /Rifai (1990) presented a class of assumed mixed finite element method which allows the systematic development of low order elements possessing good coarse mesh and distortion insensitivity properties. It's a three-field mixed formulation in terms of displacements, stresses and an enhanced strain field, which encompasses the classical method of incompatible modes. Within this framework, incompatible elements arise as particular 'compatible' mixed approximations of the enhanced strain field. The condition that the stress interpolation contain piecewise-constant functions, ensure satisfaction of the patch test and allow the elimination of the stress field from the formulation. The preceding conditions are formulated in a form particularly convenient for element design. As an illustration of the methodology three new elements are developed and shown to exhibit good performance suitable for non-linear analysis; a plane 3D elastic /plastic QUAD, and axisymmetric element and a thick plate bending QUAD. Constitutive equations in non-linear solid mechanics typically define a stress tensor in terms of a suitable conjugate strain measure. Assumed strain methods use these direct constitutive relation in three-field variational setting. Assumed stress methods, on the otherhand, employ inverse constitutive relations, which define strains in term of stress measures in the context of two-field variational formulation. Well-known and widely used constitutive model, such as finite deformation elasticity, demonstrate that explicit expressions for these inverse relations are generally not available. It was concluded that assumed strain mixed methods are much better suited than assumed stress method for non-linear analysis.

Simo /Armero (1992) presented a class of assumed strain mixed finite elements methods for fully non-linear problems in solid mechanics is presented which when restricted to geometrically linear problems encompasses the classical method of incompatible modes as a particular case. The method relies crucially on a local multiplicative decomposition of the deformation gradient into a conforming and an enhanced part, formulated in the context of a 3-field variational formulation. The resulting class of mixed methods provides a possible extension to the non-linear regime of well-known incompatible mode formulation. In addition this class of methods includes non-linear generalization of recently proposed enhanced strain interpolations for axisymmetric problems, which cannot be interpreted as incompatible modes of elements. Remarkably these methods appear to be especially well suited for problems involving localization of the deformation.

The enhanced assumed strain (EAS) method originally proposed by Simo and Rifai is used by *Andelfinger /Ramm (1993)* to develop new four-node membrane, plate and shell elements and 8-node solid elements. The equivalence of certain EAS elements with Hellinger-Reissner (HR) elements is highlighted i.e. the 7-parameter element EAS-7 with 2x2 integration is identical to the HR element of Pian and Sumihara. 8-node solid elements, which are free volumetric locking, and 4-node shell elements, which have an improved membrane and bending behavior, compared to the Bathe-Dvorkin shell element, are introduced. It has been proved that the EAS methods are well suited to improve and optimize continuum and structural finite elements. If for linear elements, the additional strains are assumed so that the total strain fields are of the same order as the displacement fields, the EAS formulation leads to elements, which are identical to optimally interpolated HR-elements. However, in order to keep the numerical effort as low as possible the number of additional strain parameters should be kept to a minimum. In shell analysis, the BD-element is improved by the EAS formulation for the membrane and bending components. Especially the stress resultants are more accurate and free of oscillations. For the transverse shear components, the ANS method is applied. However, the last test problem indicates that element with an ANS formulated transverse shear part may still exhibit shear locking when are warped. The authors concluded that EAS concept applicable to small strain plasticity required to be extended into the large deformation range where the additional variables have to be defined in terms of displacement gradients instead of strains.

Bischoff /Ramm (1997) combined the concept of assumed natural strain (ANS) and the enhanced assumed strain (EAS) techniques to derive an efficient and reliable finite elements for continuum based shell formulations. In the present study two aspects are covered. The classical 5-parameter-shell formulation with Reissner-Mindlin kinematics as discussed by *Andelfinger /Ramm (1993)* for the linear case of a four-node shell element, are extended to geometrical nonlinearities. A geometrically nonlinear version of the EAS approach is applied which is based on the enhancement of the Green-Lagrange strains instead of the displacement gradient as originally proposed by Simo /Armero(1992). It has been shown that a non-linear version of the EAS method alternative to the one proposed by Simo /Armero is possible, namely the additive decomposition of the Green-Lagrange strain tensor. In a similar way for a higher order situation, special provisions have been made to avoid artificial stiffening caused by the three dimensional displacement field and termed thickness-locking, a 7-parameter nonlinear shell formulation have been introduced.

Klinkel /Wagner (1997) presents the development of a 3D brick element with EAS for a geometrically non-linear theory. Some linear and non-linear examples show that this element can be used successfully in the whole range of solid structures including stability effects. Thin 2D and 3D beam and shell structures are calculated with few 3D elements and the results are the same as for shell or beam elements. A new enhanced strain element based on the definition of extra compatible modes of deformation added by *Cesar /Natal Jorge (1999)* to the standard 4-node finite element to improve its performance. The element is built with the objective of addressing incompressible problem and avoiding locking effects. By analyzing at the element level the deformation modes, which form a basis for the incompressible subspace, the extra modes of deformation are proposed in order to provide the maximum possible dimension to that subspace. Subsequently another new element with more degrees of freedom is formulated using a mixed method. This is done by including an extra field of variables related to the derivative of the displacement field of the extra compatible modes. The performance of the elements proposed is assessed in linear and non-linear situations.

Sousa et al. (2002), in particular focused on to improve performance of lower order 3D solid elements since they have advantages for 3D analysis due to easy mesh generation and data interpretation. However low order elements suffer from so-called volumetric locking. Reduced and SRI techniques were the first irreducible form solutions for locking problem. Mixed formulations also effectively solve problem with the apparent advantage of a sound mathematical background but Malkus and Hughes showed the equivalence under certain conditions, of mixed formulation and SRI techniques of penalty formulations. Later the B-bar method was introduced, which avoided the necessity of reduced integration and in which the shape function derivatives related to the volumetric response were replaced by approximations resulting from a mixed formulation. Simo /Rifai(1992) introduced the concept of enhanced strain element, where the strain field is enhanced with the inclusion of extra variables. With this approach volumetric locking is avoided and good accuracy is achieved even with the coarse meshes. Recently some mixed /enhanced strain formulations were introduced for the solution of elasto-plastic finite strain problems. For 2D four-node square element, by analyzing the basis of subspaces that result from the finite element solution, Cesar and Owen made evident how, under certain circumstances, the locking occurs. In this paper the same framework is utilized to explain the ability or inability of the different solution referred to avoid volumetric locking in 3D analysis, based on this methodology new enhanced strain element (for 3D analysis), based on extra compatible modes of deformation are proposed. The extension of their applicability in problems of thin shells is also presented. Conclusion;

The discussion about the number of internal variables to use in the achievement of an element free of any locking type still remains open. In fact some enhanced modes are only needed in particular situations, like the six additional deformation modes of the HCiS18 element. Improvements still can be made on these elements, aiming to improve its performance using less internal variables. However, it has been shown that, for an element free of volumetric locking, the subspace of incompressible deformation must have dimension 23. The application of the proposed element to nonlinear problems is being developed, since all the assessment made here are linear situations.

Cesar et al. (2002) worked on the degenerated approach for shell elements of Ahmad and co-workers. To avoid transverse shear locking effects in 4-node bilinear elements, an alternative formulation based on the EAS method of Simo and Rifai is proposed directed towards the transverse shear terms of the strain field. In the first part of the work the analysis of the null transverse shear strain subspace for the degenerated element and also for the selective reduced integration (SRI) and assumed natural strain (ANS) formulations is carried out. Locking effect are then justified by the inability of the null transverse shear strain subspace, implicitly defined by a given finite element, to properly reproduce the required displacement pattern. Illustrating the proposed approach, a remarkably simple single element test is described where ANS formulation fails to converge to the correct results, being characterized by the performance as the degenerated shell element. The adequate enhancement of the null transverse shear strain subspace is provided by the EAS method, enforcing Kirchoff's hypothesis for low thickness values and leading to a framework for the development of shear-locking free shell elements. Numerical linear elastic tests show improved results obtained with the proposed formulation.

Arieas et al. (2003) proposed low-order HIS solid element, which is a general-purpose element, can be applied without modifications, to various solid mechanics problems, from beam, plate and shell analysis to bulk forming and finite strain elasto-plastic analysis. Even complex implicit gradient models for modeling strain-softening behavior have been implemented with success with a variant of the present element. In terms of linear elastic accuracy, if mesh is regular, the element behavior is very good as the tests in this paper illustrate. There are 3d mixed or hybrid elements, which present higher degree of accuracy in certain linear elastic problems, but at the cost of lack of generality in the range of possible applications. For non-linear analysis, the element has a good behavior, with results extremely close to the best shell elements in a number of shell problems and also presents very accurate results in 3D solid analysis. The Newton-Raphson convergence characteristics were excellent and in the non-linear problems presented, the analysis could be easily extended to much higher values of loading Further work with this formulation is being carried out, with the goal of reducing the number of internal variables. In addition, improvements are needed to attenuate mesh sensitivity of enhanced strain elopements.

Low order elements have advantages for 3D analysis since they allow reasonable easy mesh-generation and data interpretation. However, these elements are known to suffer from so-called volumetric locking. *Sousa et al. (2003)* proposed several techniques to reduce this problem, such as the reduced integration, selective reduced integration, the B-bar method or mixed formulations. Later Simo and Rifai introduced the EAS method. With this approach volumetric locking can be avoided and good accuracy is achieved even with coarse meshes. The extension of the low order 3D elements in problems of thin plates or shells introduces one more locking problem, namely the transverse shear-locking phenomenon. Recently new EAS 3D brick elements based on extra compatible modes of deformation were proposed for near incompressible situations and thin shell problems in linear range, using subspace analysis methodology. The extension of their applicability in nonlinear problems involving near incompressibility and low thickness to length ratios is here proposed, as well as assessment and comparisons with other formulations.

Sousa et al. (2003) focuses on the development of a new EAS method based class of 8-node solid finite elements, suitable for the treatment of volumetric and transverse shear locking problems. Doing so, the proposed elements can be used efficiently for 3D and thin shell applications. The starting point of the work relies on the analysis of the subspace of incompressible deformations associated with the standard (displacement-based) fully integrated and reduced integrated hexahedral elopements. Prediction capabilities for both formulations are defined related to nearly-incompressible problems and an enhanced strain approach is developed to improve the performance of the earlier formulation in this case. With the insight into volumetric locking gained and benefiting from a recently proposed enhanced transverse shear strain procedure for shell applications, a new element conjugating both the capabilities of efficient solid and shell formulations is obtained. Using a quite simple formulation, with no stabilization or under-integration techniques, and a minimal set of additional variables, justified by the framework of subspace analysis, the HCiS12 element performed successfully in all the examples presented. Comparing with other well-known EAS solid elements, a great improvement was done. Numerical results attest the robustness and efficiency of the proposed approach, when compared to solid and shell elopements well established in the literature.

Vu-Quoc /Tan (2003) present a simple and efficient non-linear 8-node solid-shell element formulation-having only displacement DOFs and without rotational DOFs that has optimal number of parameters to pass the patch tests and thus allows for efficient and accurate analyses of large deformable multiplayer shell structures using elements at extremely high aspect ratio. The formulation of this element is based on the mixed Hu-Washiju variational principle leading to a novel enhancing strain tensor that renders the computation particularly efficient with improved in-plane and out-of-plane bending behavior (Poisson thickness locking) especially in refined analyses of composite structures involving a large number of high aspect ratio layers. It also reviewed the equivalence between various choices of the enhancing strains in tensor form and point out the relative efficiency of these choices. We discuss the EAS formulations based on green-Lagrange strain and the displacement gradient, points out the pitfalls in each approach. Shear locking and curvature thickness locking are treated with assumed natural strain (ANS) method. We provide an optimal combination of the ANS method and the minimal number of EAS parameters required to pass the out-of-plane bending patch test. Numerical examples involving static analyses of multiplayer shell structures having a large range of element aspect ratios are presented. The present solid-shell element was proven for the thick and extremely thin aspect ratio in linear and non-linear regime as well as isotropic material and composite laminates with dissimilar material layer. The present formulation can predict the through thickness effects and in particular, the inter-laminar stresses, to a high degree of accuracy.

Mijuca D. (2004) presented a new 3D multi-field finite element approach for analysis of isotropic and anisotropic materials in linear elastoplastics, derived from primal-mixed variational formulation based on Hellinger-Reissner's principle. The novel properties are stress approximation by the continuous base functions, introduction of e constraints as essential boundary conditions and initial displacement and stress /strain field capability. It has two essential contributions in accordance to the similar approaches, the stress field is approximated by continuous base functions and known stress constraints may be treated as essential boundary conditions. In addition there is possibility to apply initial displacement and stress(or strain) field. It is proven that proposed finite element HC8/27 is reliable, even in the limit problems discretised by highly distorted meshes. Consequently, it could be recommended for the use in the analysis on non-smooth model problems of arbitrary geometry in the compressible and nearly incompressible limits. In order to avoid the geometrical invariance error and to enable introduction of known displacement and stress constraints and surface forces, in an adequate coordinate system, the underlying finite element scheme is coordinate dependent.

Valente et al. (2004) extended a previously proposed solid-shell finite element based on enhanced assumed strain(EAS) formulation to account for large deformation elasto-plastic thin-shell problems and tested in large deformation elastoplastic nonlinear geometric problems for the shell elements. An optimal number of 12 enhanced (internal) variables are employed, leading to a computationally efficient performance when compared to other 3D or solid-shell enhanced elements. This low number of enhanced variables is sufficient to (directly) eliminate either volumetric and transverse shear locking, the first one arising, for instance, in the fully plastic range, whist the last appears for small thickness values. The enhanced formulation comprises an additive split of Green-Lagrange material strain tensor, turning the inclusion of nonlinear kinematics a straightforward task. The presented numerical simulations show high predictability characteristics when compared to other well established (shell and solid-shell) formulations in the literature.

Remarks

This part of literature study has been performed aiming at the utilization of most suitable 3D solid element available in the literature. In this case 3D Solid lower order elements with incompatible modes are good one, which has been developed earlier are still being used by commercial softwares. In the recent past, most elements are developed based on enhanced assumed strain method and such an element as well as its applicability in modeling concrete as parent material in the composite element is being sought for.

2.6 Summery of Literature Survey

The finite element technique being a very important tool, have received a considerable interest by various authors for the purpose of analysis of discontinuous systems in particular the RC structures. The earliest work on such an application was done by Ngo and Scordelis(1967), where simple beam model were developed with constant strain triangles and a special bond link were used to describe the bond-slip effect. It was a case of linear analysis with predefined cracks to evaluate principal stresses both in concrete and reinforcement along with bond stresses. In 1972, Nilson introduced nonlinear material properties for concrete and steel as well as nonlinear bond-slip relationship into the analysis to perform nonlinear analysis with the help of incremental load method. Attention was also given to introduce new crack direction in subsequent iterations. In line with the above, plane stress elements were also used by numerous investigators such as Nayak and Zienkiewicz(1972) etc. for the same with an emphasis on constitutive relationships of the materials, cracking and elasto-plastic behavior, the effect of temperature, creep and shrinkage, tension stiffening. The concept of smeared crack approach introduced by Kollegger and Mehlhorn(1990) was preferred by the investigators to model the cracking phenomena in nonlinear analysis of RC structures, as its implementation in finite element analysis is very straight forward than that of the discrete crack model. In this context, two different methods emerged viz. the fixed crack and the rotating crack model. In fixed crack model, cracks are supposed to form in a direction perpendicular to the principal stress direction when it exceeds concrete tensile strength and the crack direction remains unchanged in course of subsequent loading. In fact, it was well accepted by the researcher at the very early stages due to its easy formulation. Subsequent studies, however, showed that it causes numerical instability as a result of singularity in stiffness matrix and later on this difficulty was overcome by introducing variable cracked shear modulus by Balakrishnon and Murray(1988). In rotating crack model, crack direction changes with subsequent loading path depending on the current principal strain direction. Also the assumption of no shear strain in the crack plane eliminates the requirement of cracked shear modulus. This model is particularly useful in analytical studies of global behaviour of RC structures rather than the local effects in the vicinity of a crack.

As far as finite element analysis is concerned, a lot of works mainly based on two-dimensional (2D) modeling of RCC structure without reinforcements and based on various integral methods has been reported in different reputed journals in last few decades. Attempts were made to improve performance of 2D isoparametric element based formulation using reduced and selective integration schemes, B-bar method, additional incompatible modes, but to a few specific problems and also under certain conditions of mixed formulation. All these attempts were made aiming at removing inherent difficulties (locking etc.) particularly in thin structures. Even these methods can only analyze certain specific problems where it is possible to study the behaviour of the structure with necessary simplification by adopting the assumptions of 2D analysis. In applications of 3D analysis, the standard quadratic 20-noded hexahedral element has been used, though it has high number of nodes involving a large number of degrees of freedom and necessitates large computational time. Since comparatively lower order elements have the advantages for 3D analysis due to easy mesh generation, data interpretation and lower computational time, improvement of such type of element performance has drawn attention of the investigators.

Among the lower order elements, the linear isoparametric elements are the simplest constant strain elements. However it has got some well-known deficiencies as far as the finite element analysis is concerned. It cannot represent the state of stress in pure bending accurately due to inherent volumetric and transverse shear locking phenomenon. This difficulty with the associated locking phenomena has also been overcome using a different concept of Enhanced Assumed Strain Approach (EAS) by Simo and Rifai(1990) in near incompressible and bending situations, where the strain field is enhanced with inclusion of additional variables. Numerous growth in this line have been reported in the literature by Simo and Armero(1992), Andelfinger and Ramn(1993), Souza et al.(1996), Cesar et al.(2002) and Valente et al.(2002). A remarkable progress and accuracy has been obtained by the element HCiS18 introduced by Sousa et al., even with the coarser meshes. In the present case, this element has been used to model the parent material i.e. concrete of the reinforced concrete structures.

Another aspect of RC structure is that it is highly non-homogeneous due to discrete presence of the reinforcements. In general there are three methods available for modeling of reinforcement, e.g. the discrete, the smeared and the embedded approach. The first one represents reinforcements by truss elements those are connected to the mesh at the concrete/parent element nodes and hence finite element mesh generation becomes dependent on reinforcement layout. The second one (smeared) is more suitable for homogeneous or uniformly distributed reinforcements, such as wall panels. So they can't be generally applied to 3D structures. Within embedded approach, proposed by Elwi and Hrudey(1989), Barzegar and Madipuddi(1994), these restrictions were removed and even the reinforcements are superimposed as one dimensional uniaxial element with the same displacement field as parent/concrete element without any additional node /DOF. They are allowed to intersect the parent element at any location and hence mesh design becomes independent of reinforcement layout. Here the author has used the same method proposed by Cheng and Fan(1993), Gomes and

Awruch(2001) due to its simplicity to handle problems of 3D analysis of RC structures to model the reinforcement.

Accounting for interaction between parent material/concrete and the reinforcements are done to make RCC structure to behave in a more realistic way because concrete is a strong, relatively durable in compression and reinforcements are strong, ductile in tension. This composite action requires transfer of load between concrete and steel. This load transfer mechanism is referred as bond-slip, which is depicted as continuous stress field in the vicinity of steel-concrete interface. As the loading on RCC structures are gradually increased, this bond-slip increases, as result relaxation of steel stress takes place more and more and an equilibrium is set up in the domain. To account for this phenomenon, two different approaches are very common. The first approach makes use of the bond-link element as proposed by Ngo and Scordelis(1967). This bond-link element has got no physical dimension and it connects a node of a concrete /parent material with that of a steel node having the same coordinate. It has been observed by the various authors that the bond-link element cannot adequately represent the stiffness of the steel concrete interface. The second approach makes use of bond-zone element described by a material law to model the contact surface between steel and concrete. Even though many studies of the bond-slip relationship between the mating surfaces have been conducted, a considerable uncertainty about this complex phenomenon still exists because of many parameter involved.

This phenomenon of interaction between the materials are modeled within the embedded approach where nodal D.O.F.s are increased by the slip D.O.F.s for each element and as a result global stiffness matrix size is increased dramatically. In bond behaviour, slip takes place due to damage in concrete adjacent to the bars exhibited by cracking /crushing. Lundgren(1999) developed an interface model based on plasticity theory with fully three-dimensional features. For all practical analysis of engineering problem, this approach is not very appealing, as it requires extremely large computational time. Another approach was initially introduced by G. Beer(1985) using isoparametric joint /interface element and was later on used by Hartl et al.(2000), where bond slip situations are being considered introducing supplementary interface elements of zero thickness. Within this approach, global displacement field is calculated at first considering perfect bond between reinforcements and concrete and then the slip is calculated by relaxing the perfect bond at the material level.

Theoretical and experimental research on strength theory of materials under complex stress state is a general problem. Strength theory is an important foundation for research on the strength of the materials and structures, and is widely used in mechanics. It is of great importance in theoretical research and engineering applications and is also very important for the effective utilization of the materials. In particular, the actual behavior and strength of concrete materials is quite complicated. The behavior of concrete is affected much by the physical and mechanical properties of its components and as a result concrete shows a great variety of responses under different loading conditions. That's why only a single mathematical model is not expected to describe its behavior completely for all practical applications. Hence a proper definition of failure must be postulated specific to the situation to predict the failure of concrete structures and hence requires an appropriate failure criteria of concrete under combined stress states.

Considering that many of the previous models and methods have not been fully verified so far, it is the intent of this study to addresses some of the model selection issues, viz tension-stiffening, compression softening, modeling of cracking, discrete modeling of reinforcements, lower order solid elements in modeling concrete and in particular to the effect of bond-slip both in linear as well as nonlinear regime.

An attempt is essential to get the response of reinforced concrete structures considering (1) lower order solid brick element for easy and simple mesh generation as well as data interpretation, (2) reinforcements as 1D truss elements considering only the axial deformation in its exact spatial position without affecting the parent element mesh using embedded approach, (3) mutual interaction between concrete and reinforcements for entire load history including bond-slip effect using continuous interface elements without affecting the size of global stiffness matrix and (4) modeling of concrete considering both geometrical and material nonlinearity adopting appropriate failure criteria. In this context, a substantial effort to be given to develop a simple user friendly finite element program. A FE formulation has been made and a program has been developed, considering above aspects and presented in chapter 4 / Appendix.

Chapter 3

Modeling Aspects

Based on the literature survey, modeling aspects for concrete, reinforcement and their composite action in regard to material behaviour, in general, are highlighted /discussed in this chapter, which forms the basis of the employed model and finite element formulation.

3.1 General :

Reinforced concrete is made up of two materials with different characteristic features, viz. concrete and reinforcements. Reinforcements may be considered as a homogeneous material and its material properties are well defined. On the otherhand, concrete is highly non-homogeneous medium made up of hardened paste of cement mortar and aggregates. Its mechanical properties are scattered more widely and can't be defined very easily. However, for the convenience of analysis and design, concrete is often considered as homogeneous medium in a macroscopic sense. Still as a whole, reinforced concrete medium become highly non-homogeneous due to discrete presence of the reinforcements.

The various stages of behavior of reinforced concrete beam as noted in *Chen (1982)* are shown by typical load-displacement curve as shown in Fig. 3.1-1. Similar diagrams are also obtained for load-displacement relationship for other stress conditions. This highly nonlinear relationship can be roughly divided into three ranges of behaviour ; (1) the uncracked elastic stage, (2) the crack propagation and (3) the yielding of reinforcement or crushing of concrete stage.

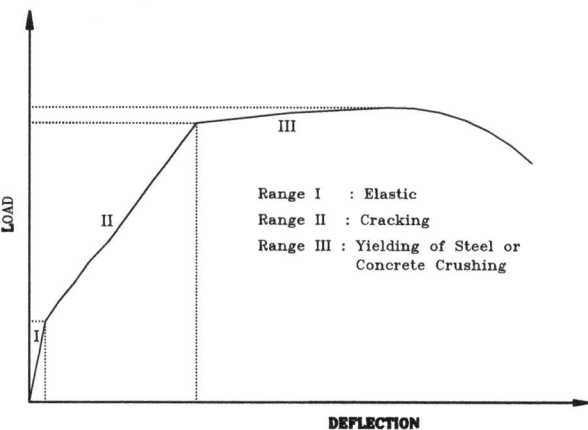

Fig. 3.1-1 : Idealized Load-displacement response of RC member

The nonlinear response of reinforced concrete is caused by two major material effects; cracking of concrete in tension and yielding of reinforcement or crushing of concrete in compression. Nonlinearities also arise from the interaction of the constituents of reinforced concrete, such as the bond-slip between the reinforcements and surrounding concrete, aggregate interlock at a crack and dowel action of the reinforcements while crossing a crack. The time-dependent effects of creep, shrinkage and temperature variation also contribute to the nonlinear behavior. Furthermore, the stress-strain relation of concrete is not only nonlinear, but is different in tension than in compression and the mechanical properties are dependent on concrete age at loading and on environmental conditions, such as ambient temperature and humidity. The material properties of concrete and reinforcement are also strain-rate dependent to some extent.

Because of this differences in short-term and long-term behavior of the constituent materials, a general purpose model of RC members and structures should be developed based on separate material models for reinforcement and concrete, which needs to be combined together through an interaction model to describe its composite behaviour. Moreover, when RCC structures are modeled based on continuum mechanics, contribution and distribution of stiffness of reinforcements should be given due importance. In general, the assumptions made in the description of material behaviour are as follows;

- The stiffness of concrete and reinforcement is formulated separately and then are superimposed to obtain the element stiffness.

- The smeared crack model is considered to describe the behaviour of cracked-concrete.

- Cracking in more than one direction is considered by a system of orthogonal cracks.

- The direction of crack may change with the loading history i.e. hypoelasticity based rotating crack concept is utilized.

- The reinforcement is assumed to carry stress along its axis only and the effect of dowel action is ignored.

- The transfer of stresses between reinforcement and concrete as well as the associated bond-slip is accounted for at the material level by introducing interface elements supplementary between reinforcement and concrete after the displacement field has been computed based on rigid bond condition.

- The geometric nonlinearity has also been included based on total Lagrangian approach.

- The lower order (8-noded) solid elements, based on recently developed enhanced assumed strain (EAS) approach, has been utilized to model parent material i.e. concrete.

3.2 Concrete :

Plain cement concrete consists of hardened cement paste with aggregates embedded in it. Hence it's highly heterogeneous medium resulting in a very complex behaviour. A considerable anisotropy is introduced by the direction of pouring concrete during the casting process. The variety of curing process also causes a complicated distribution of initial stresses. During the loading process, a nonlinear behaviour and an anisotropic material degradation /damage may also be observed. The time-dependent deformation due to creep along with shrinkage also contributes considerably towards the total deformation of the structure as well.

A considerable effort has been given by the various investigators to model the constitutive laws of concrete under different loading and unloading conditions at different stress levels. However in this work, concrete is assumed to behave linearly elastic and orthotropic even in multi-axial stress states for all engineering purpose. The proposed model includes the effect of triaxial nonlinear stress-strain law, tensile cracking, compression crushing and strain softening under monotonic loading condition. As plain cement concrete undergoes large relative displacements, only small deformation has been accounted for along with rigid body rotations. Hence a total Lagrangian formulation has been followed although with engineering stress and strain in the finite element implementation. The total secant stiffness has been used for the incremental stress-strain relations to account for strain softening at higher stress levels.

This part starts with brief overview of concrete behaviour in general followed by a classification of available concrete models. Then the employed model is discussed along with its phenomenological features and the computational implementation (refer to Art.-4.2). The five-parameter William-Warnke failure criterion is employed along with specific crack model based on hypoelasticity theory. The post peak failure mechanism (using a fracture energy principle) is also discussed. The anisotropy resulting from cracking is also taken into consideration.

3.2.1 Constitutive Behaviour :

Concrete exhibits a large number of microcracks, especially, at the interface between coarser aggregates and mortar, even before subjected to any load. The presence of these components has a great effect on the mechanical behavior of concrete, since their propagation during loading contributes to the nonlinear behaviour at low stress levels and causes volume expansion near failure. Many of these microcracks are caused by segregation, shrinkage or thermal expansion of the mortar. Some microcracks may develop during loading because of the differences in stiffness between aggregates and mortar. Since the aggregate-mortar interface has a significantly lower tensile strength than mortar, it constitutes the weakest link in the composite system. This may be considered as the good reason for the low tensile strength of concrete.

The response of a structure under load depends to a large extent on the stress-strain relation of the constituent materials and the magnitude of the stress. Since concrete is used mostly in compression, the stress-strain relation in compression is of primary interest. Such a relation can be obtained from cylinder tests of concrete as per standard specification of height to diameter ratio of 2 or from strain measurements of beams

The concrete stress-strain relation exhibits nearly linear elastic response upto about 25 to 30% of the compressive strength. This is followed by gradual softening upto the concrete compressive strength, when the material stiffness drops to zero. Beyond the peak compressive strength, the concrete stress-strain relation exhibits strain softening until failure takes place by crushing.

a) Factors influencing mechanical behavior concrete :

The performance of concrete is dependent on many factors. One of such factors is different *type of loading system* (Fig. 3.2-1), while applying compression to concrete specimen. Dry steel platens, lubricated steel plates, brush bearing plates, fluid cushion and standard triaxial test equipment are some of the arrangements followed for application of load. Devices with rigid steel plates are common. Such device induces uniform normal displacements in the direction of loading, but the respective normal stresses are non-uniformly distributed. Fluid cushion provides uniform normal stress and free lateral displacements resulting in zero shear stress in the surface. The behavior of other loading systems is ranging in between the behaviour of these two devices.

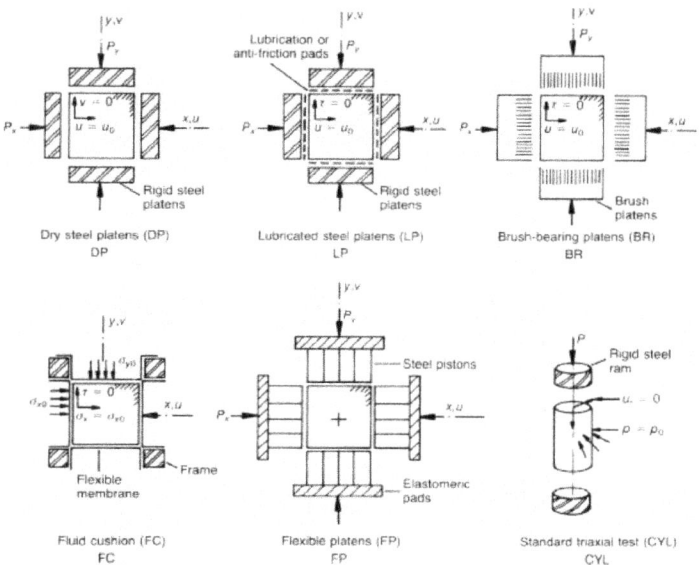

Fig. 3.2-1 : Different types of loading system

Other important factor in a standard testing apparatus is the *form and size of specimen*. Results with dry steel platens shows that compressive strength depends on the slenderness ratio of the loading system (Fig. 3.2-2) due to end restrains and resulting non-uniform strain distribution. The size of the specimen also affects the ultimate strength. Smaller specimen tested at 28 days shows to develop more strength as compared to larger ones.

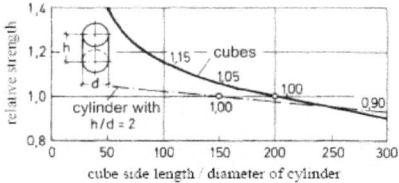

Fig. 3.2-2 : Compressive strength vs specimen slenderness

Materials of the formwork also influence the result of standard cube (15cm) test. Investigation shows that cubes cast in plastic moulds develope 6% less strength compared to cubes cast into steel moulds.

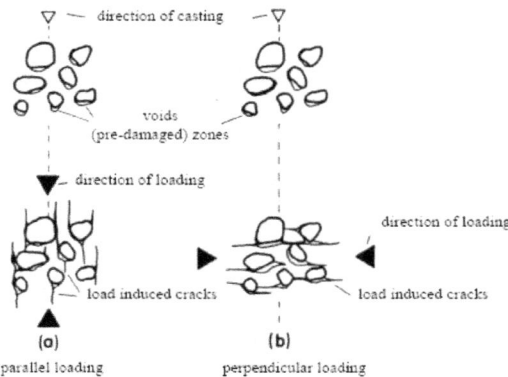

Fig. 3.2-3 : Formation of microcracks with loading direction

The casting direction plays a major role in deformability of the concrete specimen (Fig. 3.2-3). If a specimen is loaded parallel to the direction of casting, the concrete behaves 20% softer than the concrete, which is loaded perpendicular to the casting direction due to voids formed during casting prior to the loading. Investigations show that this anisotropy affects only the deformability, but the ultimate strength is hardly affected.

Moisture can reduce the strength of concrete upto 10% for standard concrete with a lower water-cement ratio. This reduction may rise upto 40% for low strength concrete with a high water cement ratio. It is assumed that water reduces the internal friction and the adhesion forces within concrete beside other effects. However, this decrease of the ultimate strength is reversible. A drying process of moist concrete re-establishes the original strength.

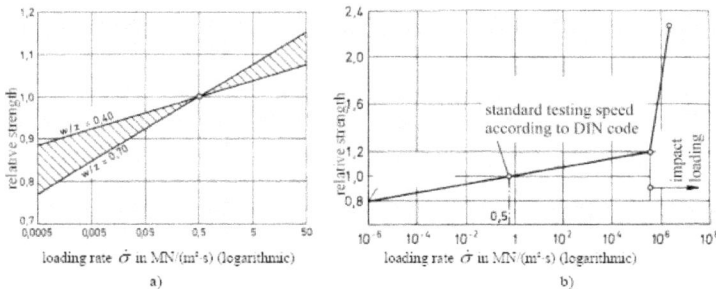

Fig. 3.2-4 : Effects of loading rate

The strength of concrete is also dependent on *rate of loading* (Fig. 3.2-4). In fact the change of strength is almost linear on a logarithmic time scale. For compression loading, the effect of increasing strength by hydration is counteracted by the decrease of strength under sustained loading. It is seen that a specimen fails at about 85% of the ultimate load with 56 days under sustained loading. It may be assumed that this effect leads to the reduction of the compressive strength to $\alpha.f_{ck}$, where $\alpha = 0.85$ for the ultimate load analysis. In a similar manner, the tensile strength also depends on the duration of loading.

b) Tensile behaviour :

Investigations show that the tensile behaviour of concrete is linear upto about two-third of the tensile strength. Beyond this limit, the pre-existing cracks start propagating. Microcrack planes develop perpendicular to the loading direction and are uniformly distributed over the specimen. Shortly before the ultimate load is reached, additional microcracks accumulate in a weak region of concrete specimen forming a microcrack bandwidth. It is characterized by the strains, which is considerably larger than the strains in the remaining part of the specimen.

Beyond the ultimate load, the crack band localizes and a softening region develops. The crack bandwidth decreases and the strain increase considerably. In the remaining part of the specimen the strains are decreasing and unloading is occurring. Hence the performance in the softening regime can be described by the sum of stress-strain relation of the two separated concrete parts and of the discrete crack width. It can be concluded that tensile cracking is an anisotropic material phenomenon similar to compressive cracking and the tensile cracking occurs in one direction, the material may still remain unaffected in the perpendicular directions.

c) **Compressive behaviour :**

The behaviour of concrete subjected to compressive loading is characterized by the development of cracks. Initial microcracks are present at the interface between the aggregates and the mortar matrix even before any external load is applied to concrete. During hydration and subsequent shrinkage, the volume of the cement matrix changes and the tensile stresses arise. These tensile stresses cause randomly distributed cracks.

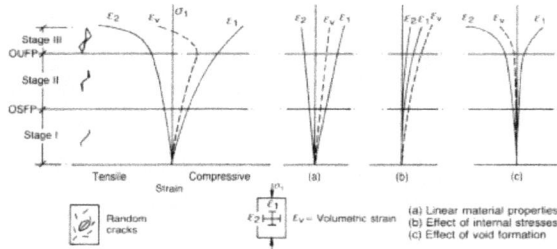

Fig. 3.2-5 : Stress-Strain diagram for triaxially loaded concrete

During loading, these microcracks will continuously propagate. On the macroscopic level, the mechanical behaviour may be considered as linear /elastic initially. With increasing load, the development of cracks causes anisotropic degradation. The stages from the onset of loading until the ultimate strength can be subdivided in three stages (Fig. 3.2-5). (1) The elastic deformation is dominant from onset of loading upto 30(for low strength concrete) to 70%(for high strength concrete) of f_c. There may be a small increase of micro-cracks and material behaviour remains approximately linear. When external load is applied, microcracks in addition to those pre-existing are formed at isolated points in the material, where tensile stress concentrations are highest in consequence of the incompatible deformations of the aggregates and the mortar.

During this stage, the microcracks remains stable and do not propagate. With the increasing load, tensile strains starts to concentrate near the crack tips and the initially stable microcracks starts to connect each other so as to initiate LFI (local fracture initiation). (2) In this stage, existing cracks starts propagating in the direction of loading in a stable manner. If the applied load is held constant, crack propagation does not continue. Thus the void formation results in an increase of volumetric strain. This is known as OSFP (onset of stable fracture propagation). (3) The degree of cracking can reach a level, at which the crack system becomes unstable and failure occurs even if the load remains constant over a relatively long period. The start of this stage is termed as OUFP (onset of unstable fracture propagation). The load can still be increased beyond this point to the ultimate surface but the amount of increase is dependent on the rate at which the load is applied.

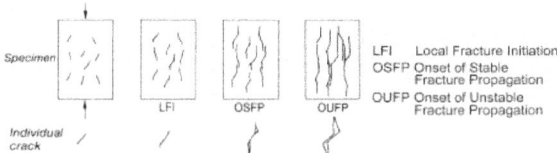

Fig. 3.2-6 : Stages of crack growth under compressive loading

Based on various investigations, it is observed that the compressive failure is initiated by an anisotropic degradation and the ultimate strength depends on the 3D stress state. With increasing confining (hydrostatic) stress the deviator stress increases considerably. The failure envelope (not the initiation of cracking) is nearly independent on the stress path along which the ultimate envelope is approached for monotonic loading. The ultimate strength is not subjected to considerable scatter for monotonic loading situations. Because of this scatter of data, a mathematical model should be considered which is capable of describing the ultimate strength considerably /reasonably well.

3.2.2 Models of Concrete Behaviour :

Intensive research work was conducted in the last few decades on constitutive laws of concrete and many mathematical models of concrete are being currently in use for the analysis of reinforced concrete structure. However there are a few models available, which may predict response of RC structures under arbitrary loading conditions. Most of the models are calibrated to fit a few experimental data. A brief description of the models is found in the literature (Chapter 2). These models may be summarized /grouped into the following major categories.

a) Elasticity based models :

Linear elasticity theory is the most commonly used material law for uncracked as well as cracked concrete. The linear elasticity models are significantly improved by various nonlinear-elastic generalizations. The elastic models can of course also be combined with criteria defining 'failure' of the material. The elastic formulation can be quite accurate for concrete sustaining proportional loading, but they fail to identify plastic deformations, a shortcoming that becomes apparent when material experiences unloading. This can to some extend be rectified by introducing unloading criteria considering either deformation theory of plasticity or flow theory of plasticity.

Isotropic linear-elastic models :

It's a very simple theory from conceptual point of view; only two material parameters are required viz. young's modulus and Poisson's ratio. It seems to be appropriate for tensile loading till the cracks are initiated and moderate for compressive loading, but its performance is very poor at high compressive stresses.

Cauchy-elastic models :

This model was proposed to model one-dimensional behaviour considering current stress (σ) as a function of current and strain tensors (ε) in the form $\sigma = f(\varepsilon)$. The elastic behaviour described by such function is both reversible and path-independent in he sense that the stresses are determined from current state of strain and vice versa. There is no dependence of the behaviour on the stress and strain histories followed to reach the current state of stress and strain. Such model may generate energy under certain loading-unloading cycles. Generating energy is admissible since it violates the laws of thermodynamics.

Green-elastic (hyperelastic) models :

This is based on the assumption of existence of a strain energy-density function (Ω) or a complementary energy-density function (Ψ) so that stress-strain relations are defined by $\sigma = \dfrac{\partial \Omega}{\partial \varepsilon}$ or $\sigma = \dfrac{\partial \Psi}{\partial \varepsilon}$. This ensures that no energy can be generated through load cycles and the laws of thermodynamics are always satisfied. This is basically a secant type formulation and therefore not capable to describe aging and history /rate dependence, also the material parameters have no physical meaning.

Incremental-elastic (hypoelastic) models :

In the above models, the total stress is expressed as a function of total strain and hence is independent of loading path to arrive at a current state. In hypoelastic (minimum elastic) models, the material behaviour is described in terms of current /incremental stresses and strains. Such models are dependent on deformation /loading history and are expressed as $d\sigma = f(d\varepsilon)$. This model is quite general and the behaviour is infinitesimally or incrementally reversible and is capable of accounting material anisotropy at high loads. Due to its simplicity and classical form, it has frequently been used by various investigators for constitutive modeling of concrete, in particular to the finite element analysis. In most of the simplified forms, the triaxial stresses and strains are being projected onto a one-dimensional equivalent scalar function such as octahedral stresses etc. and yields good agreement in monotonic loading situations.

Variable moduli models :

This model uses a different incremental stress-strain relationship, may be considered a special class hypoelastic materials in which response tensors are assumed to depend on invariants instead of stress or strain tensors itself. This different material response functions apply in initial loading and in subsequent unloading and reloading. This model employs a loading surface in order to make a distinction. Thus the model is generally irreversible even for incremental loading. These models are called variable-moduli models. Depending on loading or unloading, the nonlinear response of concrete is simulated by a piecewise linear elastic model with variable moduli. The model is therefore computationally simple and is particularly suitable for finite element calculations. In general, the variable moduli model is unable to describe accurately the behaviour of concrete under high stress and in the strain softening range.

b) Plasticity based(deformation theory based) models :

The plastic models are based on various theory related to deformation mechanics of solids consisting of yield surface, flow rule hardening rule and the failure surface. They form a big group in the literature.

Classical Plasticity models :

Such models use three cornerstones such as a yield criteria, a flow rule, a hardening rule. The mechanism of material nonlinearity in concrete is consists of both plastic slip and micro-cracking. Here total strain increment is assumed to be the sum of elastic and plastic strain increment tensors such that $d\sigma = d\sigma^e + d\sigma^p$. Hooke's law provides the necessary relationship between incremental stress and elastic strain. The plastic part of the strain increment tensor needs a flow rule to define the direction of plastic flow and a hardening rule (isotropic or kinematic hardening) to govern the phenomenon of configuration change in yield surface during the loading process.

Elasto-plastic fracture models :

In classical plasticity models, same elastic material behaviour is used to represent unloading and reloading function. It is written mathematically $\dot{\sigma} = C(\dot{\varepsilon} - \dot{\varepsilon}_{pl})$. This may be true for ductile material, but can't be applied to concrete, as it's a quasi-brittle material due to continuous microcracking during subsequent loading phases. Hence plastic fracturing theory becomes essential over the classical plasticity theory, which may account for degradation of elastic material moduli with increasing deformation. Using $\dot{\varepsilon}_{el} = (\dot{\varepsilon} - \dot{\varepsilon}_{pl})$ and $\dot{C}$ as rate of material moduli degradation, deformation law is expressed as $\dot{\sigma} = C\dot{\varepsilon}_{el} + \dot{C}\varepsilon_{el}$. This agrees better with the observed material response than classical plasticity theory.

Endochronic models :

The endochronic theory was originated by Valanis for the description of mechanical behaviour of metals. This continuous model for elastic behaviour was developed which doesn't require specific definition of yield condition and a cumbersome hardening rule. Valanis showed that by employing a pseudo time scale (intrinsic time or endochronic time), a constitutive equation in integral or differential form could be successfully used to describe metal behaviour including strain hardening, unloading and reloading, and continued cyclic straining. The formulation of endochronic models for concrete is based on an extensive set of functions, which fit experimentally observed effects like inelasticity, inelastic dilatancy, strain softening and hardening, rate dependency. Even though this model provided superior results, its popularity is restricted by its complexity. Various numerical coefficients are required for the development of a constitutive law, which are required to be estimated by curve fitting of available experimental data. However there are few experimental data existing for such purpose and it is difficult to obtain materials parameters.

c) Damage mechanics based models :

Here the modeling of progressive crack propagation and concentration of microcracks in concrete is done based on laws of thermodynamics and continuum damage mechanics. It is assumed that stiffness degradation takes place as a result of continuous material damage. In general there are two types of variables, which are used to represent material damage. One variable accounts for isotropic or scalar damage, which is related to the collapse of the microporous structure of the material. The other type accounts for anisotropic or tensorial damage, which is related to the coalescence of microcracks in the material. The fundamental assumption in this model is that the local damage in the material can be averaged and represented in the form of damage variables, which are related to the tangential stiffness tensor of the material. The models of this type can describe progressive damage of concrete occurring at the microscopic level through the variables defined at the level of macroscopic stress-strain relationship. The main advantage of this model is that it has got a sound physical background. However, it is not able to reproduce all facets of the behaviour of quasibrittle material like concrete.

d) Microplane models :

Micromechanical models attempts to develop the macroscopic stress-strain relationship from the mechanics of microstructure. These types of models project the strain tensor for a material point to numerous spatially oriented planes containing this point. The constitutive relations are formulated for each one of these planes. The macroscopic strain and stress tensors at the point under consideration are determined as a summation /integration of all these vectors on planes of various orientations (microplanes) under the assumption of static and kinematic constraint. Thus the stresses on these planes are obtained. The main advantage of microplane models is its conceptual clarity as the model is formulated in terms of vectors and the inherent nature of satisfying tensorial invariance requirements. The disadvantage in the microplane model is the huge computational work and storage requirement.

e) Crack models :

All the abovementioned models do not account for tensile behaviour of concrete in an extensive manner. Hence they are to be combined with a crack model to cater nonlinear response of reinforced concrete dominated by progressive cracking. Although cracking is the dominant source of nonlinear material behaviour in plain concrete, but in cracked reinforced concrete tensile stresses are still taken care of by the reinforcements. Hence they need to be handle with care and an adequate modeling of cracks is indispensable for accurate prediction of displacement and stresses. Fig. 3.2-9 shows /explains the distribution of stress and stiffness in a cracked concrete.

Cracking is the major source of nonlinearity in RC structures. Hence a realistic crack model is necessary in order to predict the load-deformation behaviour accurately. The selection of crack model depends on the purpose of finite element analysis. Mainly two types of crack models are available in the literature; discrete and smeared crack model. For the purpose of study of overall behaviour of concrete, the smeared crack model is a good choice where concern for crack pattern and local damage is of secondary importance.

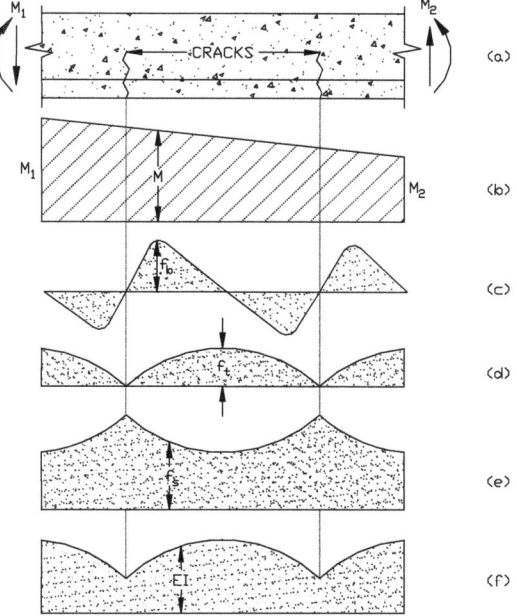

Fig. 3.2-9 : Effects of cracking in RC beam

(a) Part of a beam   (d) Distribution of tensile stress in concrete
(b) Bending moment distribution   (e) Distribution of tensile stress in reinforcement
(c) Bond stress distribution   (f) Flexural stiffness distribution in elastic range

Discrete crack model :

The first finite element analysis of RC structures, which includes the effect of cracking, was developed by *Ngo /Scordelis (1967)*. It considered linear elastic analysis of RC beams with predefined cracks by separating the nodes in the finite element mesh (Fig. 3.2-10) and thus defining a discrete crack model. In general, joint elements are introduced between the separated element nodes. The stiffness of such joint element depends on the crack width. Such discrete crack algorithm is computationally costly since the domain needs to be redefined everytime whenever a crack occurs and also bandwidth of stiffness matrix is destroyed. For this reason, discrete crack models are not popular, but it offers advantage in situations where the material behavior in the vicinity of crack i.e. localized behavior is of primary interest. They are not generally applicable and in particular to the 3D analysis.

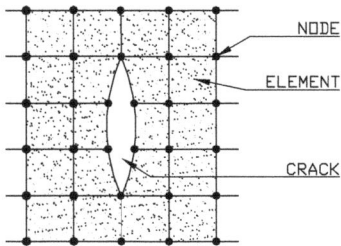

Fig. 3.2-10 : Discrete crack model

Smeared crack model :

Within the smeared crack approach, cracking is considered at the integration points. The cracks are assumed to be smeared over the proportionate regions of integration point with an assumption of only average stresses-strain relations. The concept of smeared crack model was proposed for the analysis of reinforced concrete surface structures and focused on the numerical treatment of cracked reinforced concrete in a state of plane stress, but the same may also be applied for the sake of 3D analyses due to its simplicity in numerical implementation. Also such models allow a good approximation of the global structural behaviour.

Although this approach seems to be simple to implement, it has a major drawback as long as finite element analysis is concerned. When a single element cracks, the stiffness of the entire structure is greatly reduced resulting in continuous strain increase at all other integration point in subsequent iterations. Thus leading to softening of a large portion of material in the structure and overall behaviour of the system becomes finite element mesh dependent. This difficulty can be overcome by introducing the fracture energy concept.

In this context, two different methods emerged viz. the fixed crack and the rotating crack model. In *fixed crack model*, cracks are supposed to form in a direction perpendicular to the principal stress direction when it exceeds concrete tensile strength and the crack direction remains unchanged in course of subsequent loading. In 3D problems, a maximum of three crack planes may develop at each integration point. Fixed crack models often predict wrong crack directions and hence overestimates the stiffness and ultimate load. This difficulty becomes insignificant for higher percentage of reinforcement present in the RC structure, when rotation of principal axes is small. In fact, it was well accepted by the researcher at the very early stages due to its easy formulation. Subsequent studies, however, showed that it causes numerical instability as a result of singularity in stiffness matrix and later on this difficulty was overcome by introducing variable cracked shear modulus. In *rotating crack model*, crack direction changes with subsequent loading path depending on the current principal strain direction. Also the assumption of no shear strain in the crack plane eliminates the requirement of cracked shear modulus. This model is particularly useful in analytical studies of global behavior of RC structures rather than the local effects in the vicinity of a crack. As such these models are conceptually simple. Only some models based on hypoelastic theory with rotating crack is being presented here as the proposed model is based on hypoelastic material properties.

3.3 Reinforcement :

RC structures are highly non-homogeneous medium due to discrete presence of the reinforcements. While modeling RC structures as layered structure, many authors have considered steel as a separate layer embedded and distributed evenly. Hardly a few literatures are reported, where due attention has been paid to model the reinforcing steel with different physical /mechanical properties in its exact spatial position in the respect to the element. That is to say that when RC structures are modeled based on continuum mechanics, contribution and distribution of stiffness of reinforcements should be considered appropriately and in an implicit manner. In general there are three methods available for modeling of reinforcement, e.g. the discrete, the smeared and the embedded approach.

a) Discrete approach :

In this method, reinforcements are considered as individual truss elements, which are connected to the mesh only at the concrete/parent element nodes. This approach of modeling of reinforcements is very simple and straightforward as suggested by *Ngo /Scordelis (1967)*. Bond-slip may also be included without any difficulty, as additional degrees of freedom are not introduced. Furthermore, this way of modeling of reinforcement offers FE programs to handle situations very easily as no special attention is required to be paid for element formulation for the reinforcements. The disadvantage of discrete approach is that finite element mesh generation becomes dependent on reinforcement layout. Considering small concrete cover, aspect ratio of the finite elements becomes a challenging situation to derive response of the system in general. Also number of elements present in a system increases just to take care of the presence of the reinforcements while modeling reinforced concrete structure.

b) Smeared approach :

The smeared approach is more suitable for homogeneous or uniformly distributed reinforcements, such as wall panels. In this method, it is assumed that the reinforcements are smeared as a layer (steel) of equivalent thickness, which may be modeled as a separate layer consisting of plate elements. This method was widely used for layered analysis of reinforced concrete structure, where the entire thickness is divided into layers out of which one or two is absolutely reinforcement layer of equivalent thickness. Various investigators used this method widely to solve 3D problems necessarily modeling as an equivalent 2D system where plate /plane stress elements could be used with necessary simplification. So they can't be generally applied directly to model to 3D structures and also to a situation with varying percentage of reinforcements.

c) Embedded approach :

Within embedded approach, proposed by *Elwi and Hrudey (1989), Barzegar and Madipuddi (1994)*, these restrictions were removed. In this method, reinforcements are considered to be embedded within parent element. Moreover it is no way going to affect the mesh generation of the parent material and no additional nodes are required to be introduced to in the parent element. Even the reinforcements are superimposed as one-dimensional uni-axial element with the same displacement field as parent/concrete element without any additional node /DOF. They are allowed to intersect the parent element at any location and hence mesh design becomes independent of reinforcement layout. Here the author has used the same method proposed by *Barzegar /Maddipudi (1994), Cheng /Fan (1993), Gomes /Awruch (2001)* due to it's simplicity to handle problems of 3D analysis of reinforced concrete structures in perfect bond situation, when linear behaviour is studied to model the reinforcement and as it's an appealing method for straight reinforcements in isoparametric configurations. Even bond-slip may also be taken care of without any difficulty.

3.4 Reinforcement-Concrete Interface :

Forces are transferred between concrete and reinforcement by bond due to chemical adhesion, friction and mechanical interaction at the interface. Deformed bars shows better bond than plain bars due better mechanical interlocking with the rough surface. Since bond stresses in reinforced concrete structures vary greatly due to change in the value of steel stresses along the length, it becomes very pronounced at the end anchorages as well as in the vicinity of cracks and hence controls the behaviour of RC members particularly subjected to higher stress levels. Most interestingly perfect bonding is not true throughout the loading history of a reinforced concrete structures. At the interfaces of high stress transfer, bond stress is related to the relative movement between the mating surfaces due to the presence of the cracks. Practically, strain compatibility remains no longer valid at such situations. This incompatibility and associated crack propagation gives rise to relative displacement between steel and concrete which is better known as bond-slip. However, at lower stress levels when it behaves elastically, a simplified analysis of RC structures may suffice assuming a rigid /perfect bond in between the two. In fact, perfect bonding of the reinforcements with the concrete over-predicts the shear transfer and this lead to an over or under estimation of the response of the structure depending on specific situation. Since it is the objective of the study to investigate the bond-slip behaviour of reinforcing steel in more detail, a more sophisticated bond-slip model RC structure is used in the formulation under monotonic loading.

Bond behaviour

As highlighted above, bond behaviour is considered to be result of three different mechanisms; viz. chemical adhesion, friction and mechanical interlocking between the ribs of reinforcement and concrete. The bond strength, which arises out of chemical adhesion is significantly small and is destroyed immediately as slipping between the mating surfaces starts. The inclined forces which then further generated, still continues to transfer forces and also gives rise to a longitudinal component known as bond stress together with a radial component known as normal /splitting stress.

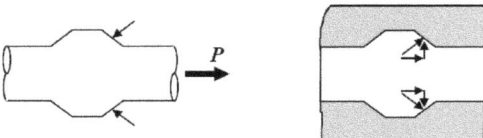

Fig. 3.4-1 : Bond stress and Splitting stress between mating surfaces

The inclined forces (refer Fig. 3.4-1) are balanced by the tensile stresses in the surrounding concrete. If this ring tensile stress is exceeds the concrete tensile strength, then longitudinal splitting cracks forms at the nearby surface of concrete parallel to the axis of the reinforcement (Fig. 3.4-2). The other type of crack that forms in the transverse direction due to the local pressure at the tip of the ribs is known as bond cracks. When splitting cracks are formed in absence of any transverse reinforcement, it is known as splitting failure. On the otherhand, when concrete surrounding the reinforcement is well confined, chances of splitting failure is reduced and a failure takes place known as pull-out bond failure. Mainly based on confinement, one of these two mechanisms is responsible for bond failure.

In general, this bond behaviour is described mathematically by relating the bond stress to the relative difference in movement between the reinforcement bar and the concrete, known as slip. The bond-slip relationship between the reinforcement and adjoining concrete depend on various parameters such as confinement, type of reinforcement, casting direction, bond condition and loading rate (Fig. 3.4-3). This behaviour is also due to the very different mechanical properties of the two materials.

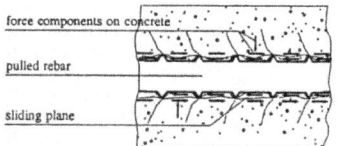
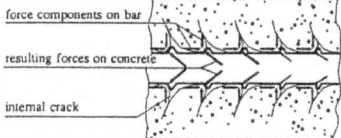

Fig. 3.4-2 : Pull-out bond failure and Splitting bond failure

The early investigations in this line were very much in evaluating the response of various parameters responsible for bond behaviour. Hence many experiments were carried out for pull-out tests. Concerning the numerical modeling of interface, efforts were made in recent years to formulate a consistent model with an objective to predict overall failure of a structure, but with help of either perfect bond model or slip. In this presentation, an attempt has been made to incorporate the gradual deterioration of concrete as a result of both rigid connection as well as considering a suitable bond model based on Modelcode90.

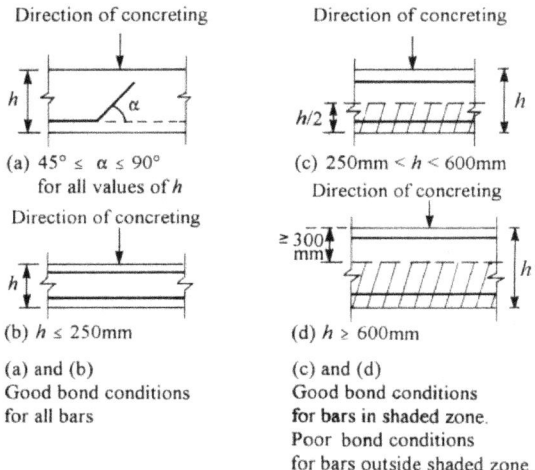

Fig. 3.4-3 : Direction of casting and bond condition

The classical embedded formulation of reinforcement implies perfect /rigid bond with the concrete, which is obtained by default. The rigid bond model is well applicable for reinforcements, where bond stress is not crucial, i.e. for stirrups, hoop bars and the minimum reinforcements, which is not provided against design forces. In art.-4.4, a brief discussion on interface material modeling along with FE modeling (using supplementary slip algorithm) has been provided to carry out numerical investigation for the main reinforcements to satisfy the purpose at hand.

3.5 FE Formulation (EAS Approach) :

The standard 20-noded hexahedral has shown robust performance in many applications. However, it has a high number of nodes, which necessitates large computational time. The linear 8-noded isoparametric elements are perhaps simplest constant strain elements. Although this standard linear quadrilateral or hexahedral elements possess least number of nodes in the elements of this type, they have shown some deficiencies in finite element analyses. They are unable to represent one of the most commonly occurring stress states, i.e. the state of bending stress.

This low order element has advantages for 3D analyses since it allow easy mesh generation and as well data interpretation. Also in order to achieve an acceptable accuracy in problems where bending is important, a large number of these element have to be used. The use of more number of elements in a finite element analyses again requires longer computational time and also computational stability will be better. It is therefore desirable to seek for an element with minimum number of nodes together with acceptable level of accuracy. Such a lower order element may be used for the purpose of analyses at hand, but after removing the deficiencies associated with the linear hexahedral element.

Several methods have been introduced previously to modify the standard linear quadrilateral and hexahedral elements. They have been discussed in length in chapter 2. The aim of this presentation is to apply one of these modifications to a linear 8-noded hexahedral element and to evaluate the efficiency as well as accuracy of the modified element by performing finite element(FE) analyses of some example problems. In particular, the source of error and the method used to modify the error /deficiencies of the standard 8-noded hexahedral linear element is discussed briefly in connection with the FE analysis of concrete structures.

One of the main causes of the deficiencies associated with lower order finite elements is their inability to represent the state of pure bending strains. The top and bottom edges of the finite element remain straight under pure bending moment. As a result, strain energy of the system generated by the normal strains $(\varepsilon_x, \varepsilon_y, \varepsilon_z)$ is increased. Since finite element stores the strain energy generated by both normal strain (ε) and shear strain (γ), a fictitious prediction of large shear strain results while approximating the state of pure bending. This unwanted shear strain is called as parasitic shear, which make an element very stiff. And this phenomenon becomes more significant for larger aspect ratio of the element. It also suffers from so-called volumetric locking. Hence this element in a FE analysis of problem that includes bending moment usually causes deflections to be grossly underestimated. In this work, 8-noded solid element HCiS18 as proposed by *Sousa et al. (2002)* based on extra compatible modes of deformation (Enhanced Assumed Strain : EAS) has been used for the analysis of RC structures.

3.6 Nonlinear Solution Techniques

Although most of the finite element software, which are commercially available, have wide range of application, they do not offer adequate material models, also suitably integrated for response /stress analysis. In this part of the presentation, a brief description has been given mainly about the integration of the model elucidated previously.

The numerical implementation of finite element model requires solution of Eq. 3.3-8. This is a system of simultaneous nonlinear equations, since components of element stiffness matrix depends on E and μ, which are a function of displacement vector. Earlier, the solution of this kind of equations is accomplished with an incremental method, where the load vector is divided into number of sufficiently small load increments, which successively applied with modification depending on solution algorithm used for the purpose.

At each load step /increment, a linear approximation of stiffness matrix is assumed and the resulting system of linear equilibrium equations is solved for displacement increments without correction. In this approach, external load does not made equal to internal resistance and hence unbalanced load is not taken care of appropriately. As a result, convergence criterion is not satisfied although displacement increments are incrementally improved and numerical solution differs from actual solution widely in successive load steps (Fig. 3.6-1).

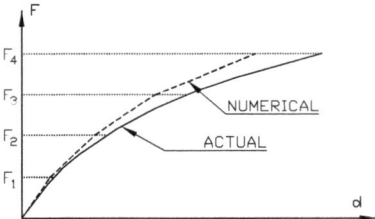

Fig. 3.6-1 : Incremental Method

Hence it is important to account for the correction phase to satisfy convergence criteria. Depending on the method followed to update the stiffness matrix during the correction phase, the iterative methods are proposed based on initial or constant stiffness method (Fig. 3.6-2a), tangent stiffness method (Fig. 3.6-2b) and the secant stiffness method (Fig. 3.6-2c).

The tangent stiffness method requires comparatively lesser number of iterations to arrive at solution, but the main disadvantage of the method is that the stiffness matrix has to be recomputed each time. As a result computation cost is increased. The initial stiffness method requires higher number of iterations, but the stiffness matrix is formed only once within the load step and hence computational cost is reduced substantially. Although tangent stiffness method is more efficient than initial stiffness method for smaller no of DOF, keeping the question of numerical stability aside. The third one, i.e. secant stiffness method is best suited for materials having softening response.

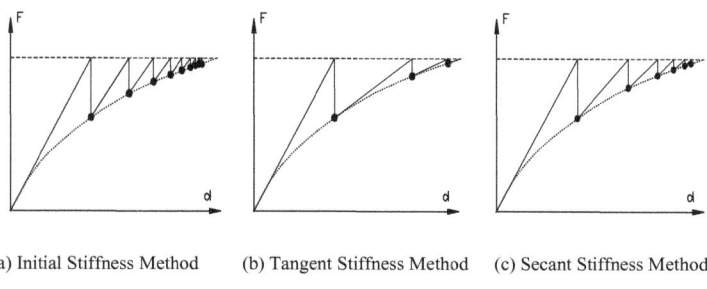

(a) Initial Stiffness Method   (b) Tangent Stiffness Method   (c) Secant Stiffness Method

Fig. 3.6-2 : Iterative Methods

In general, a method is apparent which may provide a combination of the above incremental and iterative schemes, where the load is applied incrementally and for each load increment successive iterations are performed. As a result this method provides higher accuracy. Such methods are known as step-iteration or mixed procedures.

3.7   Remarks :

The discussion on constitutive behaviour of concrete and existing models form the basis of constitutive material modeling for the entire range of load history, which has been expressed in terms of equations in the proposed FE modeling (Art. 4.2). Since, plain concrete is being considered as the medium or parent material in the reinforced concrete element, it requires also appropriate finite element modeling in three dimension under multiaxial stress state. Art. 3.5 throws some light in this line and necessitates FE formulation followed in art. 4.2.2. Modeling aspects of reinforcement and their interaction with parent material /medium i.e. concrete through bond-slip has also been discussed based on literature. Supplementary interface model is considered for the investigation work, which has been given the shape in art. 4.4. This chapter, in brief, summarizes the procedures to be adopted for the finite element implementation of the proposed model.

Chapter 4

Proposed Model
&
FE Implementation

Based on the basic modeling aspects for concrete, reinforcement and their composite action in regard to material behaviour as discussed in the previous chapter, a FE model has been prepared and employed, which uses EAS based lower order element. This chapter also includes a brief discussion on computational strategies followed and the steps of numerical implementation.

4.1   General :

In the following chapter, the behaviour of each constituent material and the derivation of the corresponding material stiffness are discussed separately. The proposed procedure utilizes 8-noded isometric solid /hexahedral elements HCiS18 with enhanced assumed strain (EAS) formulation, recently developed in the literature, to predict load-deformation and internal stresses produced in case of a simply supported RC beams and frames. It models the composite behaviour of concrete and reinforcements in rigid /perfect bond situation and their mutual interaction in bond-slip condition considering continuous interface elements at the material level. The numerical implementation of the same in both linear as well as nonlinear regime for reinforced concrete beams and frames (including the software developed for the purpose) are discussed separately and in detail. The phenomenological features and the computational implementation are presented in this chapter.

4.2   Modeling of Concrete :

In section 3.2, the constitutive behaviour of concrete and associated models is discussed. There is significant scatter in predictions of the behaviour of reinforced concrete and available experimental data under multi-axial stress conditions irrespective of the test methods. For all engineering purposes, the response of concrete under multi-axial stress states at working load condition may be considered elastic. Although an advanced model may serve as excellent tool provided concrete parameters including loading situations are known and to a specific situation. On the otherhand, a simple and robust model may provide better service while dealing with standard structures.

4.2.1   Material Modeling :

Hence a simple model has been implemented in this work. Concrete is assumed to behave linearly elastic and orthotropic even in multi-axial stress states for all engineering purpose. The proposed model includes the effect of triaxial nonlinear stress-strain law, tensile cracking, compression crushing and strain softening under monotonic loading condition. As plain cement concrete large relative displacements, only small deformation has been accounted for along with rigid body rotations. Hence a total Lagrangian formulation has been followed although with engineering stress and strain in the finite element implementation. The total secant stiffness has been used for the incremental stress-strain relations to account for strain softening at higher stress levels. To determine the strength both in compression and tension, five-parameter William and Warnke criterion is employed.

4.2.1.1   Concrete material matrix

Initially concrete is considered as an isotropic material and then it becomes anisotropic during subsequent phases of loading. Accordingly the stress at each point is defined by three principal stresses and the concrete is considered as a nonlinear orthotropic medium with the direction orthotropy coinciding with the principal stress directions (*Elwi and Murray 1979, Balan et al 1997*). In this approach, the incremental stress-strain relations of concrete in multiaxial stress state for an orthotropically anisotropic medium can be written as

$$\{d\sigma\} = [D_P]\{d\varepsilon\}$$

Eq. 4.2-1

where $\{d\sigma\}$ and $\{d\varepsilon\}$ are the vectors of stress and strain increments respectively and $[D_P]$ is the incremental concrete constitutive matrix w.r.t. the local orthotropic axes (1, 2, 3). By employing symmetry condition of the compliance tensor, the incremental stress-strain relationship of concrete in local coordinate system is expressed as

$$\begin{Bmatrix} d\sigma_1 \\ d\sigma_2 \\ d\sigma_3 \\ d\tau_{12} \\ d\tau_{23} \\ d\tau_{31} \end{Bmatrix} = \frac{1}{\Omega} \begin{bmatrix} E_1(1-\mu_{23}\mu_{32}) & E_1(\mu_{21}+\mu_{23}\mu_{32}) & E_1(\mu_{31}+\mu_{21}\mu_{32}) & 0 & 0 & 0 \\ E_2(\mu_{12}+\mu_{13}\mu_{32}) & E_2(1-\mu_{13}\mu_{31}) & E_2(\mu_{32}+\mu_{12}\mu_{31}) & 0 & 0 & 0 \\ E_3(\mu_{13}+\mu_{12}\mu_{23}) & E_3(\mu_{23}+\mu_{13}\mu_{21}) & E_3(1-\mu_{12}\mu_{21}) & 0 & 0 & 0 \\ 0 & 0 & 0 & G_{12}\Omega & 0 & 0 \\ 0 & 0 & 0 & 0 & G_{23}\Omega & 0 \\ 0 & 0 & 0 & 0 & 0 & G_{31}\Omega \end{bmatrix} \begin{Bmatrix} d\varepsilon_1 \\ d\varepsilon_2 \\ d\varepsilon_3 \\ d\gamma_{12} \\ d\gamma_{23} \\ d\gamma_{31} \end{Bmatrix}$$

Eq. 4.2-2

Where $\quad i = 1,2,3$ stands for axis of orthotropy;

$d\varepsilon_i$ = normal strain increment in i^{th} direction

$d\gamma_{ij}$ = shear strain increment in plane i-j;

$d\sigma_i$ = normal stress increment in i^{th} direction;

$d\tau_{ij}$ = shear stress increment in plane i-j;

μ_{ij} = Poisson's ratio in i^{th} direction due to stress in j^{th} direction;

$\Omega = \mu_{21}\mu_{12} - \mu_{31}\mu_{13} - \mu_{23}\mu_{32} - \mu_{12}\mu_{23}\mu_{31} - \mu_{21}\mu_{32}\mu_{13}$

E_i = total secant modulus in the ith direction of orthotropy;

G_{ij} = total secant shear modulus in plane i-j

(assumed as invariant under the transformation of coordinates)

$$= \frac{E_i.E_j}{E_i(1+\mu_{ij}) + E_j(1+\mu_{ji})}$$

Eq. 4.2-3

Since $[D_P]$, the incremental concrete constitutive matrix is defined w.r.t. the local orthotropic axes, the same has to be transformed to the global coordinate system before element stiffness matrix is formed, as also mentioned in Eq. 4.2-1 using the standard 3D transformation matrix given by;

$$T_{\sigma.gl} = \begin{bmatrix} l_1^2 & m_1^2 & n_1^2 & 2l_1m_1 & 2m_1n_1 & 2n_1l_1 \\ l_2^2 & m_1^2 & n_2^2 & 2l_2m_2 & 2m_2n_2 & 2n_2l_2 \\ l_3^2 & m_1^2 & n_3^2 & 2l_3m_3 & 2m_3n_3 & 2n_3l_3 \\ l_1l_2 & m_1m_2 & n_1n_2 & l_1m_2 + l_2m_1 & m_1n_2 + m_2n_1 & l_1n_2 + l_2n_1 \\ l_2l_3 & m_2m_3 & n_2n_3 & l_2m_3 + l_3m_2 & m_2n_3 + m_3n_2 & l_2n_3 + l_3n_2 \\ l_3l_1 & m_3m_1 & n_3n_1 & l_3m_1 + l_1m_3 & m_3n_1 + m_1n_3 & l_3n_1 + l_1n_3 \end{bmatrix} \qquad \text{Eq. 4.2-4}$$

where l_i, m_i and n_i are the direction cosines of principal stress w.r.t. global coordinate system.

4.2.1.2 Equivalent Uniaxial Strains

For the incremental concrete constitutive matrix defined in Eq. 4.2-2, the evaluation of nine incremental hypoelastic moduli must be described. In this regard, the concept of equivalent uniaxial strain as introduced by Darwin and Pecknold(1977) is adopted in the material model. The concept of equivalent uniaxial strain actually defines the variation of E_i with respect to the variation of stress. It is nothing but a fictitious strain that would occur due to uniaxial loading situation transformed from actual incremental strain and is a measure of variation of material damage parameter. The method in brief is as follows;

Eq. 4.2-2 is written as

$$\begin{Bmatrix} d\sigma_1 \\ d\sigma_2 \\ d\sigma_3 \\ d\tau_{12} \\ d\tau_{23} \\ d\tau_{31} \end{Bmatrix} = \begin{bmatrix} E_1 & 0 & 0 & 0 & 0 & 0 \\ 0 & E_2 & 0 & 0 & 0 & 0 \\ 0 & 0 & E_3 & 0 & 0 & 0 \\ 0 & 0 & 0 & G_{12} & 0 & 0 \\ 0 & 0 & 0 & 0 & G_{23} & 0 \\ 0 & 0 & 0 & 0 & 0 & G_{31} \end{bmatrix} \begin{Bmatrix} d\varepsilon_{u1} \\ d\varepsilon_{u2} \\ d\varepsilon_{u3} \\ d\gamma_{12} \\ d\gamma_{23} \\ d\gamma_{31} \end{Bmatrix} \qquad \text{Eq. 4.2-5}$$

The right hand side of the above equation can be defined as the vector of equivalent uniaxial strains, whose components may be defined in terms of actual incremental strains by comparing with the appropriate terms of the Eq. 4.2-2 as

$$\begin{Bmatrix} d\varepsilon_{u1} \\ d\varepsilon_{u2} \\ d\varepsilon_{u3} \end{Bmatrix} = \frac{1}{\Omega} \begin{bmatrix} (1-\mu_{23}\mu_{32}) & (\mu_{21}+\mu_{23}\mu_{32}) & (\mu_{31}+\mu_{21}\mu_{32}) \\ (\mu_{12}+\mu_{13}\mu_{32}) & (1-\mu_{13}\mu_{31}) & (\mu_{32}+\mu_{12}\mu_{31}) \\ (\mu_{13}+\mu_{12}\mu_{23}) & (\mu_{23}+\mu_{13}\mu_{21}) & (1-\mu_{12}\mu_{21}) \end{bmatrix} \begin{Bmatrix} d\varepsilon_1 \\ d\varepsilon_2 \\ d\varepsilon_3 \end{Bmatrix}$$

Eq. 4.2-6

The incremental equivalent uniaxial strains may be evaluated using the above equation as

$$d\varepsilon_{ui} = \frac{d\sigma_i}{E_i}, \quad (i=1,2,3) \qquad\qquad \text{Eq. 4.2-7}$$

The total equivalent uniaxial strains may be determined from Eq. 4.2-7 by integrating over the loading path as;

$$\varepsilon_{ui} = \int \frac{d\sigma_i}{E_i}, \quad (i=1,2,3) \qquad\qquad \text{Eq. 4.2-8}$$

It's obvious from the above relationship that the equivalent uniaxial strain increment represents the strain increment in i^{th} direction that the material is going to exhibit under a uniaxial stress increment with other stresses kept equal to zero. Eq. 4.2-6 is defined in the direction of principal axes of orthtropy of the material and since it is assumed to follow the current directions of principal stress, $d\varepsilon_{ui}$ must be defined with respect to the current principal axes of orthotropy. This indicates equivalence between the equivalent strain parameters of elasto-plastic theory and the present equivalent uniaxial strains. However, since ε_{ui} is not transformable, they are assumed to be defined only in the current principal stress directions. The fundamental idea behind this kind of stress-strain relation is that once the multidimensional situation is expressed in terms of uniaxial case, stress-strain curves similar to the uniaxial stress-strain response may be used.

4.2.1.3   Uniaxial Stress-Equivalent Strain Relation

A uniaxial concrete law is required to obtain the stress corresponding to ε_{ui}. *Kwon and Spacone (2002), Balan et al. (2001)* propose to use the Popovics' curve (strain hardening model), originally introduced by Darwin and Pecknold (1977), upto the peak compressive stress under monotonic loading. It assumes that the actual stresses are the functions of the current equivalent uniaxial strains, which are calculated based on the actual strain increments. For $(\varepsilon / \varepsilon_c) < 1$ i.e. compressive ascending region of concrete, the law is defined by

$$\sigma_i = R_{ci} \cdot \frac{K_i \left(\dfrac{\varepsilon_{ui}}{\varepsilon_{ci}} \right)}{1 + A_i \cdot \left(\dfrac{\varepsilon_{ui}}{\varepsilon_{ci}} \right) + B_i \cdot \left(\dfrac{\varepsilon_{ui}}{\varepsilon_{ci}} \right)^2 + C_i \cdot \left(\dfrac{\varepsilon_{ui}}{\varepsilon_{ci}} \right)^3}, \quad (i = 1,2,3) \qquad \text{Eq. 4.2-9}$$

where notations have got the following expression :

$$K_i = E_0 \cdot \frac{\varepsilon_{ci}}{R_{ci}}, \quad K_{ei} = \frac{\varepsilon_{fi}}{\varepsilon_{ci}}, \quad K_{oi} = \frac{R_{ci}}{R_{fi}}, \qquad \text{Eq. 4.2-10}$$

$$A_i = C_i + K_i - 2, \quad B_i = 1 - 2.C_i, \quad C_i = K_i \cdot \frac{(K_{oi} - 1)}{(K_{ei} - 1)^2} - \frac{1}{K_{ei}} \qquad \text{Eq. 4.2-11}$$

where E_0 = Initial modus of elasticity;

ε_{ui} = Equivalent uniaxial strain in i[th] direction;

R_{ci} = Concrete strength in i[th] direction at current principal stress ratio;

ε_{ci} = Corresponding equivalent uniaxial strain;

R_{fi}, ε_{fi} = control point /breaking point in the descending branch of the stress-strain curve.

For $(\varepsilon / \varepsilon_c) > 1$ i.e. compressive descending region of concrete, the stress is reduced linearly and concrete is assumed to crush if any point reaches at ultimate stress $R_{fi}(= k.R_{ci})$ as shown in Fig. 4.2-1. The ultimate stress of concrete was assumed to be $R_{fi} = 0.75 R_{ci}$ and the corresponding ultimate strain (ε_{fi}) was .00399.

The required incremental secant modulus could be determined directly on division of Eq. 4.2-9 by ε_{ui} according to *Elwi and Murray (1979), Balan et al. (1997)* as;

$$E_i = \frac{E_0}{1 + A_i \cdot \left(\dfrac{\varepsilon_{ui}}{\varepsilon_{ci}}\right) + B_i \cdot \left(\dfrac{\varepsilon_{ui}}{\varepsilon_{ci}}\right)^2 + C_i \cdot \left(\dfrac{\varepsilon_{ui}}{\varepsilon_{ci}}\right)^3} \qquad (i = 1,2,3) \qquad \text{Eq. 4.2-12}$$

For descending branch of the proposed curve in Fig. 4.2-1, E_{soft} has been evaluated based on Rabezuk et al.(2005) to account for strain-softening during compressive loading.

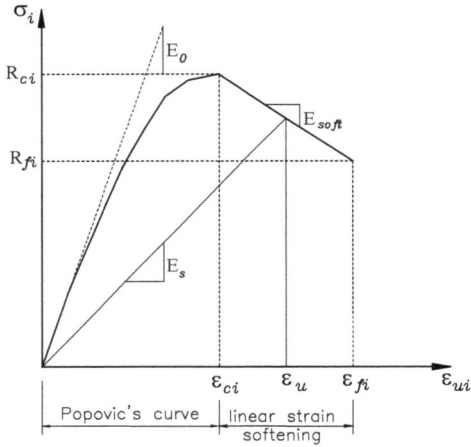

Fig. 4.2-1 : Monotonic Stress-Equivalent Uniaxial Strain Curve of Concrete

4.2.1.4 Poisson's Ratio

It is also necessary to define the variation of Poisson's ratio for implementation of the model. As suggested by Chen(1982), the variation of Poisson's ration is negligible until the stress level reaches almost 80 percent of the peak compressive stress (R_{ci}) in the ascending branch of the stress-strain curve. As the stress level further increases till it reaches R_{ci}, a subsequent volumetric expansion of concrete takes place due higher value of strain. For this region, the following expression is used to describe the variation of the same as per Balan et al.(1997)

$$\mu_{ij} = \sqrt{\mu_{ui} \cdot \mu_{uj} \cdot \frac{E_i}{E_j}} \qquad (i = 1,2,3)$$ Eq. 4.2-13

where μ_{ij} = Poisson's ratio defined as function of cubic function of equivalent uniaxial strains as

$$\mu_{ui} = \mu_0 \left[1 + A_i \cdot \left(\frac{\varepsilon_{ui}}{\varepsilon_{ci}} \right) + B_i \cdot \left(\frac{\varepsilon_{ui}}{\varepsilon_{ci}} \right)^2 + C_i \cdot \left(\frac{\varepsilon_{ui}}{\varepsilon_{ci}} \right)^3 \right], \ (i = 1,2,3)$$ Eq. 4.2-14

where μ_0 = initial Poison's ratio and other parameters are same as defined in Eq. 4.2-11 except $K_i = \frac{1}{2\mu_0}$. For the stress level R_{ci}, μ_{ij} reaches almost a constant value of 0.36 and remains constant till concrete reaches the breaking stress due to dilatancy phenomenon.

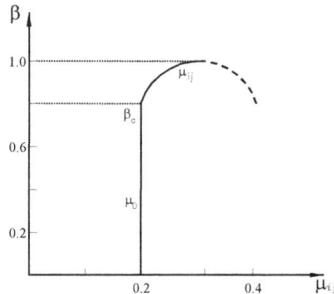

Fig. 4.2-2 : Variation of secant value of Poisson's Ratio

Chen /Saleeb (1982) suggested and as also reported by various literature against experimental investigations, the variation of the secant value of Poisson's ration is given by the following Fig. 4.2-2

Defining a term *nonlinearity index* $\beta = \dfrac{\sigma_i}{\sigma_{ci}}$ in compression and $\beta = \dfrac{\sigma_i}{\sigma_{ti}}$ in tension.

$$
\left.
\begin{aligned}
\mu_{ij} &= \mu_0 && \text{for } \beta \le \beta_a (= 0.8) \\
\mu_{ij} &= \mu_{ij}\,(\text{Eq. 4.2-13}) && \text{for } \beta_a < \beta \le 1.0 \\
\mu_{ij} &= 0.36 && \text{for } \beta > 1 \text{ till } \varepsilon_{fi} \\
\mu_{ij} &= 0.0 && \text{beyond } \varepsilon_{fi}
\end{aligned}
\right\}
\qquad \text{Eq. 4.2-15}
$$

Only little is known about the increase of Poisson's Ratio in the post failure regime (when $\beta > 1$) and hence it is assumed to be constant till it reaches breaking point and equal to zero beyond the same.

4.2.1.5 Principal Stresses

The proposed model is based on the concept of equivalent uniaxial strain and is defined on material axis of orthotropy, which is assumed to coincide with the direction of principal stress at each load step. For three-dimensional problem, the principal stresses are interpreted mathematically as eigenvalues of σ_i and the following expression used to determine principal stresses (σ_i, $i = 1,2,3$) as per *Boresi et al. (1985)*;

$$
\begin{Bmatrix} \sigma_1 \\ \sigma_2 \\ \sigma_3 \end{Bmatrix} = \begin{Bmatrix} \sigma_o \\ \sigma_o \\ \sigma_o \end{Bmatrix} + \frac{2}{\sqrt{3}}.J_2 \begin{Bmatrix} \cos(\theta) \\ \cos\left(\theta - \dfrac{2}{3}\pi\right) \\ \cos\left(\theta + \dfrac{2}{3}\pi\right) \end{Bmatrix}
\qquad \text{Eq. 4.2-16}
$$

where,

octahedral normal stress $\sigma_o = \dfrac{1}{3}\left(\sigma_{xx} + \sigma_{yy} + \sigma_{zz}\right)$,

second deviator stress invariant $J_2 = \dfrac{1}{6}\left[(\sigma_1 - \sigma_2)^2 + (\sigma_2 - \sigma_3)^2 + (\sigma_3 - \sigma_1)^2\right]$,

third deviator stress invariant $J_3 = (\sigma_1 - \sigma_o)(\sigma_2 - \sigma_o)(\sigma_3 - \sigma_o)$,

Lode angle $\theta = \frac{1}{3} Cos^{-1} \left(\frac{3\sqrt{3}}{2} \cdot \frac{J_3}{J_2^{3/2}} \right)$.

The directions of principal stresses are the associated eigenvectors of σ_i and the same is calculated using the condition $n_1^2 + n_2^2 + n_3^2 = 1$ in addition to the three equations available on projecting the stresses on three axes in a way also shown in detail in Appendix (art. 6.5).

4.2.1.6   Ultimate Surface

The evaluation of incremental variable moduli in Eq. 4.2-12 also requires the specification of the parameters defined in Eq. 4.2-10 and Eq. 4.2-11. As these parameters vary with the principal stress ratio, they are determined by defining a surface in the principal stress space to calculate three values of R_{ci} and a surface in the uniaxial strain space to calculate three values of ε_{ci} corresponding to the values of R_{ci}. Such a surface, which defines ultimate values of strength or strain for a particular stress ratio, is termed as 'failure surface'. This failure surface is more appropriately called as 'ultimate strength surface' in this case as it also takes care of strain softening of the material.

Choosing 'ultimate strength surface' for material like concrete is very crucial for prediction of its behaviour under complex multiaxial stress state. Yield criteria based on single shear stress, e.g. Tresca, Von Mises etc do not necessarily represent the real failure /yield of materials under complex stress state. The other category of yield criteria e.g. Argyris criteria etc. based on curve fitting of multi-parameter, although having complex mathematical expressions, however can simulate accurately smooth models for materials under complex stress state such as concrete.

The ultimate strength surface of concrete due to multiaxial stress state is described in this presentation by considering the five parameter surface originally proposed by Argyris, later on modified by William and Warnke for high compression zone (*Chen 1982*). In connection with three-dimensional incremental model for describing the nonlinear behavior of concrete, this five-parameter model considers the curved meridians using second order parabolic expressions and non-circular trace in the deviatoric plane using elliptical curve. As a result, it has a smooth surface with unique gradient and continuous derivative everywhere and becomes valid for all stress combinations in the range of most practical applications including tensile stresses .The surface is defined by the following equation ;

$$\frac{F}{f_{cu}} - S \geq 0$$

Eq. 4.2-17

where, F = a function of the principal stress state ($\sigma_1, \sigma_2, \sigma_3$).

$$= \frac{1}{\sqrt{15}} \left[(\sigma_1 - \sigma_2)^2 + (\sigma_2 - \sigma_3)^2 + (\sigma_3 - \sigma_1)^2 \right]^{1/2}$$

Eq. 4.2-18

S = failure surface expressed in terms of principal stresses

$$= \frac{2r_2(r_2^2 - r_1^2).Cos\theta + r_2(2r_1 - r_2).\left[4(r_2^2 - r_1^2).Cos^2\theta + 5r_1^2 - 4r_1r_2\right]^{1/2}}{4(r_2^2 - r_1^2).Cos^2\theta + (r_2 - 2r_1)^2}$$

Eq. 4.2-19

and five input parameters $f_t, f_{cu}, f_{cb}, f_1, f_2$ are as follows

  f_t = ultimate uniaxial tensile stress,

  f_{cu} = ultimate uniaxial compressive stress,

  f_{cb} = ultimate biaxial compressive stress,

  f_1 = the ultimate compressive stress point for a state of biaxial compression on tensile meridion and

  f_2 = the ultimate compressive stress point for a state of biaxial compression on compressive meridion

However this failure surface is defined in terms of two parameters viz. f_t, f_{cu} and the rest three parameters are expressed in terms of f_{cu}. Both the function 'F' and the failure surface 'S' are expressed in terms of the principal stresses ($\sigma_1, \sigma_2, \sigma_3$), where, $\sigma_1 = \max(\sigma_1, \sigma_2, \sigma_3)$, $\sigma_3 = \min(\sigma_1, \sigma_2, \sigma_3)$ and $\sigma_1 \geq \sigma_2 \geq \sigma_3$. The terms used to define 'S' are

$$Cos\theta = \frac{(2\sigma_1 - \sigma_2 - \sigma_3)}{\sqrt{2}\left[(\sigma_1 - \sigma_2)^2 + (\sigma_2 - \sigma_3)^2 + (\sigma_3 - \sigma_1)^2\right]^{1/2}}$$ Eq. 4.2-20

$$r_1 = a_0 + a_1\xi + a_2\xi^2,$$

$$r_2 = b_0 + b_1\xi + b_2\xi^2$$ Eq. 4.2-21

with $\xi = \sigma_h/f_{cu}$ and $\sigma_h = (\sigma_1 + \sigma_2 + \sigma_3)/3$

The values of the undetermined co-efficient $a_0, a_1, a_2, b_0, b_1, b_2$ may be found from the reference *Elwi /Murray (1979)* using the nondimensional values of the tensile and biaxial compression strength as $\alpha_t = f_t/f_{cu}$ and $\alpha_c = f_{cb}/f_{cu}$. The same has also been listed down in the Appendix.

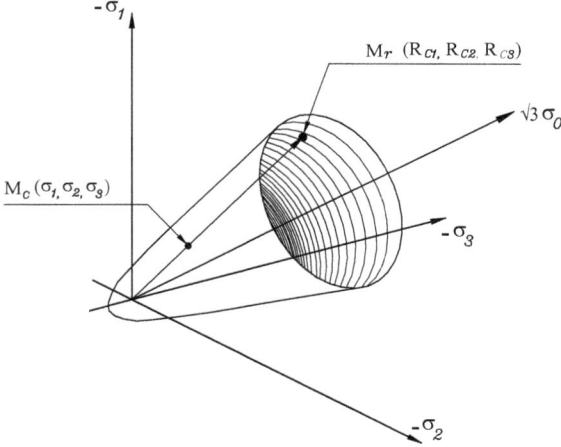

Fig. 4.2-3 : Concrete Failure Surface and Current Material Strength

Similarly, for the evaluation of the ultimate equivalent uniaxial strains ε_{ci} corresponding to ultimate strength R_{ci}, there exists a surface in the equivalent uniaxial strain space that has the same form as the ultimate strength surface defined earlier. This surface is defined by replacing $\sigma_1, \sigma_2, \sigma_3, f_t, f_{cu}$ in Eq. 4.2-17 by $\varepsilon_{u1}, \varepsilon_{u2}, \varepsilon_{u3}, \varepsilon_t, \varepsilon_{cu}$ respectively.

The current concrete strength values $R_{ci}(i = 1,2,3)$ are determined from the ultimate strength surface. For the current stress level, first the corresponding principal stress values $\sigma_1, \sigma_2, \sigma_3$ are calculated following Eq. 4.2-16. A point $M_c(\sigma_1, \sigma_2, \sigma_3)$ is considered in the principal stress space and then a line that extends from origin through M_c intersects the ultimate strength surface at $M_R(R_{c1}, R_{c2}, R_{c3})$ where R_{ci} is the required current concrete strength of concrete in the ith-direction (Fig. 4.2-3). Here this concept has been utilized to find R_{ci}, but with reference to the rendulic plane as proposed by *Elwi and Murray (1979), Bouzaiene and Massicote(1997)*.

Also the parameters σ_{fl} and ε_{fl}, on the descending branch of the stress-equivalent strain curve in Fig. 4.2-1 are to be supplied in order to calculate incremental moduli defined in Eq. 4.2-16. Since these two parameters controls the nature of descending branch and vary from case to case indicating thereby highly test dependent, it is assumed as proposed by Balan et al.(1995)

> For compression loading : $\sigma_{fl} = 0.85.R_{ci}$ and $\varepsilon_{fl} = 1.41.\varepsilon_{ci}$.
>
> For tension loading : $\sigma_{fl} = 0.25.R_{ci}$ and $\varepsilon_{fl} = 4.0.\varepsilon_{ci}$.

4.2.1.7   Concrete in tension

Nonlinear behaviour of concrete is characterized by formation and propagation of tensile cracks. To model the cracking behaviour of concrete under tensile stress, smeared crack approach is considered as proposed by *Kolleger and Mehlhorn (1987)*. According to the smeared crack approach, cracking of concrete is assumed to form at the integration points of the finite element in a plane perpendicular to the direction of maximum principal tensile stress as soon as this tensile stress reaches the specified tensile strength. Once a crack is formed, the behaviour of concrete at that integration point becomes orthotropic and it continues to remain for that load step. New crack directions are considered to be initiated at a different load step.

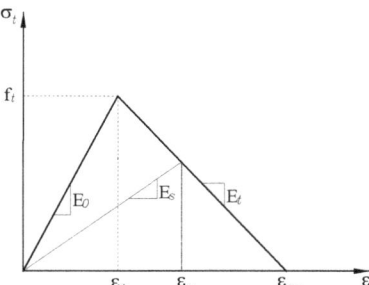

Fig. 4.2-4 : Linear strain softening model of concrete in tension

The response of concrete under tensile stress has been assumed linear until fracture surface is reached as in Fig. 4.2-4. After concrete cracking, tensile stress is not immediately set to zero but is gradually released by a linear strain softening behaviour as in *Cho et al.(2002)*. Due to bond effects, cracked concrete between the cracks carries a certain amount of tensile force normal to the crack plane. The concrete adheres to the reinforcing bars and contributes to the overall stiffness of the structure. Several approaches are there to model this tension stiffening effect. Here, the total strain increment is assumed to be consisting of two parts: the concrete strain increment and the crack strain increment. The strain softening modulus E_t is derived based on fracture energy of concrete as follows.

$$\frac{1}{E_t} = \frac{1}{E_0} + \frac{1}{C_{cr}}$$
Eq. 4.2-22

where, cracking modulus $C_{cr} = -\dfrac{f_t^2 . w_f}{2.G_f}$, w_f = crack bandwidth and G_f = fracture energy of concrete required to produce one unit of area of a continuous crack.

It has been observed from various experimental data that after formation of a crack, sufficient shear stress could be transferred across the rough surfaces of cracked concrete due to aggregate interlocking and reinforcement ratio. A common practice to consider this phenomenon in a smeared crack model is to attribute an appropriate value to cracked shear modulus G_c in terms of uncracked shear modulus G with an appropriate shear retention factor, which has been followed by many researchers. In present study, an approach similar to *Cho et al.(2002)* has been adopted, where cracked shear modulus is assumed to be reduced linearly as a function of current tensile strain (ε) when it exceeds tensile strain (ε_t).

$$G_c = \alpha_c . G \left(1 - \frac{\varepsilon}{\varepsilon_m} \right), \text{ for } \varepsilon_t \le \varepsilon \le \varepsilon_m \qquad \text{Eq. 4.2-23}$$

where α_c is used as 0.5 for one crack, 0.25 for more than one crack and ε_m is used as 0.004.

When a crack is formed, the material stiffness is reduced in the failure plane in the direction normal and parallel to the crack and the Poisson's ratios (μ_{12}, μ_{31}) become equal to zero in the crack plane and the stress normal to the crack is equal to zero. Thus the material starts to strain soften in the principal stress direction. Gradually σ_1 reduces to zero and the material looses stiffness in that direction. In this light, the generalized stress-strain relation defined in Eq. 4.2-2 needs to be modified for cracked concrete as along with associated terms ;

$$\begin{Bmatrix} d\sigma_1 \\ d\sigma_2 \\ d\sigma_3 \\ d\tau_{12} \\ d\tau_{23} \\ d\tau_{31} \end{Bmatrix} = \frac{1}{\Omega} \begin{bmatrix} E_1(1-\mu_{23}\mu_{32}) & 0 & 0 & 0 & 0 & 0 \\ 0 & E_2 & E_3.\mu_{32} & 0 & 0 & 0 \\ 0 & E_3.\mu_{23} & E_3 & 0 & 0 & 0 \\ 0 & 0 & 0 & G_{12}\Omega & 0 & 0 \\ 0 & 0 & 0 & 0 & G_{23}\Omega & 0 \\ 0 & 0 & 0 & 0 & 0 & G_{31}\Omega \end{bmatrix} \begin{Bmatrix} d\varepsilon_1 \\ d\varepsilon_2 \\ d\varepsilon_3 \\ d\gamma_{12} \\ d\gamma_{23} \\ d\gamma_{31} \end{Bmatrix}$$

$$\text{Eq. 4.2-24}$$

When σ_1 becomes equal to zero, the corresponding diagonal term is actually equal to zero. However to avoid the numerical difficulty, the same element in the constitutive matrix is provided with a small value equal to unity.

4.2.1.8 Compression Crushing

The above procedure is set to identify the failure due to the cracking phenomenon in the tensile regime. However under multiaxial stress condition, compression crushing may also take place, which is identified with the help of ultimate strength envelope as the current stress level reaches ultimate compressive strength R_{ci}. With reference to the Fig. 4.2-1, the descending branch of the curve during strain softening is considered as linear. As the material reaches the peak value of stress level at the onset compression crushing, strain softening in all direction start until minimum stress reaches a value equal to σ_{fi}. With the assumption that Poisson's ratio μ_{ij} is equal to zero after compression crushing, the constitutive relation takes the form ;

$$\begin{Bmatrix} d\sigma_1 \\ d\sigma_2 \\ d\sigma_3 \\ d\tau_{12} \\ d\tau_{23} \\ d\tau_{31} \end{Bmatrix} = \begin{bmatrix} E_1 & 0 & 0 & 0 & 0 & 0 \\ 0 & E_2 & 0 & 0 & 0 & 0 \\ 0 & 0 & E_3 & 0 & 0 & 0 \\ 0 & 0 & 0 & G_{12} & 0 & 0 \\ 0 & 0 & 0 & 0 & G_{23} & 0 \\ 0 & 0 & 0 & 0 & 0 & G_{31} \end{bmatrix} \begin{Bmatrix} d\varepsilon_1 \\ d\varepsilon_2 \\ d\varepsilon_3 \\ d\gamma_{12} \\ d\gamma_{23} \\ d\gamma_{31} \end{Bmatrix}$$ Eq. 4.2-25

where, $G_{12} = \dfrac{E_1.E_2}{(E_1 + E_2)}$, $G_{23} = \dfrac{E_2.E_3}{(E_2 + E_3)}$, $G_{31} = \dfrac{E_3.E_1}{(E_3 + E_1)}$ and E_i is the total secant modulus at the descending branch of the stress strain curve as shown in Fig. 4.2-1, may be calculated as proposed by Rabczuk(2005) ;

$$E_i = \frac{\sigma_{ci}}{\varepsilon_{ui}} + E_{soft} \cdot \left(\frac{\varepsilon_{ui} - \varepsilon_{ci}}{\varepsilon_{ui}} \right)$$ Eq. 4.2-26

where, E_{soft} is the softening modulus of concrete in the descending portion of the curve, which in again may be calculated, based on the ultimate values of stress and strain parameters. It may be noted that crack activation (either active or passive) is required only for the cyclic loads. Loading and unloading function is to be defined for load reversals or cyclic loads. There is hardly any possibility that the cracks may be activated by a very little amount for monotonic load only during successive cycles. From this perspective, no loading-unloading function has been considered, as it's a case of monotonic load.

4.2.2   FE Formulation (EAS Approach) :

A classical displacement based isometric formulation is followed with three translational degrees of freedom at each node of 8-noded solid hexahedral elements to model the parent material (concrete) of the reinforced concrete. Using the standard elasticity matrix for the parent material D_P (Eq. 8.3-5 for linear analysis and Eq. 4.2-2), strain displacement matrix B_P (Eq. 8.3-3), 3D transformation matrix $T_{\sigma,gl}$ (Eq. 8.4-4), volume considered V_P, p is the subscript to denote the parent material and their usual interrelationships for the continuum in 3D stress state, the element stiffness is derived in a very straightforward way, very similar to Eq. 4.3-14.

$$K_P^e = \sum_P B_P^T . \left[T_{\sigma,gl}^T\right] D_P . \left[T_{\sigma,gl}\right] B_P . dV_P .$$ Eq. 4.2-27

The following is the shape or interpolation function (refer Fig. 4.2-5)

$$\left\{N_i^P\right\} = \frac{1}{8}(1 + \xi.\xi_i).(1 + \eta.\eta_i).(1 + \varsigma.\varsigma_i), \ i=1 \ to \ 8$$ Eq. 4.2-28

with ξ, η, ς being the intrinsic co-ordinates for the 8-noded Serendipity (parent) element, utilized for the purpose. Fig. 4.2-5 shows the assumed displacements of a typical isoparametric eight-node solid element in global and natural coordinate system as per *Cook et al. (2003)*.

However, the element stiffness matrix (size 24x24) formulated thus can not infer about the internal stresses set up due to it's inability to represent the state of pure bending strains and due to fictitious inclusion of large shear strains (parasitic shear). This effect of parasitic shear strain together with volumetric locking becomes significant with large aspect ratio of the element and hence structural response (deflection) is grossly underestimated as well as become dependent on mesh design. Several methods have been proposed to remove this deficiency of linear 8-noded isoparametric solid elements. Here an enhanced strain formulation proposed by *Sousa et. al (2002)* is incorporated based on extra compatible modes of deformation which don't have physical meaning and are eliminated at the element level by static condensation method. The details of this category of element have been discussed in the Appendix. The most interesting part in these category of elements is that only enhance assumed strain(EAS) is employed for both the treatment of volumetric as well as transverse shear locking in an unified way.

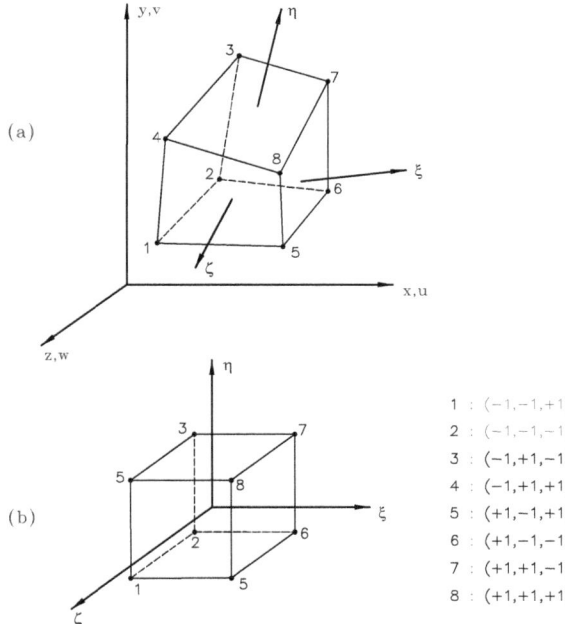

Fig. 4.2-5: Typical 8-node solid element;

(a) Global coordinate system, (b) Natural coordinate system

In particular, the element designated as HCiS18 has been used here, where 18 nos. of new extra variables are associated in addition to the usual strain field and the augmented strain matrix becomes with 'w' being the displacement field (subscript p corresponding to usual DOF of parent element and α corresponding to DOF against enhanced nodes) ;

$$\{\varepsilon_P^{'}\} = \{\varepsilon_P\} + \{\varepsilon_\alpha\} = [B_P \quad B_\alpha]\begin{Bmatrix} w_P \\ w_\alpha \end{Bmatrix}$$

Eq. 4.2-29

Making use of the bubble function, $N_\alpha = \dfrac{1}{2}(1-\xi^2).(1-\eta^2).(1-\varsigma^2)$

Eq. 4.2-30

The enhanced part of the strain matrix becomes

$$B_\alpha = \dfrac{|J_0|}{|J|}.T_0.M_{18}^e$$

Eq. 4.2-31

where J_0 and J is the Jacobian determinant evaluated respectively at $\xi = \eta = \varsigma = 0$ and at each Gauss points, T is the transformation matrix and M_{18}^e is obtained from the *Sousa et al (2003)* /Eq. 8.6-9 as

$$M_{18}^e = \begin{bmatrix} \frac{\partial N_\alpha}{\partial \xi} & 0 & 0 & 0 & 0 & 0 & 0 & 0 & 0 & \frac{\partial^2 N_\alpha}{\partial \xi \partial \eta} & \frac{\partial^2 N_\alpha}{\partial \xi \partial \varsigma} & \frac{\partial^2 N_\alpha}{\partial \eta \partial \varsigma} & 0 & 0 & 0 & 0 & 0 & 0 \\ 0 & \frac{\partial N_\alpha}{\partial \eta} & 0 & 0 & 0 & 0 & 0 & 0 & 0 & \frac{\partial^2 N_\alpha}{\partial \xi \partial \eta} & \frac{\partial^2 N_\alpha}{\partial \xi \partial \varsigma} & \frac{\partial^2 N_\alpha}{\partial \eta \partial \varsigma} & 0 & 0 & 0 & 0 & 0 & 0 \\ 0 & 0 & \frac{\partial N_\alpha}{\partial \varsigma} & 0 & 0 & 0 & 0 & 0 & 0 & \frac{\partial^2 N_\alpha}{\partial \xi \partial \eta} & \frac{\partial^2 N_\alpha}{\partial \xi \partial \varsigma} & \frac{\partial^2 N_\alpha}{\partial \eta \partial \varsigma} & 0 & 0 & 0 & 0 & 0 & 0 \\ 0 & 0 & 0 & \frac{\partial N_\alpha}{\partial \xi} & \frac{\partial N_\alpha}{\partial \eta} & 0 & 0 & 0 & 0 & 0 & 0 & 0 & \frac{\partial^2 N_\alpha}{\partial \xi \partial \eta} & \frac{\partial^2 N_\alpha}{\partial \eta \partial \varsigma} & 0 & 0 & 0 & 0 \\ 0 & 0 & 0 & 0 & \frac{\partial N_\alpha}{\partial \xi} & \frac{\partial N_\alpha}{\partial \varsigma} & 0 & 0 & 0 & 0 & 0 & 0 & \frac{\partial^2 N_\alpha}{\partial \xi \partial \eta} & \frac{\partial^2 N_\alpha}{\partial \eta \partial \varsigma} & 0 & 0 & 0 & 0 \\ 0 & 0 & 0 & 0 & 0 & 0 & 0 & \frac{\partial N_\alpha}{\partial \eta} & \frac{\partial N_\alpha}{\partial \varsigma} & 0 & 0 & 0 & 0 & 0 & 0 & 0 & \frac{\partial^2 N_\alpha}{\partial \xi \partial \eta} & \frac{\partial^2 N_\alpha}{\partial \xi \partial \varsigma} \end{bmatrix}$$

Eq. 4.2-32

With this enhanced strain components, total DOF becomes 24+18=42 and accordingly, the size of the element stiffness matrix becomes 42x42, which is reduced to 24x24 by static condensation from *Cook et al. (2003)*. It is well established and has also proved its worth in evaluating the performance of the reinforced concrete structures in the present investigation. To demonstrate the accuracy and potentiality of the modified element thus, finite element solution of simply supported RC beams and frames are compared in Chapter-5.

Both the geometric as well as material nonlinearity have been taken into account for the proposed formulation to simulate the problem in hand. The first category of nonlinearity due to large displacements enters through kinematic relations between strain and displacements. The most appropriate formulation for numerical solution depends on the type of analysis being considered. For the 3D solid elements employed in this work, a total Lagrangian formulation is adopted in which large deflection and moderate rotations are accounted for, where the current stress and strain fields are referred to the original geometric configuration and displacement field. The strain-displacement matrix is calculated once during the nonlinear process and its nonlinear part is updated using current displacements by a simple matrix multiplication. The constitutive relations defined herin in terms of engineering stresses (2nd Piola-Kirchoff stress) and strains (Green's strain) are considered valid for the new stress /strain values in current configuration.

4.3 Modeling of Reinforcement :

In art.-3.3 various existing methods and their utilities are being highlighted to evaluate the contributions of reinforcement reinforced concrete medium. Hence when RCC structures are modeled based on continuum mechanics, contribution and distribution of stiffness of reinforcements has been given due importance as per the following modeling considerations ;

4.3.1 Material Modeling :

Unlike concrete, the properties of reinforcing steel are generally not dependent on environmental conditions and hence are considered as much durable than the concrete. Hence a single stress-strain diagram is adequate to define the material properties required for the sake of analysis of reinforced concrete structures in all possible load ranges (*Kwak et at. 1997*). For all practical engineering purposes, steel exhibits the same stress-strain curve both in tension and compression. In general, it shows linear elastic portion, a yield plateau and a strain hardening range in which stress again increases with strain and finally, a range which the stress drops at the breaking point as shown in Fig. 4.3-1.

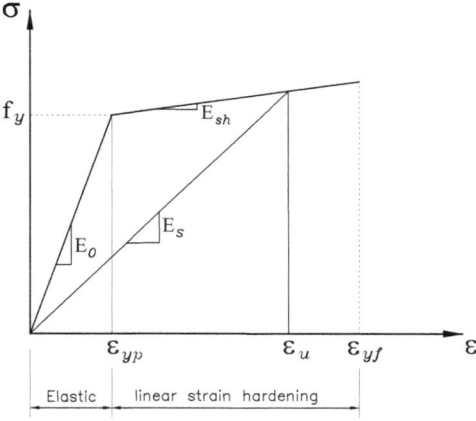

Fig. 4.3-1 : Steel Stress-Strain Relation

     Since reinforcement is used in reinforced concrete construction in the from of bars, its not at all necessary to consider further complexities of three-dimensional constitutive relations. For computational ease, it is sufficient to idealize the one dimensional stress-strain relation for reinforcements. As the following figure states, the first part is linear till yielding and the second part is rising linearly with a very mild slope considering the strength increase due to strain hardening. Although it contradict the basic assumptions made in IS code of practice, it has been assumed for (1) computational convenience and (2) the behaviour of RC members is widely affected by the yielding of reinforcing bars when the structure is subjected to monotonic bending moments. Also the yielding followed by strain hardening behaviour of steel improves the numerical stability of the problem.

     In this study, for computational convenience reinforcement is idealized as one-dimensional element for which above diagram is adequate to fulfill the purpose at hand. The first idealization neglects the strength increase due to strain hardening and it is modeled as a linear material till the yield point as per various codes of national and international codes of practice. The second idealization of linear strain hardening is particularly useful for achieving numerical convergence /stability. Thus it is particularly useful for computational convenience and also the behaviour of RC members are not greatly affected by when the structure is loaded monotonically. Such idealization has been effectively used by many researchers (*Ngo and scordelis 1967* etc.). The following equations are being utilized here to determine secant modulus for the corresponding strain ranges ;

$$E_s = E_0, \qquad\qquad \text{for } \varepsilon \leq \varepsilon_{yp} \text{ and} \qquad\qquad \text{Eq. 4.3-1}$$

$$E_s = \frac{f_y}{\varepsilon_u} + \frac{\left(\varepsilon_u - \varepsilon_{yp}\right)E_{sh}}{\varepsilon_u}, \qquad \text{for } \varepsilon_{yp} \leq \varepsilon \leq \varepsilon_{yf}. \qquad \text{Eq. 4.3-2}$$

4.3.2 FE Formulation (Embedded):

The reinforcement represents a discontinuity of the stiffness distribution within a reinforced concrete member. When such a domain is discretised by finite elements, only in a few situations the domain is subdivided to take care of the stiffness of the reinforcements in position appropriately. Hence a formulation is needed to account both concrete and reinforcement in an implicit manner.

In this study, the straight reinforcement bars are modeled utilizing classical embedded approach proposed by *Elwi /Hrudey (1989), Cheng /Fan (1993)* and *Hartl et al.(2000)*, where the same displacement field of the parent element is assigned. It allows discrete presentation of reinforcements at their exact spatial position without increasing the size of the global stiffness matrix if the perfect bond is assumed. In fact this approach may also be extended in bond-slip situations without increasing the parent element nodes as well as element stiffness matrix.

The reinforcements are embedded into the parent concrete element (Fig. 4.3-2). Hence in the structural domain, the reinforcement layout remains independent of element mesh. The only requirement is to identify the elements with reinforcement(s) and their sectional properties together with its orientation, which may be taken care of by a preprocessing subroutine. The reinforcement nodes are generated independently of the element nodes within the respective element. The obtained strain field from computed displacement field applies to the parent elements and to the reinforcement elements. Once it is identified it becomes very simple to handle problems of three-dimensional RC structures in perfect bond situations. Since the reinforcement nodes do not introduce additional degrees of freedom to the vector of nodal parent element displacements, size of the stiffness matrix remains unaltered.

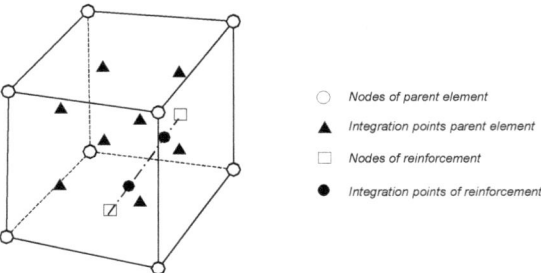

Fig. 4.3-2 : Parent element embedded with reinforcements

The stiffness of the reinforcements is calculated as one-dimensional elements embedded in the space of parent element and is then super-imposed on the stiffness of the parent element. The same strain displacement matrix B_P (used for the parent element) is utilized to evaluate the stiffness of the reinforcements. Since the reinforcement is considered as one-dimensional, the stiffness (integration) is to be evaluated along the path of the reinforcement(s). In order to integrate the stiffness contribution of the reinforcement(s) the strain displacement matrix has been computed at the respective gauss point(s) of the reinforcements expressed in terms of the intrinsic coordinates of the parent element. A Newton root finding algorithm in 3D is used for this purpose, where the known integration points of reinforcement in global coordinates are computed in local coordinates using an inverse mapping procedure based on iterative method by *Barzegar /Madipuddi (1994).* Thus the stiffness contribution of reinforcement towards the element becomes

$$K_R^e = \sum_{RB} B_P^T . T_{\varepsilon,gl}^T . D_R . T_{\varepsilon,gl} . B_P . dV_R ,$$ Eq. 4.3-3

where, RB is the number of reinforcement elements within the parent element and R is the subscript used to denote reinforcement. D_R is the elasticity matrix for the reinforcement due to uniaxial tension /compression in local coordinates given by the following expression ;

$$D_R = \begin{bmatrix} E_s & 0 & 0 & 0 & 0 & 0 \\ 0 & 0 & 0 & 0 & 0 & 0 \\ 0 & 0 & 0 & 0 & 0 & 0 \\ 0 & 0 & 0 & 0 & 0 & 0 \\ 0 & 0 & 0 & 0 & 0 & 0 \\ 0 & 0 & 0 & 0 & 0 & 0 \end{bmatrix}$$

Eq. 4.3-4

E_s is the initial modulus of elasticity of reinforcement $= 5000\sqrt{f_{cu}}$ in Mpa as per the IS code of practice.

Once the integration points within the local coordinates are known, the element stiffness matrix may be computed simply by adding Eq. 4.3-3 with the contribution of parent element (Eq. 4.2-27) in perfect bond situation.

Transformation of local integration point of Reinforcement to Parent element

Within the structural domain, details of reinforcement elements (diameter, numbers etc.) are to be identified within each parent element (concrete) at first. Once it is completed, the coordinates of starting node and the ending node of reinforcement elements within a parent element are known. When shape /interpolation function for one dimensional element is employed, the local coordinates of integration points are known, viz. $\xi = \pm 0.5773503$ for two Gauss points. The global coordinates of these points may be computed using

$$x = N^e_{r,g(\xi)} \cdot x^e_{r,g}$$

Eq. 4.3-5

To evaluate stiffness contribution of reinforcement as per Eq. 4.2-32, the strain-displacement matrix B has to be computed at the integration points of the reinforcement. Hence these Gauss points are to be expressed in terms of intrinsic co-ordinate of the parent element using the following method. The conventional way of mapping local coordinates to global coordinates is

$$x = N^e_{p(\xi,\eta,\zeta)} . x^e_p \qquad\qquad \text{Eq. 4.3-6}$$

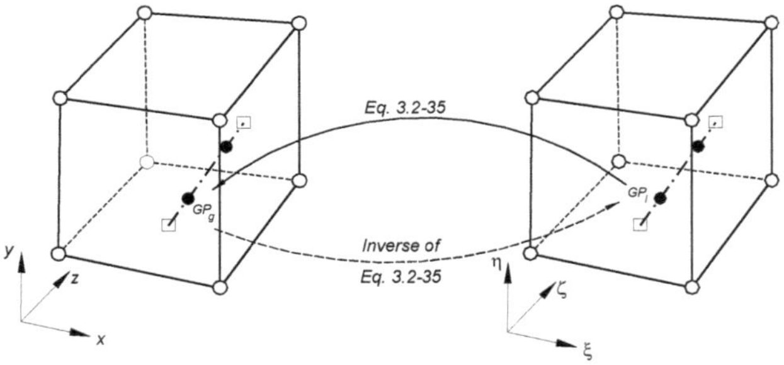

Fig. 4.3-3 : Mapping between local (ξ,η,ζ) and global (x,y,z) configuration

Now for the known global coordinates, an inverse relationship is required for finding intrinsic coordinates. This may be achieved in two ways numerically *Elwi /Hrudey (1989)*; viz. an integration (Runge-Kutta) method and an iterative method. The iterative method is followed here based on Newton root finding algorithm applicable to n-dimensional case. Using J_n as the Jacobian matrix, the iterative equation for intrinsic coordinates may be expressed as

$$\xi_{p,n+1} = \xi_{p,n} + J_n^{T^{-1}} . (x_p - x_{p,n}) \qquad\qquad \text{Eq. 4.3-7}$$

The details of the numerical procedure may be found in the above-mentioned reference. Eq. 4.3-7 is implemented with a subroutine NEWRAPH, where no difficulty is encountered as far as the convergence is concerned for a well-conditioned Jacobian matrix.

Stiffness of Reinforcement Element :

The virtual work and the virtual strains are computed in a common way as follows;

$$\delta W = \int_V \delta \varepsilon^T . \sigma . dV \qquad\qquad \text{Eq. 4.3-8}$$

$$\delta\varepsilon = B^e.\delta u^e$$ Eq. 4.3-9

In general, the stresses (σ) and the strains (ε) are related to each other in a nonlinear way. By linearising this relation, the incremental stresses become;

$$\Delta\sigma = D.\Delta\varepsilon = D.B^e.\Delta u^T$$ Eq. 4.3-10

where, D is the tangent material matrix. Using Eq. 4.3-9, the incremental virtual work can be computed by

$$\Delta\delta W = \int_V (B^e.\delta u^e)^T.(D.B^e.\Delta u^e).dV$$ Eq. 4.3-11

In the above equation both incremental strain and incremental stress are expressed in global coordinate system. Since the material matrix is always expressed in local set of axes, converting the Eq. 4.3-11 in local system using $\varepsilon_{\xi\eta\varsigma} = T_{\varepsilon,gl}.\varepsilon_{xyz}$

$$\Delta\delta W = \int_V \left(T_{\varepsilon,gl}.(B^e.\delta u)\right)^T.D_{local}.\left(T_{\varepsilon,gl}.(B^e.\Delta u)\right)dV$$ Eq. 4.3-12

By rearranging the terms, we have

$$\Delta\delta W = \int_V \delta u^T \left(T_{\varepsilon,gl}^T.B^{eT}.D_{local}.T_{\varepsilon,gl}.B^e \right).\Delta u.dV$$ Eq. 4.3-13

The terms inside the bracket contributes to the stiffness of reinforcement element, which should be multiplied by the appropriate volume at the integration point under consideration. If the cross-sectional area (A_R) is being supplied, the stiffness of reinforcement (similar to Eq. 4.3-3) may be expressed as

$$K_R^e = \sum_{RB} A_R. \sum_{GP} B_P^T.T_{\varepsilon,gl}^T.D_R.T_{\varepsilon,gl}.B_P.l_R$$ Eq. 4.3-14

It may be noted that the orientation of the reinforcement as well as identification of reinforcement elements inside the parent element along with intersection of reinforcement with the surface of the parent element has been avoided. Since only low order elements with straight edges are being used for the presentation and very simple straight reinforcement are only used, these complicacies are avoided intentionally. Data are being supplied as an input to the system.

4.4   Modeling of Reinforcement-Concrete Interface :

In rigid or perfect bond condition and in the cases where bond stresses are not crucial(e.g. stirrups), this aspect of interaction between the two i.e. concrete and reinforcement does not play any significant role. But in case of main reinforcement this modeling of interface phenomenon effectively modifies the overall response of such structures particularly in non-linear regime. The various factors for the same has been discussed in Art.-3.4 and the modeling issues are being taken care in finite element implementation as follows ;

4.4.1 Material Modeling

The supplementary slip algorithm may be effectively applied to incorporate the effect of bond-slip provided the value of the tangent modulus of interface element 'k' is available. Thus a bond stress versus slip relation is needed to implement the bond-slip algorithm. Various experimental investigations viz. ASTM pullout test etc suggest that the bond-slip relation depends on the position of reinforcements, the surface condition of bar, the loading state, the boundary condition i.e. the surrounding concrete, the confinement level and the anchorage length of the bar. In this study, a simple bond stress-slip model as per Modelcode-90 [MC90] is adopted shown in Fig. 4.4-1, as it shows good approximation of the actual behaviour in cases of monotonic loading.

The monotonic envelope consists of an initial nonlinear relation due to adhesion stage in which the ribs of the deformed bars penetrate into the mortar matrix resulting in local crushing and microcracking. This ascending branch is given by

$$\tau = \tau_{max} \cdot \left(\frac{s}{s_1}\right)^{\alpha} \text{ for } 0 \leq s \leq s_1 = s_2 \qquad \text{Eq. 4.4-1}$$

where, α is a parameter that controls the curvature of the curve depending on the value of slip(s) and reflects reinforcement-concrete interface properties depending on bond condition and confined /unconfined concrete.

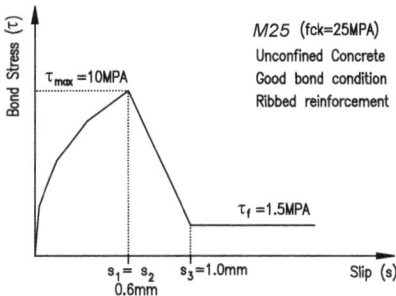

Fig. 4.4-1 : Bond-slip Relation

The tangent modulus of the interface stiffness may be calculated by taking first derivative of the above equation as ;

$$k = \frac{\tau_{\max}}{s_1^{\alpha}}.\alpha.s^{\alpha-1}$$

Eq. 4.4-2

The second part of the curve bond stress(τ) decreases linearly to the ultimate value of frictional bond resistance(τ_f) due to reduction in bond resistance because of splitting cracks along the reinforcement upto s_3, i.e. residual bond capacity.

In the present study, for deformed ribbed reinforcement in good bond condition for confined concrete the following values have been assumed ; $s_1 = s_2 = 0.6mm$, $s_3 = 1.0mm$, $\alpha = 0.4$, $\tau_{\max} = 2.0\sqrt{f_{cu}}$, and $\tau_f = 0.30\sqrt{f_{cu}}$.

4.4.2 FE Formulation (Supplementary Interface Model)

Accounting for interaction between parent material/concrete and the reinforcements are done to make RCC structure to behave in a more realistic way because concrete is a strong, relatively durable in compression and reinforcements are strong, ductile in tension. This composite action requires transfer of load between concrete and steel. As the loading on RCC structures are gradually increased, this bond-slip increases, as result relaxation of steel stress takes place more and more and an equilibrium is set up in the domain. This phenomenon of interaction between the materials are modeled within the embedded approach where nodal D.O.F.s are increased by the slip D.O.F.s for each element and as a result global stiffness matrix size is increased dramatically.

In bond behaviour, slip takes place due to damage in concrete adjacent to the bars exhibited by cracking /crushing. In this respect, bond-link element was introduced by *Ngo & Scordelis (1967)* at first, later on bond-zone element was introduced *Groot(1981)* and subsequently contact elements by *Mehlhorn(1987)*. *Lundgren (1999)* developed an interface model based on plasticity theory with fully three-dimensional features. For all practical analysis of engineering problem, this approach is not very appealing, as it requires extremely large computational time. As per the literature review, recommendations are given to modify the constitutive law of either concrete or reinforcements, which can't be implemented within the embedded approach. Another approach was initially introduced by *G. Beer (1985)* using isoparametric joint /interface element and was later on used by *Hartl et al (2000)*, where bond slip situations are being considered introducing supplementary interface elements of zero thickness. Within this approach, global displacement field is calculated at first considering perfect bond between reinforcements and concrete and then the slip is calculated by relaxing the perfect bond at the material level.

The basic concept of supplementary slip algorithm is similar to that of a truss analogy as shown in Fig. 4.4-2, when the reinforcements are embedded in a classical way in the parent element without slip degrees of freedom (D.O.F). The truss members are the reinforcements and the supports are the concrete. The end points of the reinforcements are connected to the psudo node on the concrete treated as support by bond spring, which are considered as continuous interface elements. Once the global

---

A 3D Hypoelastic Model of RC Structure using lower order EAS elements.

displacement field is known, the strains along the reinforcement may be integrated and the same are referred as prescribed displacement of the supports. These support displacements get transferred to the end points of the reinforcements depending on the characteristic property of the bond spring. Thus the relative displacement of the reinforcement support node and the adjacent reinforcement end node is referred as bond-slip. The difference of the reinforcement force computed thus with respect to the same considering perfect bond are mapped back as residual nodal forces to the parent element.

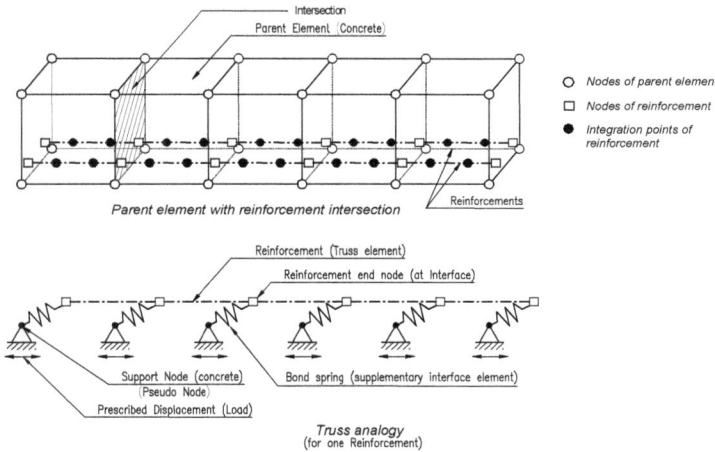

Fig. 4.4-2 : Supplementary Interface model

In order to calculate slip, truss model is analyzed considering the stiffness of the reinforcement element as

$$K_R = A_R \sum_l B_{rl}^T . E_S . B_{rl} . dl_R ,$$ Eq. 4.4-3

where, E_S is the secant modulus of reinforcements, B_{rl} is the strain displacement matrix for 1D reinforcement along its length given by Eq. 8.3-2, l_R is the length of the reinforcement element under consideration and A_R is the cross sectional area of each reinforcements.

Considering S as the surface area of interface element, the incremental virtual work of the interface element is given by

$$\Delta \delta W_{\text{int}} = \int_S \delta u_{slip} . \Delta \tau . dS \qquad \qquad \text{Eq. 4.4-4}$$

The incremental interface stress $(\Delta \tau)$ is calculated as $\Delta \tau = k . \Delta u_{slip}$ with k as the stiffness of interface given by Eq. 4.4-2 with u_{slip} is the vector of nodal slip displacements for interface (joint) element derived as $u_{slip} = N_{r,l} . u_{slip}^e$, $N_{r,l}$ is given by Eq. 8.3-11, u_{slip}^e given by Eq. 8.3-19.

With the above definition, Eq. 4.4-4 may be rewritten as

$$\Delta \delta W_{\text{int}} = \int_S \delta u_{slip}^{eT} . N_{r,l}^T . k . N_{r,l} . dS . \Delta u_{slip}^e \qquad \qquad \text{Eq. 4.4-5}$$

In the present case, the slip is the difference between concrete displacement along the bar and the displacement at reinforcement node. Utilizing the Eq. 4.4-5 and strain displacement matrix B_j for the joint element, the stiffness of the continuous interface element is computed as ;

$$K_j = \sum_S B_j^T . k . B_j . dS \qquad \qquad \text{Eq. 4.4-6}$$

where, the joint strain-displacement matrix B_j is given by Eq. 8.3-4 and k is the tangent modulus of interface element derived from bond-slip diagram depending on magnitude of slip.

Once the stiffness of the reinforcement and the interface element is derived, they may be suitably placed in a matrix form as

$$\begin{Bmatrix} F_f \\ F_s \end{Bmatrix} = \begin{bmatrix} K_{ff} & K_{fs} \\ K_{sf} & K_{ss} \end{bmatrix} \begin{Bmatrix} u_f \\ u_s \end{Bmatrix} \qquad \qquad \text{Eq. 4.4-7}$$

where, $u_f = \begin{bmatrix} u_{1r} & u_{2r} \end{bmatrix}$ with 'f' as free node and $u_s = \begin{bmatrix} u_{1p} & u_{2p} \end{bmatrix}$ with 's' as support node as shown in Fig. 4.4-3.

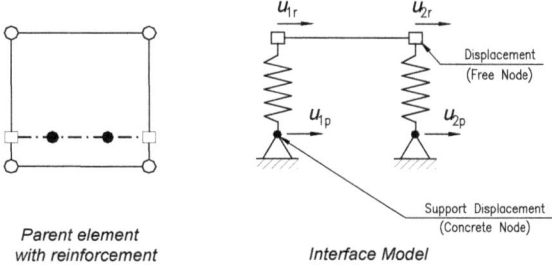

**Parent element
with reinforcement**   **Interface Model**

Fig. 4.4-3 : Interface model Sketch

It is to be noted that here an iteration is a must to obtain a convergent value of tangent stiffness as reinforcement-concrete interface behaviour is non-linear from the beginning of loading even when both concrete and steel remains in the elastic range. The end conditions are specified in terms of prescribed displacements (u_s) as Dirichlet boundary condition. Once these displacements at the free nodes (u_f) are calculated, the same set of equations are again solved for the revised slip until a good convergence is obtained with sufficient accuracy and then the relative displacements($u_{slip} = N_j^e.u_j^e$) of the nodes along with the steel stress due to bond slip are calculated.

The strain in the reinforcement bar only due to slip is calculated as

$$\varepsilon_{slip} = B_{r,l}.u_{slip} \qquad\qquad \text{Eq. 4.4-8}$$

The strain at the same point due to perfect bond is calculated on basis of parent element displacement vector as

$$\varepsilon_{rigid} = T_{\varepsilon,gl}.B_p.u_p \qquad\qquad \text{Eq. 4.4-9}$$

The total strain in the reinforcement undergoes slip becomes $\varepsilon = \varepsilon_{slip} + \varepsilon_{rigid}$. Then the stresses in the reinforcement are computed by relating this strain with constitutive relation of reinforcement. The difference of these stresses $(\Delta\sigma_r)$ for the strain given by Eq. 4.4-8 and Eq. 4.4-9 is calculated. Finally this stress is mapped back as residual nodal forces $(R_p = \int_{RB} B_p^T.\Delta\sigma_r.dl)$ of the respective parent element. Within this supplementary interface model, incremental strain update is inevitable. It is implemented by assuming linearly elastic behaviour of the reinforcements within the iterative scheme of the supplementary algorithm. As the slip converges to a stable solution, the stress in reinforcement is updated by the constitutive relation of the same.

4.5   Aspect of Nonlinear Formulation :

The basis of this formulation is the enhanced assumed strain (EAS) method. Its linearised version is very simple, originally discussed by *Simo /Rifai (1990)*. This aspect has been dealt with in detail in art-4.2.2. While dealing with nonlinearities, the approach maintains the original framework as by *Andelfinger /Ramm (1993), Bischoff /Ramm (1997), Klinkel /Wagner (1997)* and most recently by *Vu-Quoc /Tan (2003), Valente et al. (2004)*. In fact this method is simpler compared to *Simo /Armero (1992)* and may be referred to *Valente et al. (2004)* for details. Using the Hu-Washizu-de Veubeke principle applicable for static loads

$$\Pi^{HWV}(u,\varepsilon,\sigma) = \int_V W_u(\varepsilon)dV + \int_V \sigma : \left[\frac{1}{2}(F^T F - I_2) - \varepsilon\right]dV - \Pi^{ext} \qquad \text{Eq. 4.5-1}$$

$$\Pi^{ext} = \int_V u.\overline{b}.\rho.dV + \int_S u.\overline{t}.dS \qquad \text{Eq. 4.5-2}$$

where, u is the displacement, ε is the Green-Lagrange strain, σ is the 2nd Piola-Kirchhoff stress, W_u is the displacement-driven strain energy, S and V are the control area and control volume respectively, (ρb) and t are the body forces and traction forces respectively including the prescribed values marked by upper bar. It may be noted that the above equations do not include boundary conditions as they are referred to the reference configuration.

The total strain (ε) is assumed to be consists of a compatible (displacement based) ε^u and an incompatible parts (enhanced) ε^α as defined in Eq. 4.2-28

$$\varepsilon = \varepsilon^u + \varepsilon^\alpha = B_u.u + B_\alpha \alpha \qquad\qquad \text{Eq. 4.5-3}$$

On substitution of Eq. 4.5-3 and the orthogonality condition given by $\int_V \sigma.\varepsilon^\alpha .dV = 0$

into Eq. 4.5-1 and Eq. 4.5-2, number of independent variables reduces to two and the weak form modified functional in variation becomes

$$\delta\Pi(u,\varepsilon^\alpha) = \delta\Pi^{int} - \delta\Pi^{ext} \qquad\qquad \text{Eq. 4.5-4}$$

$$\delta\Pi^{int} = \int_V (\delta\varepsilon^u + \delta\varepsilon^\alpha) : \frac{\partial W_s(\varepsilon^u + \varepsilon^\alpha)}{\partial(\varepsilon^u + \varepsilon^\alpha)} .dV \qquad\qquad \text{Eq. 4.5-4a}$$

$$\delta\Pi^{ext} = \int_V \delta u.\overline{b}.\rho.dV + \int_s \delta u.\overline{t}.ds \qquad\qquad \text{Eq. 4.5-4b}$$

The above weak form may now be expanded using truncated Taylor series to relate kth state to (k+1)th state with finite variation using operator Δ. In each element's domain the displacement field (including corresponding variation and increment) is interpolated as

$$u \approx u^h = N(\xi).d \,, \ \delta u \approx \delta u^h = N(\xi).\delta d \,, \ \Delta u \approx \Delta u^h = N(\xi).\Delta d \qquad \text{Eq. 4.5-5}$$

In a similar way, Green-Lagrange strain tensor and its enhanced counterpart may be defined

$$\varepsilon^u = B_u(\xi).d \,, \ \delta\varepsilon^u = B_u(\xi).\delta d \,, \ \Delta\varepsilon^u = B_u(\xi).\Delta d \qquad\qquad \text{Eq. 4.5-6}$$

$$\varepsilon^\alpha = B_\alpha(\xi).\alpha \,, \ \delta\varepsilon^\alpha = B_\alpha(\xi).\delta\alpha \,, \ \Delta\varepsilon^\alpha = B_\alpha(\xi).\Delta\alpha \qquad\qquad \text{Eq. 4.5-7}$$

where, the enhanced operator B_α (defined in art. 3.2.1.2) involves a set of internal variables α, which are discontinuous between elements and are eliminated using static condensation at each element level.

Now Eq. 4.5-5, 6 and 7 may be substituted in Eq. 4.5-4 and focusing on variation whole potential, we may have the system of equation simply as extension of linear case.

$$\begin{bmatrix} K_{uu} & K_{u\alpha} \\ K_{\alpha u} & K_{\alpha\alpha} \end{bmatrix} \begin{Bmatrix} \Delta u \\ \Delta \alpha \end{Bmatrix} = \begin{Bmatrix} F_u \\ F_\alpha \end{Bmatrix}$$

Eq. 4.5-8

$$K_{uu} = K_{uu}^{\lg} + K_{uu}^{n\lg}$$

Eq. 4.5-8a

$$F_u = \int_V N^T . \overline{b} . \rho . dV + \int_S N^T . \overline{t} . dS - \int_V B_u^T . \sigma . dV$$

Eq. 4.5-8b

$$F_\alpha = -\int_V B_\alpha^T . \sigma . dV$$

Eq. 4.5-8c

The internal force vector due to resulting displacement is given by $\int_V B_u^T . \sigma . dV$

and due to enhanced field is given by $\int_V B_\alpha^T . \sigma . dV$. The linear and nonlinear geometric

stiffness matrices are $K_{uu}^{\lg}, K_{uu}^{n\lg}$. $K_{uu}^{\lg}$ is defined in Eq. 4.2-26. The details of geometric

nonlinearity and its computational aspects of $K_{uu}^{n\lg}$ in three dimensions is discussed in

art. 6.7. Furthermore, the coupling stiffness matrices $(K_{u\alpha}, K_{\alpha u})$ along with the fully

enhanced stiffness matrix $(K_{\alpha\alpha})$ is also introduced in nonlinear situation as in

Eq. 4.5-8.

Apart from these geometric aspects, the constitutive update of the stress tensor

needs a specific treatment arising out of material nonlinearity, which is explained in

art.- 4.2 following hypoelastic formulation. The formulation of various stiffnesses

involved in the presentation, applicable to continuum in three dimensions, has been

dealt with sufficient details. With the definition of displacement vector at any point

within the structure $\{u\} = [N]\{d^e\}$, strain displacement relation $\{\varepsilon\} = [B]\{d^e\}$, stress

computation $\{\sigma\} = [D]\{\varepsilon\}$, the various nodal forces may be calculated as

The nodal forces due to surface traction

$$\{F_t\} = -\sum_e \int [N]^T . \{p\} dV$$

Eq. 4.5-9a

The nodal forces due to body forces

$$\{F_b\} = -\sum_e \int [N]^T . \{f\} dV$$

Eq. 4.5-9b

The nodal forces due to initial strains

$$\{F_{\varepsilon_0}\} = -\sum_e \int [B]^T.[D]\{\varepsilon_0\}dV \qquad\qquad \text{Eq. 4.5-9c}$$

The nodal forces due to initial stresses

$$\{F_{\sigma_0}\} = -\sum_e \int [B]^T.\{\sigma_0\}dV \qquad\qquad \text{Eq. 4.5-9d}$$

the vector for externally applied nodal forces may calculated by appropriately summing up components of Eq. 4.5-9.

4.6   Numerical Implementation :

a) Solution Algorithm

For any nonlinear solution algorithm, the basic steps are; the formation of current stiffness matrix, the solution of the equilibrium equations for the displacement increments, the determination of state for all elements and finally the convergence check. Here the step-iteration procedure is followed with current (secant) stiffness calculated only once at the beginning of each load step and also the crack direction remains unaltered during the entire load step. New crack direction are only assumed to form at subsequent load steps. It has also been assumed that since initially concrete does not show prominent nonlinearity during its uncracked elastic stage of loading approximately upto 25 percent of failure stress, no iterative solution is sought for two load steps at the very beginning of solution. For each problem, solutions are started with initial control parameters E_0, μ_0, f_{cu} and the material constants /parameters of the failure surface. In absence of any data modulus of elasticity of concrete is calculated by default as $E_0 = 5000.\sqrt{f_{cu}}$ and the same for reinforcement $E_s = 2.0E + 06$ MPa. The various default parameters assumed are as follows;

- Various Strength Parameters of concrete (MPA)

  Ultimate uniaxial tensile strength $f_t = 0.10\, f_{cu}$
  Ultimate biaxial compressive strength $f_{cb} = 1.15\, f_{cu}$

- Various Strain Parameters (mm)

    Concrete
    Ult. Uniaxial Compressive (Cracking) Strain ε_{cu} = 0.00283
    Ult. Uniaxial Compressive (Failure) Strain ε_{cm} = 1.41 ε_{cu}
    Ult. Uniaxial Tensile (Cracking) Strain ε_{t} = 0.045 ε_{cu}
    Ult. Uniaxial Tensile (Failure) Strain ε_{m} = 4.0 ε_{t}
    Ult. Uniaxial Biaxial Compressive Strain ε_{cb} = 1.30 ε_{cu}
    Reinforcements
    Ult. Uniaxial Tensile (yielding) Strain ε_{yp} = 0.0020
    Ult. Uniaxial Tensile (Failure) Strain ε_{yf} = 5.0 ε_{yp}

- Various Softening Moduli (MPa)

    With crack band width w_{f} = 15mm and fracture energy G_{f} = 180N/m,
    Softening Modulus of concrete in Tension E_{crack} = 822 Mpa
    Softening Modulus concrete in Compression E_{soft} = 0.15f_{cu}/0.41 ε_{cu}
    Softening Modulus of Reinforcement E_{sh} = 0.014E_{0}

A brief summery of the steps of the nonlinear solution algorithm with complete reference to the theoretical formulation presented herewith along with list of subroutines prepared for the purpose.

1. Form the element (secant) stiffness matrix of concrete (parent material) at the current displacement level ($E = E_{0}, \mu = \mu_{0}$ at the 1st load increment) using LHS of Eq. 4.2-27 (include K_{uu}^{nlg} using Eq. 8.8-4 in case of large deformation).

2. Condense additional enhanced modes using standard method of static condensation.

3. Compute element stiffness matrix of reinforcement at the current displacement level ($E = E_{s}, \mu = \mu_{s}$) using Eq. 4.3-3. Add step-2 to calculate total element stiffness of RC element.

4. For a given load factor, compute load increment vector.

5. For current load increment, determine current displacement increment and total displacement.

6. Compute strains parent /concrete element and subsequently stress assuming $E = E_{0}, \mu = \mu_{0}$.

7. Compute principal stress and associated direction using equation Eq. 8.6-5 and Eq. 8.6-15 respectively.

8. Check for stress state and corresponding ultimate surface using Eq. 4.2-17

9. Compute incremental secant value of E, μ of concrete from Eq. 4.2-12 and Eq. 4.2-13 at the current stress level.

10. With the above values compute residual forces (equivalent nodal) for concrete and similarly for reinforcements with perfect bond.

11. Unbalanced forces are to be determined, followed by a static condensation.

12. Step 1-11 are to be repeated until convergence occurs as Eq. 4.6-1.

b) **List of Subroutines** (*NACON.for*)

1. Subroutine **MESGENPB** ()

2. Subroutine **MESGENPF** ()

3. Subroutine **GRAPHFRM** ()

4. Subroutine **GRAPH** (JSCALE,XA,YA,XB,YB)

5. Subroutine **INDATAP** (NRF,ISLIP,NEtype,NATR)

6. Subroutine **CHECKP** (NB,NERR)

7. Subroutine **INDATAR** (NRF)

8. Subroutine **DPMAT** ()

9. Subroutine **TRANFMS** (TFM,TFMG)

10. Subroutine **DRMAT** ()

11. Subroutine **TRANFME** (TFM,TFMG)

12. Subroutine **INVERT** (CC,B,n)

13. Subroutine **MULT**(A,B,C,D,n)

14. Subroutine **GAUSS**(NGP,A,H)

15. Subroutine **SHAP** (ZX,ZY,ZZ,SFN,SDR)

16. Subroutine **ESHAP** (ZX,ZY,ZZ,SDR9)

17. Subroutine **SHAPR** (ZX,kgpr,SFNR,SDRR,ECORDR,DTJACR,GPCODR)

18. Subroutine **JACOBP** (iel,kgp,SFN,SDR,ECORD,DTJAC,CARTD)

19. Subroutine **BPMAT**(CARTD,BPMT)

20. Subroutine **EBPMAT** (NEtype,ECORD,DTJAC,iel,SDR9,BPMT,EBPMT)

21. Subroutine **DBMATP** (n,n1,D,B,DB)

22. Subroutine **MESSGENR**(irf,RCORDST,RCORDEND)

23. Subroutine **NEWTRAPH** (GPCODR,ECORD,kgpr,GPRP)

24. Subroutine **STIFL**(NEtype,NRF)

25. Subroutine **LOAD**(ELOAD,RLOAD,DLOAD,Ntype)

26. Subroutine **SOLVBND**(ELOAD,DISP,DISPINC,TDISP,TREAC)

27. Subroutine **SOLV1**(GSM,GLOAD,DISP)

28. Subroutine **PRNOUT** (incs,MITER,TFAC,NATR,DISP,DISPINC,TDISP,TREAC,
kdefln)

29. Subroutine **MAXDIS** (DISP,MND,DISMAX)

30. Subroutine **PRNDISP** (DISP)

31. Subroutine **RESERROR**(GGSM,GGLOAD,DISP)

32. Subroutine **STRES** (DISP,NRF)

33. Subroutine **BONDSLIP** (NRF,ELOAD,DISP)

34. Subroutine **SLIP** (DISP,NRF,SIG)

35. Subroutine **DISPSLIP** (iel,irf,ELONGR,ECORDR,BSM,EDISB)

36. Subroutine **LDISP** (CARTD,ETDISP,GMATX,BPMT)

37. Subroutine **GEOMETK** (Dvolm,AKP,GMATX,STRNP,DPH)

38. Subroutine **INCREM** (incs,TFAC,DLOAD,RLOAD,ELOAD,TLOAD)

39. Subroutine **STIFNL** (incs,NEtype,LARGE,NRF,KSYSFAIL,STRSG,STRG,
STRSR, DISPINC,DISPIN,TDISP)

40. Subroutine **HYPODRMT** (incs,kgp,STRNR,STRS,DRH)

41. Subroutine **DRHYPO** (Es,Theta,DRH)

42. Subroutine **HYPODPMT** (incs,iel,kgp,STRNP,STRES,DPH)

43. Subroutine **PRINSTR** (SIGMA,SIG,SIGDR)

44. Subroutine **EIGENJACOB** (A,V)

45. Subroutine **DPHYPO** (Alfa,Econ,ANU,Thett,DPH)

46. Subroutine **MODULII** (KCstr,EpslnU,EpslnC,Rc,Econ,ANU)

47. Subroutine **LOADID** (Rc,ICASE)

48. Subroutine **FAILURE**(incs,iel,kgp,ICASE,SIG,EpslnU,beta,KTstr,KCstr)

49. Subroutine **ARGYRIS** (SIG,Rc,EpslnU,EpslnC)

50. Subroutine **PARAMTR** ()

51. Subroutine **RESTRES** (incs,MITER,LARGE,NRF,DISP,DISPIN,TDISP,STRSG,
STRG,STRSR,EQLOAD)

52. Subroutine **CONVDISP** (incs,KITER,DISP,TDISP,ELOAD,EQLOAD,NCHECK)

53. Subroutine **ZERO** (ELOAD,TLOAD,DISP,DISPINC,TDISP,STRSG,STRG,
STRSR,TREAC)

The following is the flow diagram included here (Fig. 4.6-1) to depict the procedure to execute the bond-slip model discussed in art.-4.4 .

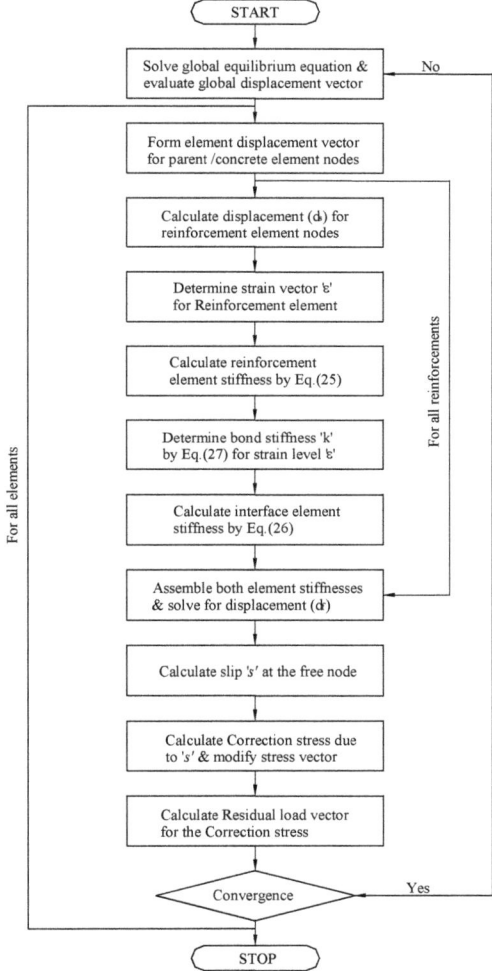

Fig. 4.6-1 : Solution algorithm for bond-slip

Load steps are restricted to 10 percent of failure load in each case till crack initiation and afterwards it is reduced to 5 percent to avoid initiation of unrealistic numerical cracking. The incremental material constitutive matrix is calculated following specified stress path as per the model issues discussed earlier. The integrated element stiffness of concrete including contribution of reinforcement (if present in the parent element) is calculated at the beginning of each load step and the equilibrium equation is solved for using banded matrix solution.

c) Convergence Criterion

The criteria for the convergence of iterative solution within the load step is based the accuracy of satisfying global equilibrium equation or on the accuracy of determining total displacements. The accuracy of satisfying nodal displacements is controlled by the value of additional displacement increment after each iteration within the load step as

$$E_{d,error} = \frac{\left[\sum_j \Delta d_j^i \right]^{1/2}}{\left[\sum_j d_j^i \right]^{1/2}} \le Toler \qquad \text{Eq. 4.6-1}$$

where, summation is carried over all degrees of freedom j, d_j is the displacement corresponding to degrees of freedom j, and $\sum d_j$ is the corresponding increment after iteration i and *TOLER* is the specified tolerance. The failure load is assumed to occur at the load step, which requires higher number of iterations to satisfy equilibrium for convergence i.e. when it undergoes large strain under the applied load. For this study maximum no of iterations is set to 30 and *TOLER* is 1 percent.

4.7   Remarks :

The analytical (FE) formulation for all the constituent materials and their implementation both in linear as well nonlinear situations have been dealt with in this chapter. A FORTRAN computer code has been developed to analyze simple problems beams and frame discussed in chapter-5.

Chapter 5

Results and Discussion

In this chapter, the existing experimental results available in the past literature are compared with the results obtained by proposed FE formulation presented in Chapter-4. Few analytical cases are also presented to evaluate the performance of the proposed FE model.

5.1 General :

A number of correlation studies are presented in this chapter with an objective of establishing the ability of the proposed three-dimensional hypoelastic model to simulate the response of the reinforced concrete beams and frames. The effective utility of the lower order EAS element HCiS18 in modeling the parent material i.e. concrete has been tested. The contribution of reinforcement in the overall response /behaviour of reinforced concrete has been given due attention using embedded approach only at the tension zone of the RC structures. The interaction between concrete and reinforcement i.e. bond-slip has also been paid attention [**Samanta /Ghosh** (2008a, 2008b, 2008c, 2009a)] in evaluating gross estimation such response both in linear as well as nonlinear regime.

5.2 Implementation in Elastic Range :

5.2.1 Single Span Simply Supported RC Beam :

The formulation followed has been implemented with FORTRAN computer program. A single span simply supported RC beam with the geometrical properties as shown Fig. 5.2-1 is investigated, which is subjected to only uniformly distributed load

(w) of 1.6 ton/m-run over the entire span. The beam is 5.0m long (L) and the cross-section 200(b) x 400(D) with 2 nos. 20dia ordinary ribbed reinforcing steel (A_{st}) placed at 40mm(d') above the bottom, i.e. the effective cover. The concrete has the characteristic strength (f_{ck}) of 25 MPa, elastic modulus E_c = 25000MPa, Poisson's ratio μ = 0.15 and the reinforcement bar has the elastic modulus Es = 200000 MPa.

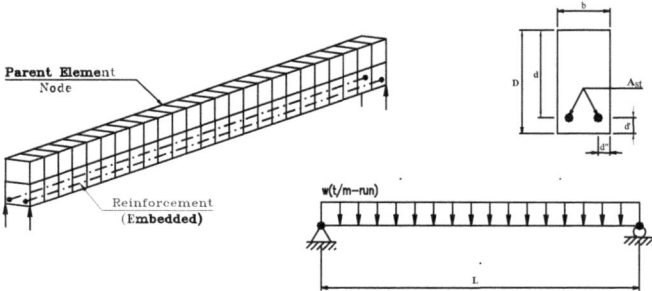

Fig. 5.2-1 : Single span RC beam system.

Both the parent material /concrete and the reinforcement are assumed to be linear elastic within the specified load range. The mesh of 50 elements of size 200 cube is generated with a preprocessing subroutine for the parent material, where 8-noded solid isoparametric elements with EAS formulation are implemented. With the supplied end points /profile of the reinforcements in the beam, the reinforcement mesh is also generated within each element for which stiffness contribution is added to the stiffness of the parent element.

Considering the material perfectly elastic and linear within the load range, the above sample problem was solved and the following stress diagram has been obtained ;

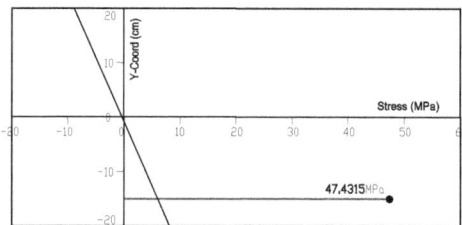

Fig. 5.2-2 : Stress Distribution Diagram (Perfect Bond)

It is assumed that concrete is unconfined as per the considered configuration and the bond condition is good. Accordingly the bond-slip parameters are assumed as $\tau_{max} = 2.0\sqrt{f_{ck}} = 10.0 MPa$, $s_1 = 0.6$ mm, $\alpha = 0.4$ (refer art.-4.4.1 and Fig. 4.4-1) and the derived stress distribution diagram are shown in Fig. 5.2-3.

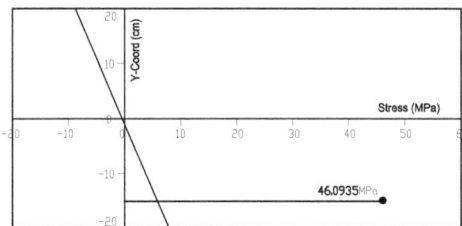

Fig. 5.2-3 : Stress Distribution Diagram (With Bond-Slip)

One of the main objectives was to assess the performance of the element HCiS18 in evaluating the bending situations considering incompressibility. With the following illustration of single span RC beam, it has been seen from the tab. 1 and Fig. 8 that the element shows results with 1.11% error only with element size 200x200x200.

Table 5.2-1 : Comparison of Deflection & Stress

Description of Items	ϕ25-2Nos. P_t=1.364 %		ϕ20-2Nos. P_t=0.872 %		ϕ16-2Nos. P_t=0.559 %		ϕ12-2Nos. P_t=0.314 %		ϕ10-2Nos. P_t=0.218 %	
	(A)	(B)	(A)	(B)	(A)	(B)	(A)	(B)	(A)	(B)
Mid-span deflection (mm)	4.2673	4.1686	4.4394	4.3640	4.5725	4.5238	4.6288	4.6023	4.6802	4.6625
Maxm. Stress at mid-span (MPa) — Top-most layer	8.6892	8.5804	8.8639	8.7860	8.9895	8.9357	9.0346	9.0053	9.1299	9.1098
Maxm. Stress at mid-span (MPa) — Bottom-most layer	7.6446	7.3662	8.1195	7.9161	8.5299	8.3891	8.6980	8.6205	8.8567	8.8043
Maxm. Stress at mid-span (MPa) — Reinf.	44.017	42.443	47.431	46.093	50.165	49.238	51.290	50.780	52.263	51.919

(A) : Without considering bond-slip
(B) : With considering bond-slip

The accuracy of the prediction in deflection using the same element has also been checked by considering a cross section 200mm x 400mm for various span, with and without a consideration for bond slip. As far as the bond slip is concerned, the scheme of the supplementary interface algorithm starts from the perfect bond analysis of reinforcement strains, which is obtained from global solution. Thus the stress is overestimated at the nodes which experiences highest strain increment. With the present iteration of the supplementary interface algorithm, due to continuous unloading no problem is encountered as long as reinforcement stress does not exceed its elastic limit.

From Fig. 5.2-4, it is observed that the mid-span deflection reduces with higher percentage of tension reinforcement both in case of perfect bond as well as bond-slip condition, although it is small in terms of percentage. It is also observed that the difference in mid-span deflection for different values of p_t increases with higher dia bars as the interface area of concrete and reinforcement increases and bond-slip effect on deflection is found more in case of reinforcement having higher diameter, which is quite expected. It may be inferred that the element type shows good results even with coarser meshes, being almost accurate as best as the analytical case. So the same may be used for other engineering purposes. As the present study provides a basic step towards the better understanding of a very complex behaviour of reinforced concrete structure in its entire range of stress history before it collapses, these analysis results in its linear elastic regime may be considered as milestone towards the same.

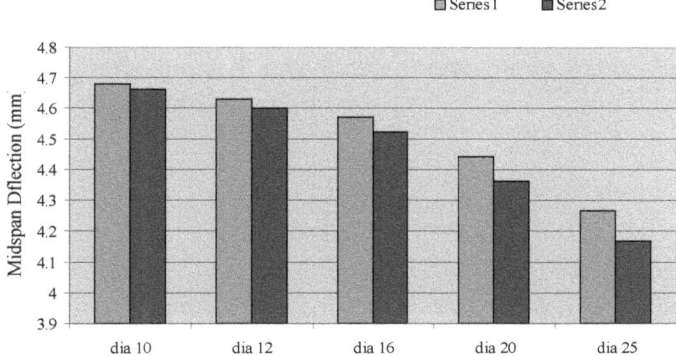

Fig. 5.2-4 : Reinforcement Vs Deflection
Series1 : Perfect Bond Condition
Series2 : With Bond-Slip

Experimental verification :

Three simply supported RC beams have been investigated from various references to validate the present model in the elastic regime. The first example has been taken from the test series of Shegg and Decanini, 1971 (mkd as RC-75-1) referred by Gomesand Awruch (2001), second one from the experiment reported by Burns, et al, 1966 (mkd as Burn-Siess beam) referred by Cho and Hotta (2002) and the third one by Bresler and Scordelis, 1963 (mkd as beam A-1) referred by Kwak and Filippou (1997).

All these experiments were performed to obtain better understanding of load-deflection behaviour of RC beams loaded to failure level primarily. The maximum load in the linear range has been considered as equal to 25% of the failure load as reported by the literature. As shown in Fig. 5.2-5, these beams have only two numbers tensile reinforcement, but no longitudinal compressive or transverse shear reinforcements. The geometry, reinforcement details, finite element mesh and material properties are noted in Table 5.2-2, which shall be read in conjunction with Fig. 5.2-5

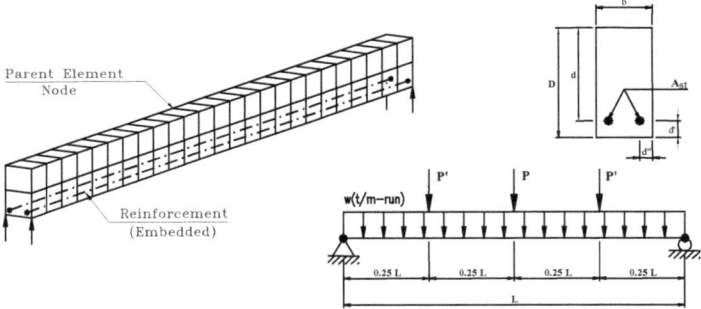

Fig. 5.2-5 : Single span RC beam system

Tab. 5.2-2 also includes the values of mid-span deflections from the present model to compare the same with experimental observations for specific values of the loads. In order to study the effect of finite element mesh on present model with enhanced strain approach, two different categories of mesh configurations were considered. The comment in this regard is exactly same as done in case of pure analytical cases. Coarser meshes are producing better results; in fact more close the experimental values.

Table 5.2-2 : Geometrical and Material properties used

Beam mkd.	RC-75-1		Burn-Siess beam		Beam : A - 1	
b (mm)	153		152.4		305	
D (mm)	246		304.8		553	
L (mm)	3,000		2,743.2		3,677	
d' (mm)	25		50.8		63	
d" (mm)	25		25		40	
"w" - self wt (ton/m)	0.094		0.116		0.422	
P (ton)	0.00		1.00		11.25	
P' (ton)	0.78		0		0	
A_{st} (cm^2)	2.35		2.65		10.20	
F_{ck} (MPa)	31.1		18.2		24.5	
E_c (MPa)	30,653		21,000		23,674	
μ	0.15		0.19		0.17	
F_y (MPa)	550		310		566	
E_s (MPa)	200,000		155,000		222,180	
Midspan deflection (mm) — Experimental	1.250		0.690		1.275	
Midspan deflection (mm) — Mesh size (b x d x L)	1 x 2 x 20	2 x 3 x 40	1 x 2 x 18	2 x 4 x 36	1 x 2 x 12	2 x 4 x 24
Midspan deflection (mm) — Present study	1.139	1.077	0.661	0.649	1.213	1.177
Error (%)	8.89	13.88	4.14	5.93	4.83	7.66

5.2.2 Single Bay Substitute Frame :

In this part of the case study, a single bay substitute frame as shown in Fig. 5.2-6 with column section 125(b)x250(d) and beam section 125(b)x200(d) has been analyzed using the computer code developed. Such configuration has been adopted for analytical study of overall response of beam-frame structure, where it considers all possible modes of deformations including in-plane force effect in addition to conventional frame analysis. In general, conventional frame analysis underestimates the flexural load carrying capacity and the corresponding response. The in-plane force effect primarily depends on percentage tension reinforcement, extent of edge restriction /movement (ratio of column stiffness to beam stiffness) due to the columns in the substitute frame as well as the loading condition. This effect is more predominant in frame beams having lower percentage of tension reinforcements and higher span-depth ratio.

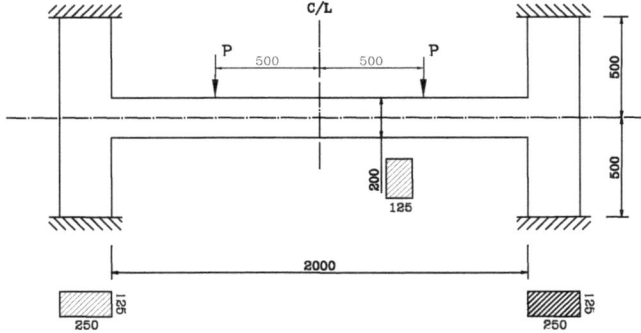

Fig. 5.2-6 : Single Bay Substitute Frame

The basic configuration has been shown in Fig. 5.2-6. It subjected to two point loads (4.0 MT each) at quarter span of the beam only apart from its self-weight. The material properties considered remain same as in the case of previous one i.e. simply-supported RC beam. Both the parent material /concrete and the reinforcement are assumed to be linear elastic within the specified load range. The mesh of 80 elements (20 nos. for each of the columns and 40 nos. for the beam) is generated with a preprocessing subroutine for the parent material, where 8-noded solid isoparametric elements with EAS formulation are implemented. The mess layout along with details of the nodes /members are shown in Fig. 5.2-7 and the deformed configuration has been shown in Fig. 5.2-8.

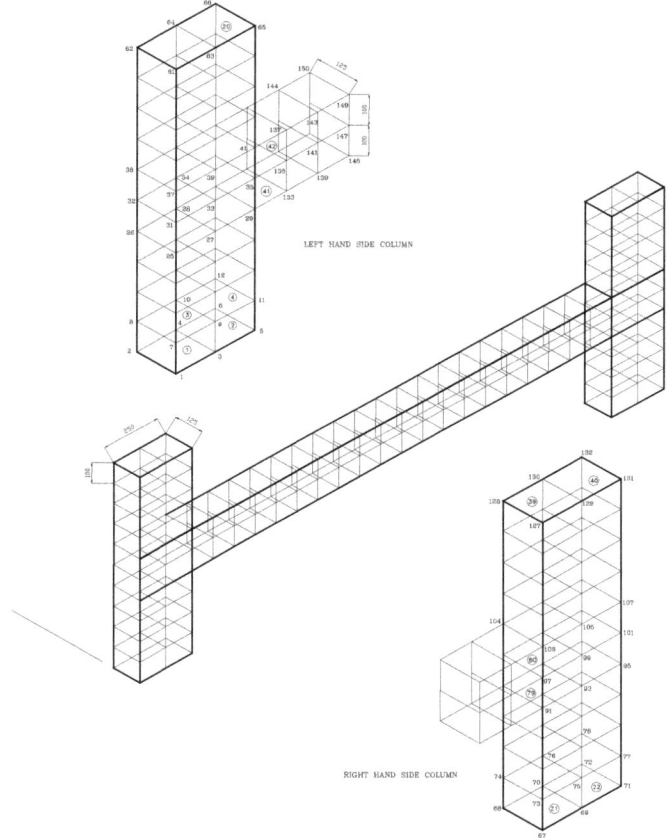

Fig. 5.2-7 : Mess Layout of Substitute Frame

The central /mid-span deflection of the beam using the developed code has been obtained as 1.1717mm, whereas conventional frame (using line element along the center-line of the frame) analysis provides a value of 1.7457mm for the same against the same loading condition. It is may be inferred that conventional frame analysis overestimates the stress and deformation much on conservative side (approx. by 49%)

leading to the section uneconomic. Also it fails to capture appropriate in-plane rigidity at the beam-column junction.

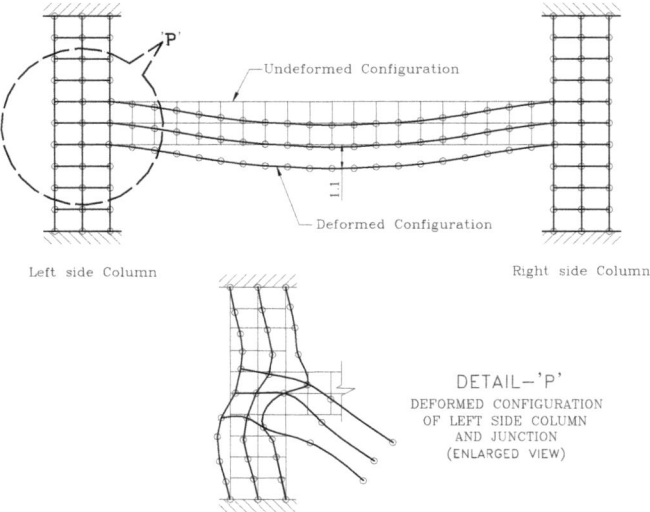

Fig. 5.2-8 : Deformed Configuration of Frame

It is interesting to note that the beam (from the configuration of the frame) having span equal to 2.0m has also been analyzed for Case-I: fixed end and Case-II: simply supported end condition. The maximum mid-span deflection for Case-I is found to be 1.9056mm, whereas for Case-II the same is 0.9036mm. As per the developed code the maximum mid-span deflection from the frame analysis (i.e. 1.1717mm) necessarily depict a kind of end restraining effect in between the simply-supported and fixed end conditions. Also the nature of end restraining (deformation pattern) has been shown in the enlarged view of beam-column junction in Fig. 5.2-8.

The above substitute frame has also been analyzed using the FEM software ABAQUS to validate the prediction of load-deformation response and the output of the computer code, the author has developed for the purpose. This commercial software is well established for the stress analysis in three-dimensional domain. The element mess was generated by aspect ratio close to unity and deviation factor equal to 0.1 and all input were in mm and N (SI). Such a procedure divides the width (250mm) of the column into 3 equal divisions, height(1000mm) of the column into 10 equal divisions, depth(200mm) of the beam into 2 equal divisions and length(1000mm) of the beam into 20 equal divisions. Thus it generates total 290 nodes and 100 elements. Fig. 5.2-9 shows the mess layout along with node levels and Fig. 5.2-10 shows the element incidences. It uses the lower order hexahedral and linear 3D stress elements (type C3D8I) using the incompatible mode. The column ends have been considered with fixed boundary condition. The frame has only been analyzed for linear elastic condition using concrete with material properties; modulus of elasticity E = 25000 MPa and Poison's ratio μ = 0.17 (for M25 grade of concrete).

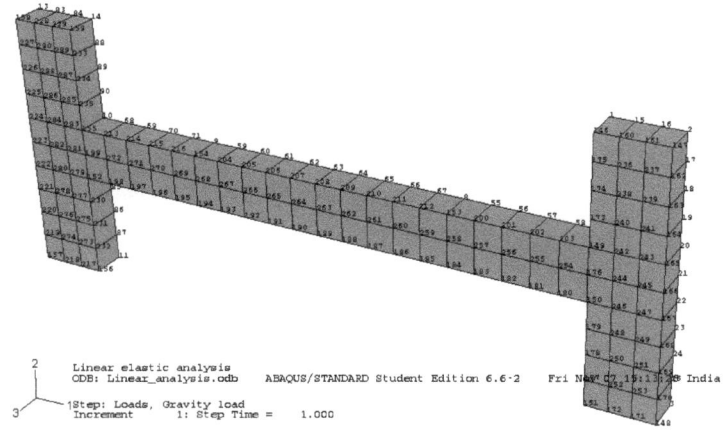

Fig. 5.2-9 : Mess Layout of Frame (ABAQUS) : node levels

A 3D Hypoelastic Model of RC Structure using lower order EAS elements.

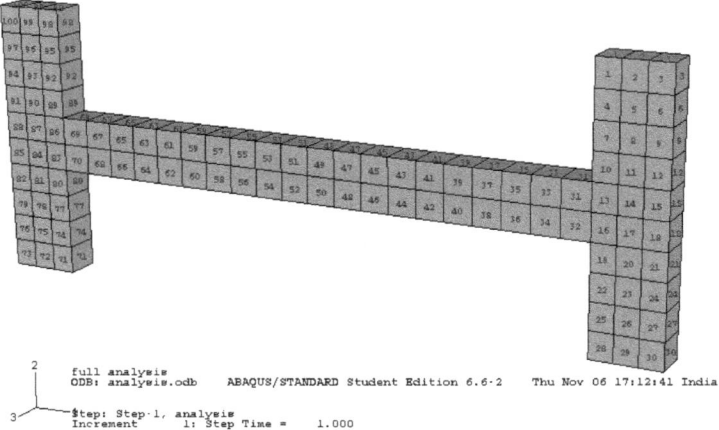

Fig. 5.2-10 : Mess Layout of Frame (ABAQUS) : element levels.

As far as loading is concerned, only self-weight /gravity load along with the point loads as shown in Fig. 5.2-6, has been taken into consideration to validate the formulation author has taken up in the elastic regime using ABAQUS. The frame material has been considered as isotropic /homogeneous and the rebar contribution has not been included in the analysis. The deformed configuration with the deflection (vertical) spectrum and stress contours have been plotted in Fig. 5.2-11 and Fig. 5.2-12 respectively. The maximum mid-span deflection from the ABAQUS frame analysis has been noted as 1.164 mm, which is within ±0.94 % when compared to analysis output of the computer code (with EAS based hexahedral lower order element) the author has developed. Also it clearly depicts that the beam is stressed most at and near the supports of the beam (12.67 MPa), although the maximum deflection is taking place at the center of the beam.

For the sake of comparison, Table 5.2-3 has been prepared which shows the deflection of a number of point along the center line of the frame beam following conventional method of analysis (STAADPro), ABAQUS and the proposed model.

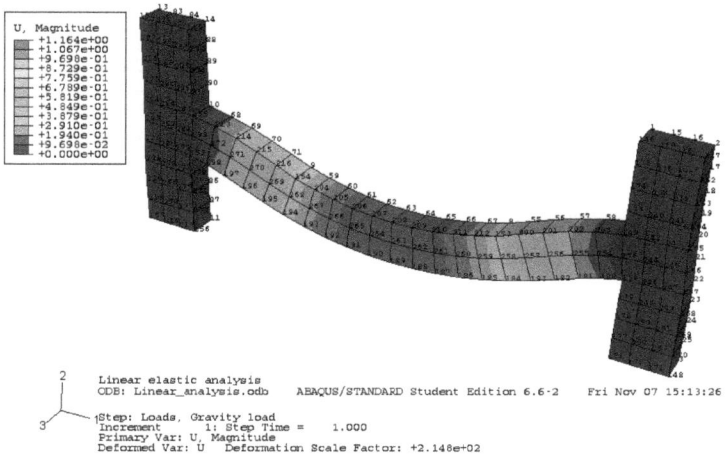

U, Magnitude
+1.164e+00
+1.067e+00
+9.698e-01
+8.729e-01
+7.759e-01
+6.789e-01
+5.819e-01
+4.849e-01
+3.879e-01
+2.910e-01
+1.940e-01
+9.698e-02
+0.000e+00

Linear elastic analysis
ODB: Linear_analysis.odb   ABAQUS/STANDARD Student Edition 6.6-2   Fri Nov 07 15:13:26

Step: Loads, Gravity load
Increment   1: Step Time =   1.000
Primary Var: U, Magnitude
Deformed Var: U   Deformation Scale Factor: +2.148e+02

Fig. 5.2-11 : Deformed Configuration of Frame (ABAQUS) : Deflection

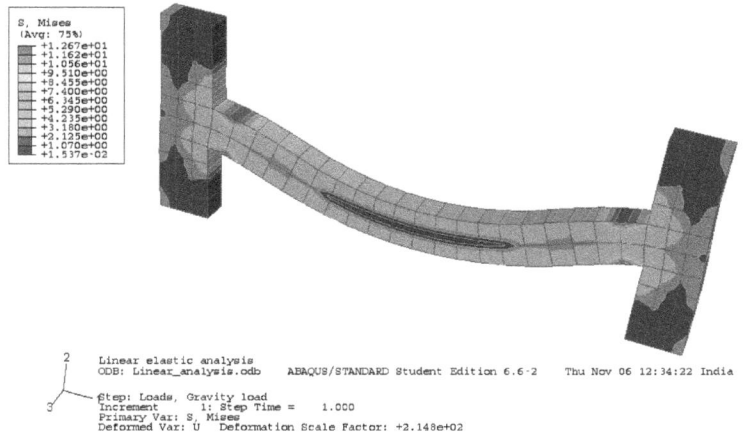

S, Mises
(Avg: 75%)
+1.267e+01
+1.162e+01
+1.056e+01
+9.510e+00
+8.455e+00
+7.400e+00
+6.345e+00
+5.290e+00
+4.235e+00
+3.180e+00
+2.125e+00
+1.070e+00
+1.537e-02

Linear elastic analysis
ODB: Linear_analysis.odb   ABAQUS/STANDARD Student Edition 6.6-2   Thu Nov 06 12:34:22 India

Step: Loads, Gravity load
Increment   1: Step Time =   1.000
Primary Var: S, Mises
Deformed Var: U   Deformation Scale Factor: +2.148e+02

Fig. 5.2-12 : Deformed Configuration of Frame (ABAQUS) : Stress

Table 5.2-3 : Comparison of Deflection of frame beam :

sl no.	STAADPro l = 2250 mm		ABAQUS l = 2000 mm		NACON (Proposed Model) l = 2000 mm	
	length (mm)	deflection (mm)	length (mm)	deflection (mm)	length (mm)	deflection (mm)
1	0	-0.015	125	-0.0628	125	-0.0391
2	112.5	-0.115	225	-0.152	225	-0.1276
3	225	-0.305	325	-0.2895	325	-0.2738
4	337.5	-0.553	425	-0.4592	425	-0.446
5	450	-0.827	525	-0.6532	525	-0.6294
6	562.5	-1.097	625	-0.8226	625	-0.7983
7	675	-1.334	725	-0.9359	725	-0.9351
8	787.5	-1.52	825	-1.0492	825	-1.0379
9	900	-1.654	925	-1.0982	925	-1.1124
10	1012.5	-1.734	1025	-1.163	1025	-1.1568
11	**1125**	**-1.7457**	**1125**	**-1.164**	**1125**	**-1.1717**
12	1237.5	-1.734	1225	-1.163	1225	-1.1568
13	1350	-1.654	1325	-1.0982	1325	-1.1124
14	1462.5	-1.52	1425	-1.0492	1425	-1.0379
15	1575	-1.334	1525	-0.9359	1525	-0.9351
16	1687.5	-1.097	1625	-0.8226	1625	-0.7983
17	1800	-0.827	1725	-0.6532	1725	-0.6294
18	1912.5	-0.553	1825	-0.4592	1825	-0.446
19	2025	-0.305	1925	-0.2895	1925	-0.2738
20	2137.5	-0.115	2025	-0.152	2025	-0.1276
21	2250	-0.015	2125	-0.0628	2125	-0.0391

Also Fig. 5.2-13 shows the same comparison pictorially and it is observed that the Proposed model predictions are very close to the solution provided by ABAQUS, at the same time they differs substantially from conventional analysis outputs.

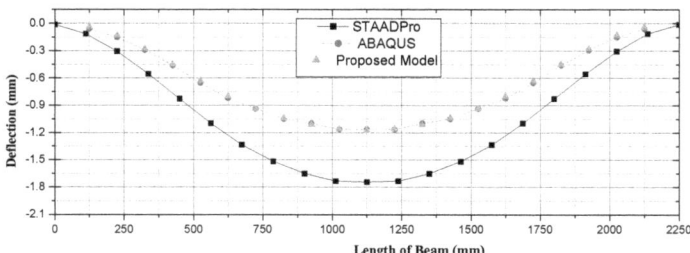

Fig. 5.2-13 : Deflection plot of frame beam

5.3   Implementation in Nonlinear Range :

The nonlinear problem is solved by modified Newton-Raphson method. The tangential stiffness matrix is recalculated only at the beginning of each load increment. In order to establish the potentiality of the model, a few benchmark examples (single span simply supported RC beam) have been taken from the literature and solved using the proposed model considering both material nonlinearity as well geometrical nonlinearity. The material nonlinearity is handled by hypoelastic formulation in three dimensions and the geometrical nonlinearity is taken care of by a Total Lagrangian formulation.

The accuracy of the prediction in load-deflection response using the proposed model has also been checked different mesh density with and without a considering bond slip. As far as the bond slip is concerned, the scheme of the supplementary interface algorithm starts from the perfect bond analysis of reinforcement strains, which is obtained from global solution. Thus the stress is overestimated at the nodes which experiences highest strain increment. With the present iteration of the supplementary interface algorithm, due to continuous unloading no problem is encountered as long as reinforcement stress does not exceed its elastic limit.

The simple beam analyzed here is subjected to only uniformly distributed load (w) due to itself weight over the entire span along with point loads. The ordinary ribbed reinforcing steel(A_{st}) is placed at the bottom, which is in tension due to transverse loads. Provisions are not made to account for the effect of shear reinforcements. The concrete has the characteristic strength f_{ck} is assumed to be same as ultimate uniaxial compressive strength f_{cu}.

Both the parent material /concrete and the reinforcement are assumed to be initially linear elastic within first few load steps. With the supplied end points /profile of the reinforcements in the beam, the reinforcement mesh is also generated within each element for which stiffness contribution is added to the stiffness of the parent element. One of the main objectives was to assess the performance of the element HCiS18 in evaluating the response in bending situations considering incompressibility. To validate the integrated model proposed, comparisons have been made with experimental results of a few simply-supported beams from the literature. All these experiments were performed to obtain better understanding of load-deflection behaviour of RC beams loaded to failure level primarily. The maximum load in the linear range has been considered as equal to 25% of the failure load as reported by the various literatures.

The values (default) of different input parameters related to properties of concrete and reinforcement were taken either from the literature or the Indian code of practice as follows.

For Concrete :

$$E_0 = 5000\sqrt{f_{cu}}$$ E_0 = Initial Young's modulus of concrete.
  f_{cu} = Ultimate Uniaxial compressive strength.

$$f_t = 0.1 f_{cu}$$ f_t = Ultimate tensile strength of concrete.

$$f_{cb} = 1.15 f_{cu}$$ f_{cb} = Ultimate Biaxial compressive strength.

$$G_f = 180 \text{ N/m}$$ G_f = Fracture energy.

$$\varepsilon_{cu} = 0.00283$$ ε_{cu} = Ultimate uniaxial compressive cracking Strain.

$$\varepsilon_{cm} = 1.41\varepsilon_{cu} = 0.00399$$ ε_{cm} = Ultimate uniaxial compressive failure Strain.

$$\varepsilon_t = 0.045\varepsilon_{cu} = 0.00013$$ ε_t = Ultimate uniaxial tensile cracking Strain.

$$\varepsilon_m = 4\varepsilon_t = 0.00052$$ ε_m = Ultimate uniaxial tensile failure Strain.

$$\varepsilon_{cb} = 1.3\varepsilon_{cu} = 0.00368$$ ε_{cb} = Ultimate biaxial compressive Strain.

$$w_f = 15.0 \text{mm}$$ Crack Bandwidth.

$$k_f = 0.75$$ Breaking stress factor (R_c / R_f).

For Reinforcement :

$$E_s = 200000 \text{ MPa}$$ E_s = Initial Young's modulus.

$$E_{sh} = 1.4\% E_s$$ E_{sh} = Strain hardening Modulus.

$$\varepsilon_{yp} = 0.002$$ ε_{yp} = Ultimate uniaxial tensile yielding Strain.

$$\varepsilon_{yf} = 5\varepsilon_{yp} = 0.010$$ ε_{cm} = Ultimate uniaxial tensile failure Strain.

5.3.1 Beam # 1 : *(RC-75-1, Shegg-Decanini Beam, 1971)*

This example model of simply supported RC beam marked as RC-75-1 subjected to two point loads at quarter span tested by Shegg-Decanini(1971) was analyzed. The experimental results show the failure of this beam is due to yielding of tensile reinforcements, which was used by *Gomes /Awruch* (2001) for comparison. This beam has only two longitudinal tensile reinforcements, but has got no longitudinal compressive and transverse shear reinforcements. Basically it's a singly reinforced and over-reinforced section.

The geometry, reinforcement details and its finite element mesh are illustrated in Fig. 5.3.1-1. The beam is 153mm by 246mm in cross-section, with a span between the simple supports of 3000mm. The beam is symmetrically loaded and the finite element mesh 1x2x20, as shown the following figure, was considered for the proposed numerical analysis.

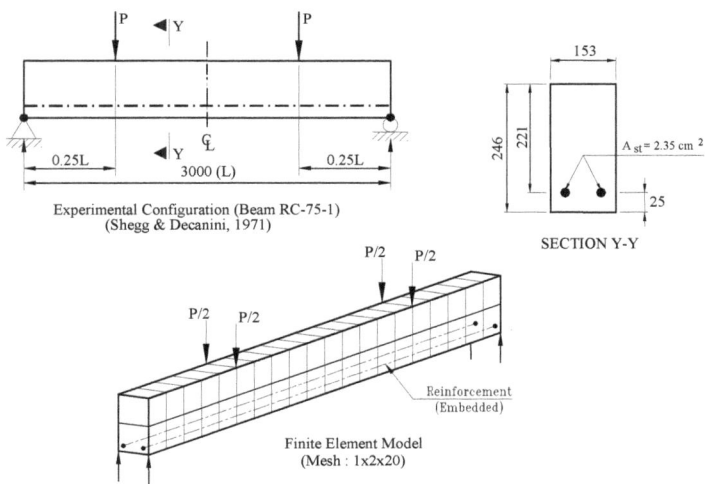

Fig. 5.3.1-1 : Details of RC beam (RC-75-1)

Other parameters related to geometry are as follows $d'' = 25mm$, $\omega = 0.094$ ton/m-run, $E_{soft} = 6700$ MPa and $E_{crack} = 165$ MPa. Based on experimental data, the following parameters related to geometry and material properties of concrete and reinforcements were considered ;

Table 5.3.1-1 : Material Properties and load used for Beam # 1

f_{cu} (MPa)	f_t (MPa)	E_0 (MPa)	μ_0	A_{st} (mm²)	f_y (MPa)	G_f (N/m)	P (ton)
31.1	2.15	30,653	0.15	235	550	210	3.25

The magnitude of fracture energy is derived using the expression $\varepsilon_0 = \dfrac{2.G_f}{f_t.w_f}$. With tensile fracture strain $\varepsilon_0 = 0.013\%$ and values of f_t and w_f as above, G_f becomes equal to 210.0 N/m. The following alternatives of finite element mesh were considered for the proposed numerical analysis to study the convergence criteria in regard to the element (HCiS18) and its behaviour considered in the proposed model.

Width(B) x Depth(D) x Length(L) = 153x246x3000				
Sl No.	Mesh designation	Mesh density (N_B x N_D x N_L)	Total number of elements.	Element Size.
1	Mesh-1	1x2x20	40	153x123x150
2	Mesh-2	1x2x24	48	153x123x125
3	Mesh-3	2x3x36	216	76.5x82x83.3
4	Mesh-4	2x3x40	240	76.5x82x75

As the load-deflection diagram (Fig. 5.3.1-2) indicates that there is a large gap in predicting the response between Mesh-1,2 and Mesh-3,4 indicating thereby the effect of mesh density and the general applicability of coarse mesh using HciS18. In fact the response of Mesh-1 (1x2x20) is still comparable and close to the experimental data.

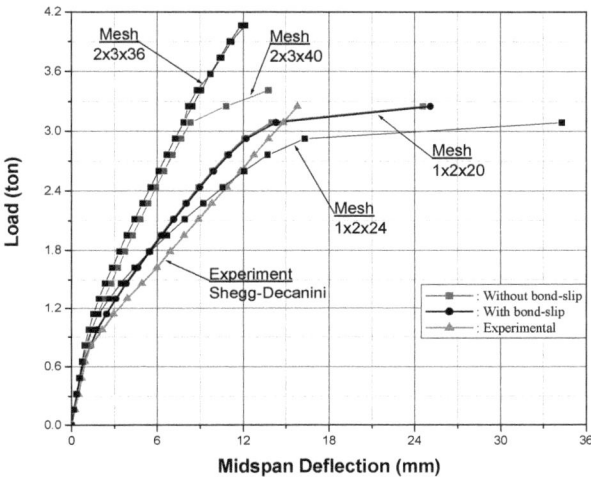

Fig. 5.3.1-2 : Load-deflection response (RC-75-1)

As far as the effect of bond-slip is concerned, its contribution is also not very significant in predicting the load displacement response of the system due to the fact that the beam is over-reinforced. In fact, in some of the load steps maximum deflection assuming perfect bond between concrete and reinforcement is similar to the same while relaxing the bond conditions. An exhaustive list of load vs. deflection for different mesh size has been shown in Table 5.3.1-2 for comparison. It is important to note that the response of the system using NACON (which uses the solid element HCiS18) is better for coarser mesh (1x2x20) than the finer mesh (2x3x40). The central deflection predicted considering the bond-slip is on higher side for the similar load, which an expected one, but the difference is very low. The reason could be attributed to the presence of almost double the percentage reinforcement required for a balanced singly reinforced section of similar mechanical and physical properties.

Table 5.3.1-2 : Load vs Deflection of beam RC-75-1(with & without bond-slip)

Sl No.	Load (ton)	Midspan Deflection (mm)				
		Experimental	Mesh 1x2x20		Mesh 2x3x40	
			Without bond-slip	With bond-slip	Without bond-slip	With bond-slip
1	0	0	0	0	0	0
2	0.1625	0.2370	0.1607	0.1607	0.1508	0.1508
3	0.3250	0.4740	0.3641	0.3641	0.3414	0.3414
4	0.4875	0.7110	0.5676	0.5676	0.5320	0.5320
5	0.6500	0.9480	0.8298	0.8298	0.7735	0.7735
6	0.8125	1.3247	1.3342	1.3342	1.0910	1.0910
7	0.9750	2.1546	1.7879	1.7905	1.4226	1.4226
8	1.1375	2.9459	2.4355	2.4426	1.8308	1.8308
9	1.3000	3.9076	3.0848	3.0980	2.2671	2.2672
10	1.4625	4.9444	3.8202	3.8404	2.7460	2.7470
11	1.6250	5.9812	4.6042	4.6342	3.2388	3.2387
12	1.7875	6.9051	5.4188	5.4584	3.7539	3.7533
13	1.9500	7.8844	6.2472	6.2967	4.2825	4.2812
14	2.1125	8.8838	7.1005	7.1602	4.8254	4.8247
15	2.2750	9.8072	7.9735	8.0428	5.3719	5.3727
16	2.4375	10.8630	8.8888	8.9729	5.9253	5.9264
17	2.6000	11.8247	9.8510	9.9487	6.4896	6.4925
18	2.7625	12.7555	10.8762	10.9919	7.0695	7.0728
19	2.9250	13.8154	12.0771	12.2078	7.6708	7.6748
20	3.0875	14.8189	13.9943	14.3137	8.3170	8.3249
21	3.2500	15.8165	24.5742	25.1042	10.8224	10.8221

The bending stresses (both compressive and tensile) at the midspan of the beam have been plotted in Fig. 5.3.1-3. The non-linear material behaviour of concrete in compression may be noted. Also the tensile behaviour of concrete shows that the level of stress in tension is much lower compared to the same in compression and the stress value does change much beyond a very small value of strain in tension in concrete. The variation of stress in reinforcement in tension is shown in Fig. 5.3.1-4. The yielding of reinforcement, obtained in case using the proposed model with bond-slip, is also supported by the numerical study performed by *Gomes /Awruch* (2001).

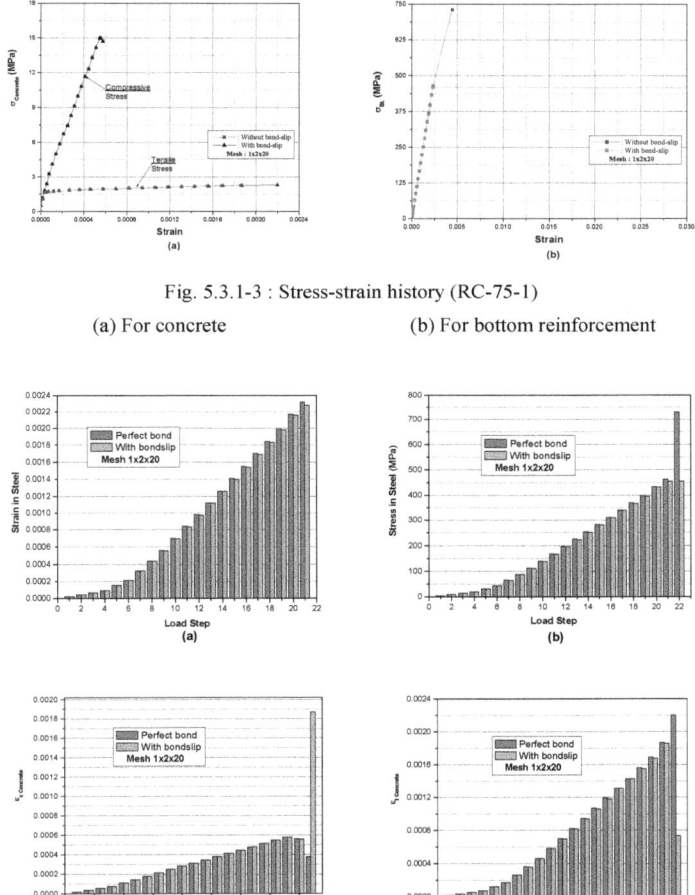

Fig. 5.3.1-3 : Stress-strain history (RC-75-1)

(a) For concrete   (b) For bottom reinforcement

Fig. 5.3.1-4 : Effect of bond-slip (RC-75-1)

(a) Strain in bottom reinforcement   (b) Stress in bottom reinforcement
(c) Compressive strain in concrete   (d) Tensile strain in concrete

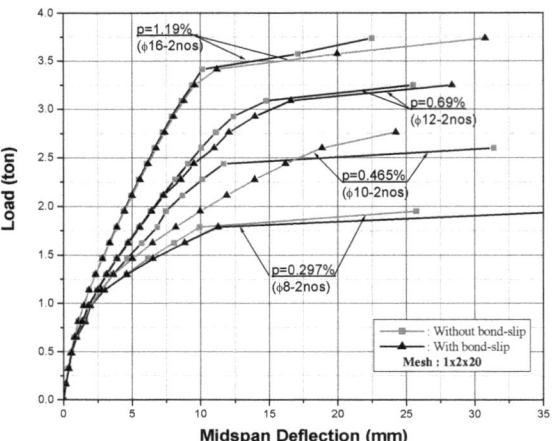

Fig. 5.3.1-5 : Effect of Reinforcement ratio (RC-75-1)

The above diagram shows load-deflection response with the variation of percentage reinforcement in tension. All the values of 'p' corresponds to the over-reinforced section except p=0.297 i.e. considering Φ8-2 nos. Hence yielding of reinforcement is observed at higher load level only except for p=0.297. The total range of strain at yielding is more for the under-reinforced situation only, but the same is low for over-reinforced cases as it is accompanied by crushing of concrete. It may also be noted that the effect of bond-slip is not effectively contributing much in predicting the overall response till 50% to 60% of the ultimate load and also in particular to the over-reinforced cases.

5.3.2 Beam # 2 : *(OA-1, Bresler-Scordelis Beam, 1963)*

This example model of simply-supported RC beam marked as OA-1 subjected to point load at midspan, tested by Bresler-Scordelis(1963) was analyzed. The experimental result shows the failure of this beam is due to yielding of tensile reinforcements, which was used by *Gomes /Awruch* (2001) for comparison. This beam has only longitudinal tensile reinforcements, but has got no longitudinal compressive and transverse shear reinforcements. The geometry, reinforcement details and its finite element mesh are illustrated in Fig. 5.3.2-1. The beam is 310mm by 556mm in cross-section, with a span between the simple supports of 3628mm. The response obtained from the experiment fails to predict the post-yield behaviour of the beam. The mode of failure observed in this test seems to be sudden after formation of cracks at critical zones like the support and the point of application of loads. The cracks at support may be attributed due to absence of shear reinforcements and failure at the point of application of load due to crushing of concrete in compression, as the section is heavily over-reinforced.

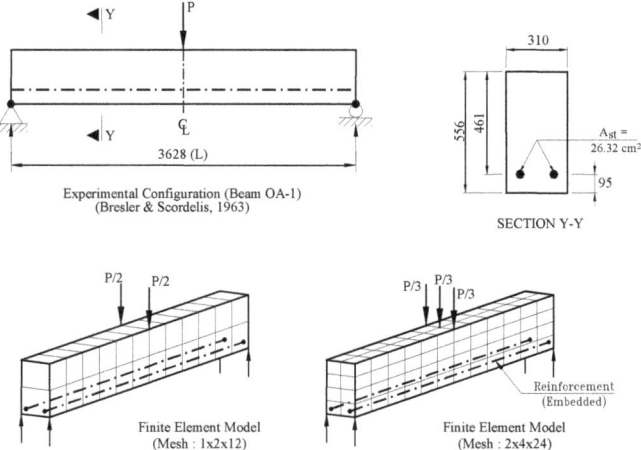

Fig. 5.3.2-1 : Details of RC beam (OA-1)

Other parameters related to geometry are as follows $d'' = 25$mm, $\omega = 0.431$ ton/m-run, $E_{soft} = 4850$ MPa and $E_{crack} = 215$ MPa. Remaining parameters were derived as discussed in the beginning of art-5.3. Based on experimental data, the following parameters related to geometry and material properties of concrete and reinforcements were considered ;

Table 5.3.2-1 : Material Properties and load used for Beam # 2

f_{cu} (MPa)	E_0 (MPa)	μ_0	A_{st} (mm^2)	f_y (MPa)	P (ton)
22.5	28,192	0.15	2632	555	33.3

The transverse load-deflection responses both in experiment as well as the present model using the finite element mesh 1x2x12 are presented in Fig. 5.3.2-2. The failure load was 33.3 ton (total) as per the experimental results. The response using the proposed model found to be very similar to the experimental values, which is able to capture the fact that the beam is over-reinforced.

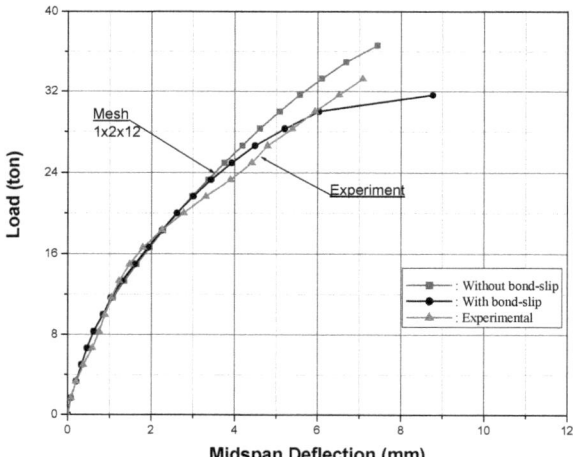

Fig. 5.3.2-2 : Load-deflection response (OA-1)

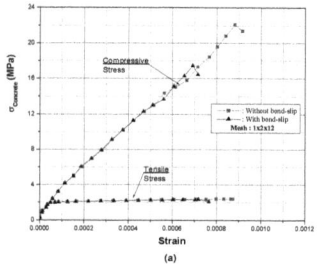 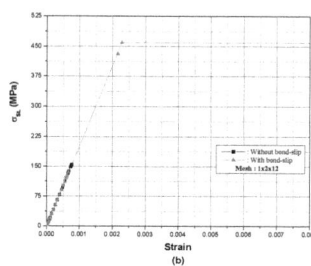

Fig. 5.3.2-3 : Stress-strain history (OA-1)

(a) For concrete   (b) For bottom reinforcement

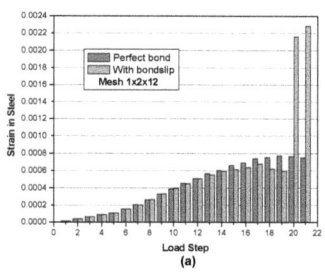 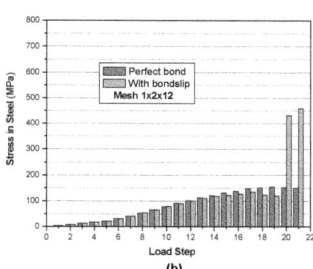

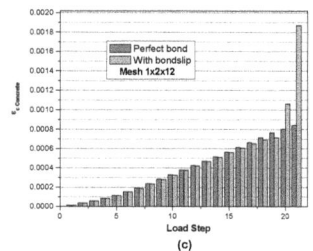 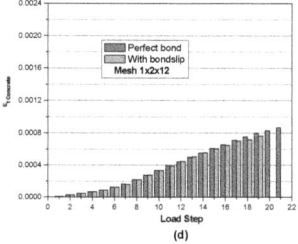

Fig. 5.3.2-4 : Effect of bond-slip (OA-1)

(a) Strain in bottom reinforcement   (b) Stress in bottom reinforcement
(c) Compressive strain in concrete   (d) Tensile strain in concrete

In fact the first crushing takes place at a load equal to 37.0 ton, when the perfect bond is assumed, while the same is around 30.0 ton if the bond slip is being considered using the proposed model. The prediction of failure mode matches more close to the response considering bond-slip. From the Fig. 5.3.2-4, the yielding of longitudinal tensile reinforcement was observed at a value of 0.00228. The beam being heavily over-reinforced, the bond-slip effects are not very significant upto 60 % of the failure load predicted by the proposed model.

5.3.3 Beam # 3 : *(Alvares, 1993)*

This example model of simply supported RC beam subjected to two point loads at quarter span, tested by Alvares(1993) was analyzed. This benchmark experimental result was used by Oliveira et. al. (2008) to show the post-yield behaviour and capability of the analytical model. This beam has three longitudinal tensile reinforcements and two longitudinal compressive reinforcements, but no transverse shear reinforcements.

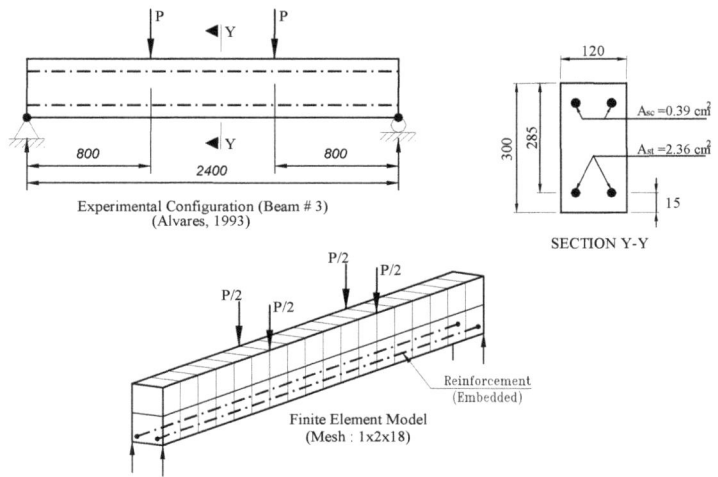

Fig. 5.3.3-1 : Details of RC beam (Alvares, 1993)

The geometry, boundary condition, reinforcement details and its finite element mesh are illustrated in Fig. 5.3.3-1. The beam is 120mm by 300mm in cross-section, with a span between the simple supports of 2400mm. This study has been done to validate the proposed numerical model developed for the purpose.

Other parameters related to geometry are as follows $d'' = 15$mm, $\omega = 0.09$ ton/m-run, $E_{soft} = 5495$ MPa and $E_{crack} = 175$ MPa. Based on experimental data, the following parameters related to geometry and material properties of concrete and reinforcements were considered ;

Table 5.3.3-1 : Material Properties and load used for Beam # 3

f_{cu} (MPa)	f_t (MPa)	E_0 (MPa)	μ_0	A_{st} (mm^2)	f_y (MPa)	E_s (MPa)	P (ton)
25.5	2.044	29,200	0.17	236	500	196,000	4.20

The following alternatives of finite element mesh were considered for the proposed numerical analysis to study the convergence criteria in regard to the element (HCiS18) and its behaviour considered in the proposed model.

Width(B) x Depth(D) x Length(L) = 120x300x2400				
Sl No.	Mesh designation	Mesh density (N_B x N_D x N_L)	Total number of elements.	Element Size.
1	Mesh-1	1x2x18	36	120x150x133.3
2	Mesh-2	2x4x36	288	60x75x66.7

Fig. 5.3.3-2 shows the correlation between the measured load-deflection response of the beam and the proposed model. The results are presented with the above finite element mesh densities and the ratio of sides of the solid element may be consistently maintained close to 1.0 for better response. The response of test data shows that the sudden failure of the beam took place and it fails to pick up the definite yield plateau. The analytical study the main longitudinal reinforcements in compression were not considered. A satisfactory agreement between analysis and experiment was observed. As Fig. 5.3.3-2 clearly indicates that although the mesh is coarse one, the yielding and the failure of the beam fairly agrees with the experimental values.

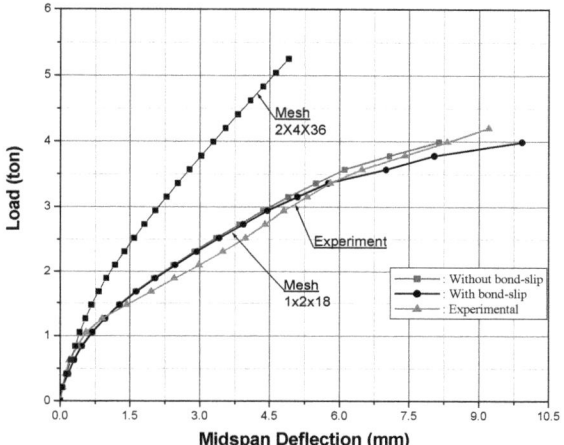

Fig. 5.3.3-2 : Load-deflection response (*Alvares, 1993*)

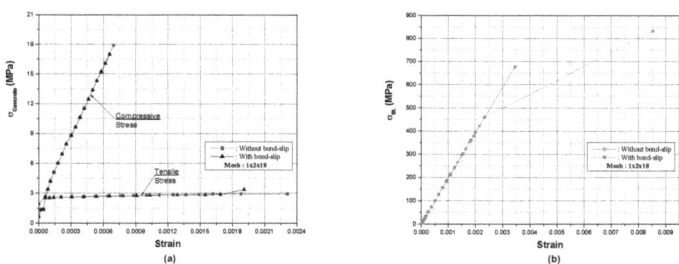

Fig. 5.3.3-3 : Stress-strain history (*Alvares, 1993*)

(a) For concrete   (b) For bottom reinforcement

Fig. 5.3.3-3(a) shows the variation of stresses both in compression fibre in the topmost layer as well as tension fibre in bottom-most fibre. Both the stresses are limited at perfect bond condition and less than the maximum value of stress considering bond-slip due to redistribution /relaxation of stress. Fig. 5.3.3-3(b) shows only the development of stresses in tensile reinforcements.

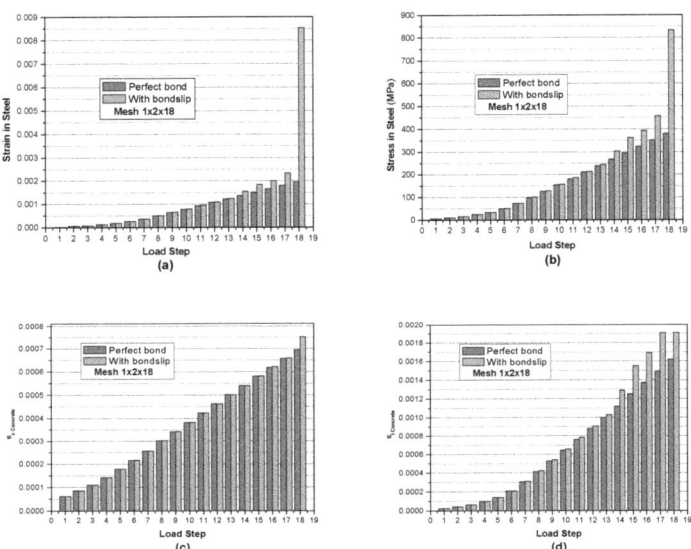

Fig. 5.3.3-4 : Effect of bond-slip (*Alvares, 1993*)

(a) Strain in bottom reinforcement   (b) Stress in bottom reinforcement
(c) Compressive strain in concrete   (d) Tensile strain in concrete

In perfect bond condition, the maximum value of stress at failure is again less than the same while considering bond-slip. Of course, it is interesting to note that there is yielding of reinforcement predicted by this model, in case the effect of bond-slip is taken into consideration and it is also very similar to the assumed stress-strain diagram of steel in the proposed model. As noted in Fig. 5.3.3-4, the stress and strain of reinforcement as inferred by this model have been redistributed /increased due to bond-slip, also the tensile strain in concrete, but he compressive strain in concrete is not much affected by the same.

5.3.4 Beam # 4 : *(TIMA, Gaston-Siess-Newmark Beam, 1972)*

This example model of simply-supported RC beam marked as TIMA subjected to two point loads at one-third span, tested by Gaston-Siess-Newmark(1972) was analyzed with an aim of establishing the ability of the proposed model in simulating the response of reinforced concrete beams. This benchmark experimental result was used by Kwak-Kim, 2001 to validate their developed numerical model. This beam has only two longitudinal tensile reinforcements, but no longitudinal compressive reinforcements and transverse shear reinforcements, indicating thereby singly-reinforced one.

The geometry, boundary conditions, reinforcement details and its finite element mesh are illustrated in Fig. 5.3.4-1. The beam is 152.4mm by 304.8mm(6 inch by 12 inch) in cross-section, with a span between the simple supports of 2743.2mm (9 ft). The details show that the beam section is highly under-reinforced.

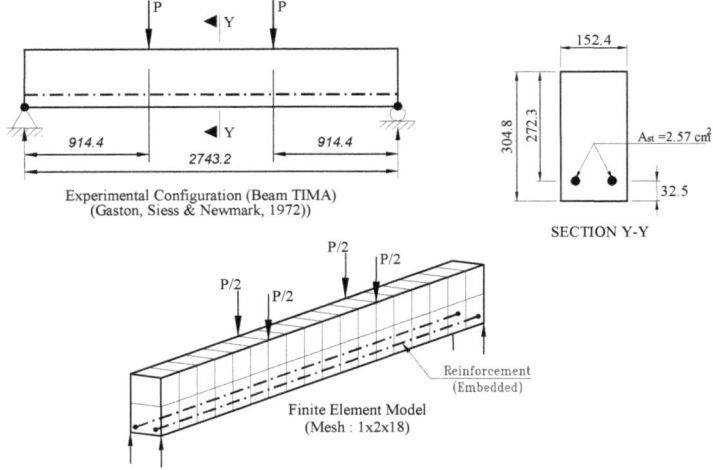

Fig. 5.3.4-1 : Details of RC beam (TIMA)

Other parameters related to geometry are as follows $d'' = 25$mm, $\omega = 0.166$ ton/m-run, $E_{soft} = 4190$ MPa and $E_{crack} = 185$ MPa. Based on experimental data, the following parameters related to geometry and material properties of concrete and reinforcements were considered ;

Table 5.3.4-1 : Material Properties and load used for Beam # 4

f_{cu} (MPa)	E_0 (MPa)	μ_0	A_{st} (mm^2)	f_y (MPa)	E_s (MPa)	P (ton)
32.4	27,158	0.15	257	324	198,407	4.70

The following alternatives of finite element mesh were considered for the proposed numerical analysis to study the convergence criteria in regard to the element (HCiS18) and its behaviour considered in the proposed model.

Width(B) x Depth(D) x Length(L) = 152.4x304.8x2743.2				
Sl No.	Mesh designation	Mesh density (N_B x N_D x N_L)	Total number of elements.	Element Size.
1	Mesh-1	1x2x18	36	152.4 cube
2	Mesh-2	2x4x36	288	76.2 cube

Fig. 5.3.4-2 compares the analytical results with the measured load-deflection relation of the specimen. The results are presented with mesh density 1x2x18. As per the experimental result first crushing takes place at a load of 4.5 ton, whereas as per the proposed model the same takes place at slightly higher load. This may be due to the fact that some more practical aspects like initial cracking, shrinkage etc. needs to be incorporated to the proposed model to simulate the actual behaviour. However the response considering the bond slip is very similar to the experimental values in the post-yield region, although prediction of failure load is on higher side in both cases of analytical investigations. However, it may also be noted that the coarse mesh option with bond-slip may only predict the yielding behaviour of this highly under-reinforced section.

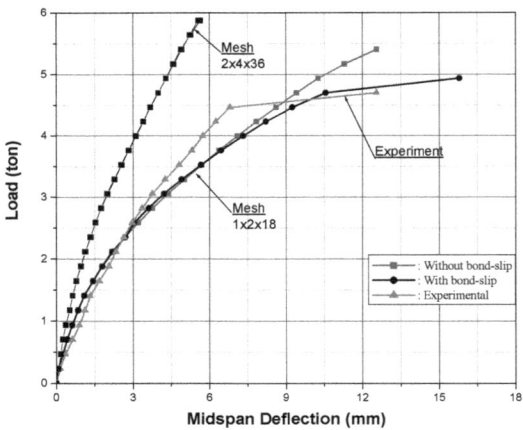

Fig. 5.3.4-2 : Load-deflection response (TIMA)

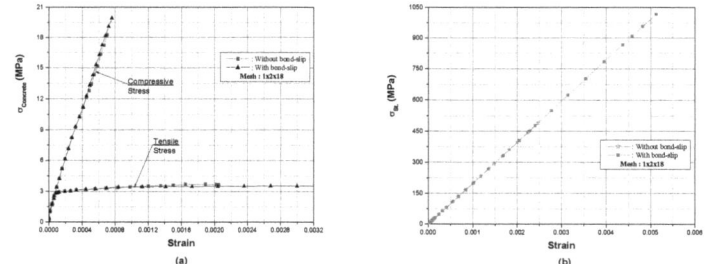

Fig. 5.3.4-3 : Stress-strain history (TIMA)

(a) For concrete   (b) For bottom reinforcement

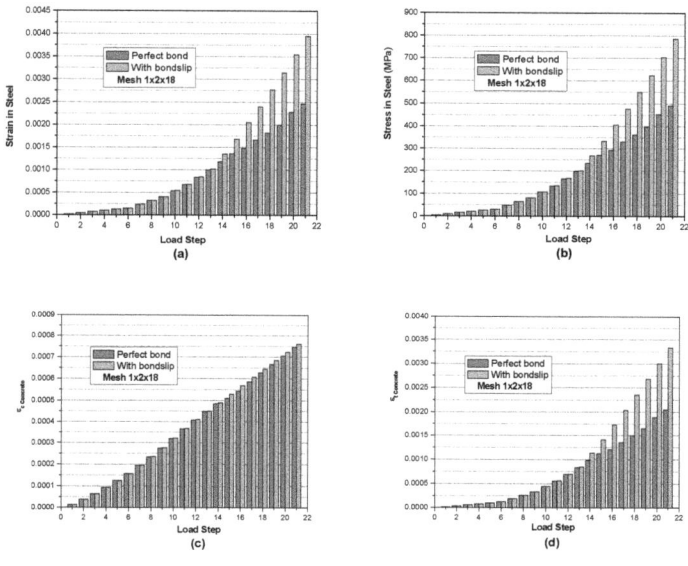

Fig. 5.3.4-4 : Effect of bond-slip (TIMA)

(a) Strain in bottom reinforcement   (b) Stress in bottom reinforcement

(c) Compressive strain in concrete   (d) Tensile strain in concrete

Fig. 5.3.4-3(a) shows the variation of stresses both in compression fibre in the topmost layer as well as tension fibre in bottom-most fibre. Both the stresses are limited at perfect bond condition and less than the maximum value of stress considering bond-slip due to redistribution /relaxation of stress. Fig. 5.3.4-3(b) shows only the development of stresses in tensile reinforcements. In perfect bond condition, the maximum value of stress at failure is again less than the same while considering bond-slip. Of course it may be noted that there is no yielding region of reinforcement predicted by this model irrespective of the bond history. As noted in Fig. 5.3.4-4, all the stresses and strains of concrete and reinforcement as inferred by this model have been redistributed due to bond-slip except the tensile stress in concrete, which is comparable.

5.3.5 Beam # 5 : *(Burn-Siess Beam, 1966)*

A benchmark example model of simply-supported RC beam subjected to central load using concrete pedestal tested by Burn-Siess (1966) is analyzed. The experiment of this beam was conducted at the university of Illinois. The results of this beam (simply supported) is considered very reliable, as also used by *Cho /Hotta* (2002). This beam has two longitudinal tensile reinforcements (ϕ13 -2nos), but no longitudinal compressive and transverse shear reinforcements. This clearly a case of singly-reinforced beam with slightly over-reinforced section. This experiment was conducted to obtain a better understanding of the load-deflection behaviour of reinforced concrete beams till the failure. The geometry, reinforcement details and its finite element mesh are illustrated in Fig. 5.3.5-1. The beam is 152.4mm by 304.8mm (6 inch by 12 inch) in cross-section, with a clear span of 2743.2mm (9 ft) between the simple supports.

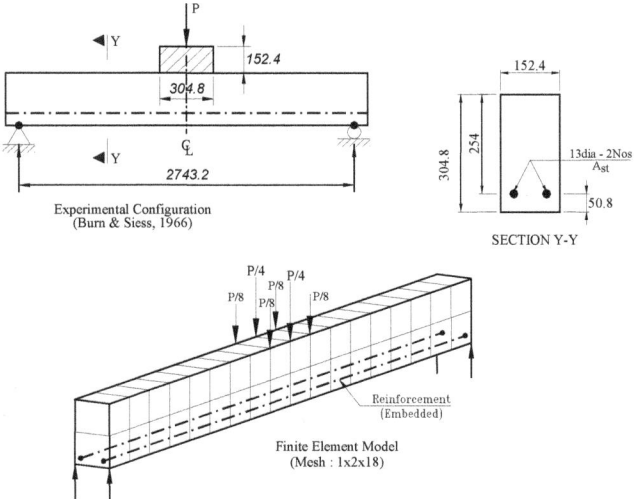

Fig. 5.3.5-1 : Details of RC beam (Burns and Siess, 1966)

Other parameters related to geometry are as follows ; d'' (side cover to main reinforcements) = 25mm, ω (self-weight of the beam) = 0.116 ton/m-run, E_{soft} (softening modulus in compression) = 3920 MPa and E_{crack} (softening modulus in tension) = 140 MPa. Based on experimental data, the following material parameters listed in Table-5.3.5-1 were considered for the purpose of analysis using the Fortran code 'NACON'. It has also been assumed that $R_{fl} = 0.75R_{ci}$ as described in Fig. 3.2-11.

Table 5.3.5-1 : Material Properties and load used for Beam # 5

f_{cu} (MPa)	E_0 (MPa)	μ_0	A_{st} (mm^2)	f_y (MPa)	E_s (MPa)	P (ton)
18.2	21000	0.19	265	310	155000	4.00

The following alternatives of finite element mesh were considered for the proposed numerical analysis to study the convergence criteria in regard to the element (HCiS18) and its behaviour, considered in the proposed model.

Width(B) x Depth(D) x Length(L) = 152.4x304.8x2743.2				
Sl No.	Mesh designation	Mesh density (N_B x N_D x N_L)	Total number of elements.	Element Size.
1	Mesh-1	1x2x18	36	152.4 cube
2	Mesh-2	2x4x36	288	76.2 cube

The transverse load-deflection responses both in experiment as well as the present model using the above finite element mesh densities are shown in Fig. 5.3.5-2. As far as the load-deflection response is concerned, it may be noted that the response of the beam becomes stiff as the mesh density or the number of elements are increased. It may be noted that the response with lower number of elements i.e. coarse mesh density produces even better response using the element HciS18.

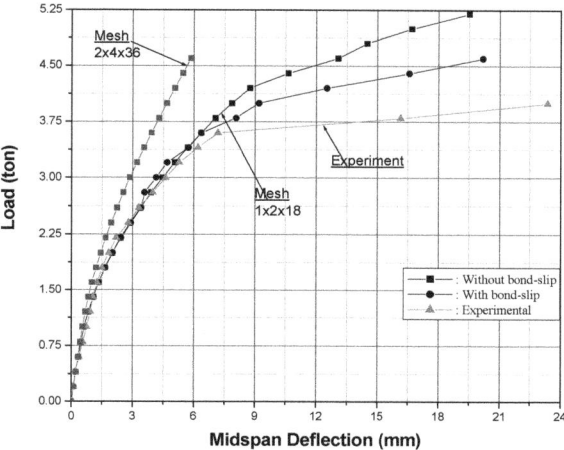

Fig. 5.3.5-2 : Load-deflection response (Burns and Siess, 1966)

Beam failure in the experiment followed plastic hinge formation, which resulted from the crushing of concrete at top fibre at the location of pedestal (load point application). The ultimate load carrying capacity was 4.01 ton, whereas the first crushing point load was noticed at 3.78 ton with a mid-span deflection of 7.3mm as per the experimental results. As per the proposed model using the mesh 1x2x18, the first crushing point is noticed at slightly higher load equal to approximately 4.0 ton and failure load is noticed at 5.0 ton. However the response of the beam in this case follows the pattern same as the experimental results till 3.5 ton (87.5% of the predicted failure load), but beyond that point it is on higher side. Of course the response considering bond-slip is more close to the experimental results. As the Fig. 5.3.5-3 indicates that since the section is over-reinforced one, there is no significant role of bond slip to play with till the first crushing point and the same is prominent beyond the same. For the load steps beyond the first crushing, the strain is more in subsequent load steps due to bond-slip and becomes more close to the experimental values.

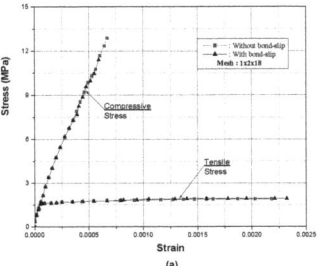 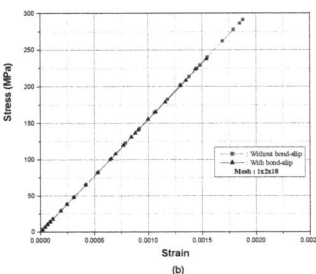

Fig. 5.3.5-3 : Stress-strain history (Kostovos, 1982)

(a) For concrete   (b) For bottom reinforcement

5.3.6 Beam # 6 :*(Kostovos, 1982)*

Another example model of simply supported RC beam subjected to two point loads at one-third span tested by Kostovos(1982) was analyzed. The results of this beam are also used by *Cho /Hotta* (2002) for comparison. This beam has two longitudinal tensile reinforcements ($\phi 6$ -2nos); the same was used also in compression but not between the point loads. The same tension reinforcements (at bottom) were extended to the top in the form of 'U' so as to develop sufficient bond length in the flexural zones, particularly in tension, the length of the beam being very small. It had also the transverse shear reinforcements but except the portion of length between the point loads.

The geometry, reinforcement details and its finite element mesh are illustrated in Fig. 5.3.6-1. The beam is 51mm by 102mm in cross-section, with a clear span between the simple supports of 915mm, total length of the beam being 1017mm. This experiment was conducted to obtain the load-deflection behaviour as well as the growth of crack pattern of reinforced concrete beams till the failure. In the numerical analysis using the proposed model, the effect of compression as well as transverse reinforcements were not considered.

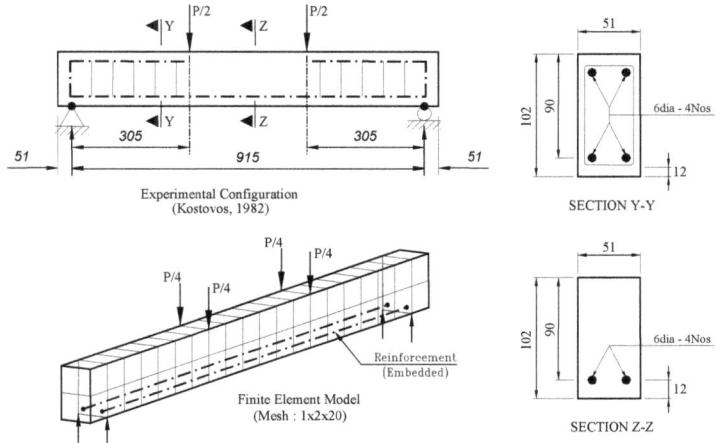

Fig. 5.3.6-1 : Details of RC beam (Kostovos, 1982)

Other parameters related to geometry are as follows $d'' = 17$mm, $\omega = 0.013$ ton/m-run, $E_{soft} = 8145$ MPa and $E_{crack} = 610$ MPa. Based on experimental data, the following parameters related to geometry and material properties of concrete and reinforcements were considered ;

Table 5.3.6-1 : Material Properties and load used for Beam # 6

f_{cu} (MPa)	E_0 (MPa)	μ_0	A_{st} (mm^2)	f_y (MPa)	E_s (MPa)	P (ton)
37.8	29,000	0.19	56.55	417	200,000	1.35

The following alternatives of finite element mesh were considered for the proposed numerical analysis to study the convergence criteria in regard to the element (HCiS18) and its behaviour, considered in the proposed model.

Width(B) x Depth(D) x Length(L) = 51x102x1017				
Sl No.	Mesh designation	Mesh density $(N_B \times N_D \times N_L)$	Total number of elements.	Element Size.
1	Mesh-1	1x2x20	40	51x51x50.8
2	Mesh-2	2x4x40	320	25.5x25.5x25.4

The flexural failure of the beam was observed in the experiment with numerous cracking mainly at the midspan (between the point of application of load) of the beam. Only yielding of longitudinal tensile reinforcement was observed with a maximum value of 0.0056, but no yielding took place in the longitudinal compressive and shear reinforcements. The transverse load-deflection responses both in experiment as well as the present model using finite element mesh 1x2x20 and 2x4x40 are shown in Fig. 5.3.6-2. As usual, the response of high-density mesh (2x4x40) does not support the actual /experimental response at all due higher stiffness attributed to it. The failure load was 1.35 ton (total) applied at each one-third span as per the experimental results. As per the proposed model, the response of the mesh 1x2x20 is very similar till total load reaches a value equal to 1.30 ton irrespective of the fact that whether bond-slip has been considered or not. But beyond that point it is on higher side and fails to capture the crushing point, the breaking load as well as the yielding behaviour of the beam, as it over-reinforced. In that sense, relative differences were found between numerical and experimental results beyond the first crushing point, although it expected to have the similar response in case of an over-reinforced section. It may also be noted that bond slip does occur significantly before first crushing, although there is higher strain at similar and higher load steps.

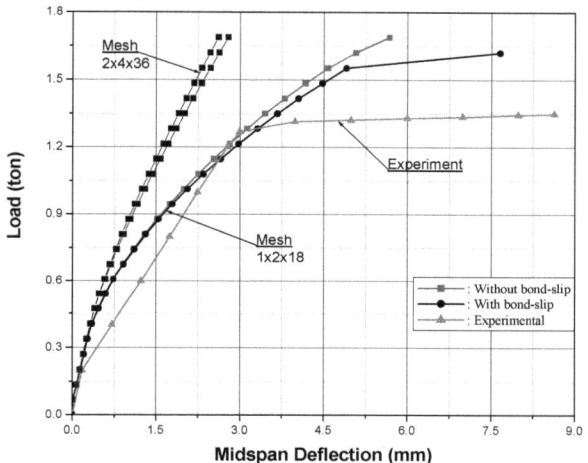

Fig. 5.3.6-2 : Load-deflection response (Kostovos, 1982)

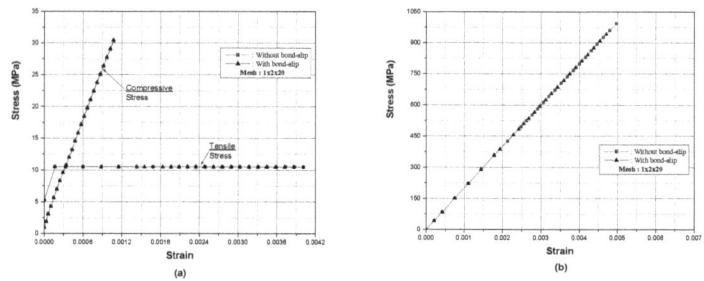

Fig. 5.3.6-3 : Stress-strain history (Kostovos, 1982)

(a) For concrete   (b) For bottom reinforcement

5.3.7 Beam # 7 : *(J-4, Burn-Siess Beam, 1962)*

This example model of simply supported RC beam marked as J-4 subjected to a concentrated load at mid-span, tested by Burn-Siess (1962) was analyzed. This benchmark experimental result was used by numerous authors (Kwak-Fillipou, 1997, Kwak-Kim, 2001 etc.) to validate the proposed numerical models developed from time to time. This beam has only two longitudinal tensile reinforcements, but has got no longitudinal compressive and transverse shear reinforcements indicating thereby that the beam section is singly reinforced one.

The geometry, support conditions, reinforcement details and its finite element mesh is illustrated in Fig. 5.3.7-1. The beam is 152.4 mm by 508mm in cross-section, with a span between the simple supports of 3657.6mm (12 ft). As the area of reinforcement in tension indicated that the beam is highly over-reinforced. This experiment was conducted to obtain the ultimate load behaviour and the crack pattern of reinforced concrete beams till the failure.

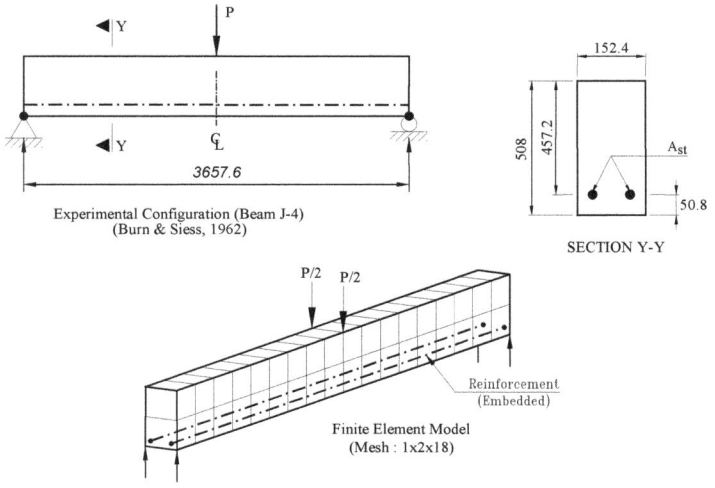

Fig. 5.3.7-1 : Details of RC beam (J-4)

Other parameters related to geometry are as follows $d'' = 50.8$mm, $\omega = 0.258$ ton/m-run, $E_{soft} = 7325$ MPa and $E_{crack} = 490$ MPa. Based on experimental data, the following parameters related to geometry and material properties of concrete and reinforcements were considered ;

Table 5.3.7-1 : Material Properties and load used for Beam # 7

f_{cu} (MPa)	E_0 (MPa)	μ_0	A_{st} (mm^2)	f_y (MPa)	E_s (MPa)	P (ton)
34	26,718	0.17	920	316	207,415	16.32

The following alternatives of finite element mesh were considered for the proposed numerical analysis to study the convergence criteria in regard to the element (HCiS18) and its behaviour considered in the proposed model.

Width(B) x Depth(D) x Length(L) = 203.2x508x3657.6				
Sl No.	Mesh designation	Mesh density (N_B x N_D x N_L)	Total number of elements.	Element Size.
1	Mesh-1	1x2x18	36	152.4x254x203.2
2	Mesh-2	1x3x24	72	152.4x169.3x152.4

The correlation between the experimentally measured load-deflection response of the beam and the proposed model using the said finite element mesh densities are shown in Fig. 5.3.7-2. Although there is no marked difference in predicting the response between the two mesh densities, but for each mesh density difference in predictions have been noted for considering bond-slip and without considering bond-slip. In general, the response using the mesh 1x2x18 produces better agreement with experimental values till the first crushing failure. Although the first crushing takes place at a load of 20.4 ton, the failure load was 16.4 ton (total) as per the experimental data available.

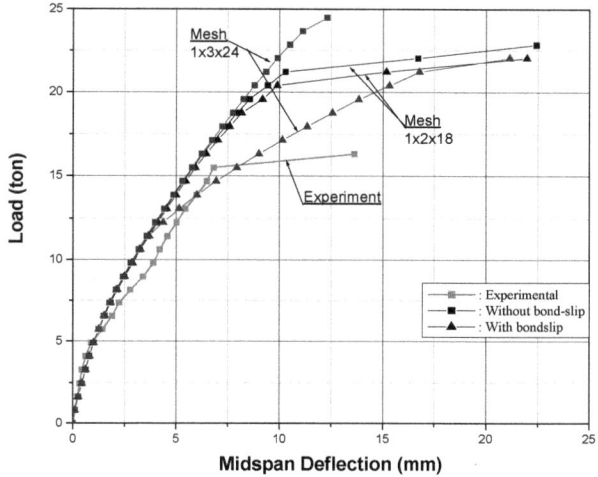

Fig. 5.3.7-2 : Load-deflection response (J-4)

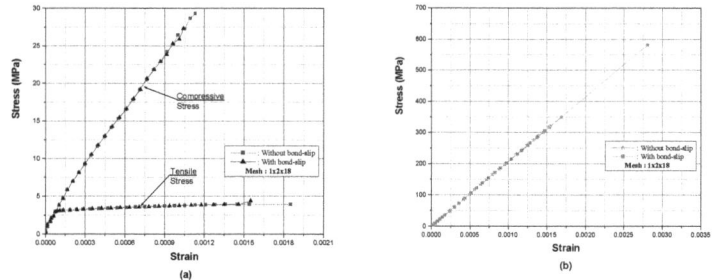

Fig. 5.3.6-3 : Stress-strain history (J-4)

(a) For concrete   (b) For bottom reinforcement

Table 5.3.7-2 : Load vs Deflection of beam J-4(with & without bond-slip)

Sl No.	Load (ton)	Experi-mental	Midspan Deflection (mm)			
			Mesh 1x2x18		Mesh 1x3x24	
			Without bond-slip	With bond-slip	Without bond-slip	With bond-slip
1	0	0	0	0	0	0
2	0.8160	0.1118	0.0926	0.0926	0.0937	0.0937
3	1.6320	0.2236	0.2643	0.2643	0.2674	0.2674
4	2.4480	0.3353	0.4364	0.4364	0.4414	0.4414
5	3.2640	0.4471	0.6116	0.6116	0.6218	0.6218
6	4.0800	0.6304	0.7915	0.7915	0.8037	0.8037
7	4.8960	0.8777	0.9909	0.992	1.0104	1.0145
8	5.7120	1.4421	1.2512	1.255	1.2441	1.2509
9	6.5280	1.8924	1.5247	1.5351	1.4914	1.5014
10	7.3440	2.2476	1.8122	1.8262	1.7758	1.7905
11	8.1600	2.7691	2.1186	2.1468	2.0805	2.1016
12	8.9760	3.4033	2.4733	2.5091	2.4225	2.4596
13	9.7920	3.8917	2.8443	2.886	2.7895	2.8365
14	10.6080	4.2088	3.2366	3.2845	3.1746	3.2341
15	11.4240	4.5825	3.6354	3.6903	3.5759	3.6472
16	12.2400	5.0207	4.0474	4.1081	3.991	4.3735
17	13.0560	5.4509	4.4668	4.5393	4.4226	5.1461
18	13.8720	5.9949	4.9123	4.9906	4.8586	6.0097
19	14.6880	6.4820	5.3624	5.4684	5.3062	6.9317
20	15.5040	6.8102	5.8262	5.939	5.7658	7.9362
21	16.3200	13.6247	6.2963	6.4577	6.2419	8.9993

The detail output of load-deflection data with the said mesh densities are also listed in Table 5.3.7-2, which clearly indicates that the coarse mesh option in this case yields fairly better agreement with the experimental values along with the post yield predictions, whereas the finer mesh fails to predict the same being without yield plateau. The sensitivity of the second mesh is very high and it may be attributed to a large gap between the number of elements in those two cases.

5.3.8 Beam # 8 :*(A-1, Bresler-Scordelis Beam, 1963)*

This example model of simply supported RC beam marked as A-1 subjected to a concentrated load at mid-span, tested by Bresler-Scordelis(1963) was analyzed. This benchmark experimental result was used by Kwak-Fillipou, 1997 to validate the proposed numerical models developed from time to time. This beam has four longitudinal tensile reinforcements distributed in two layers, two longitudinal compressive reinforcements and two-legged transverse shear reinforcements. The geometry, reinforcement details and its finite element mesh are illustrated in Fig. 5.3.8-1. The beam is 305mm(12inch) by 553mm in cross-section, with a span between the simple supports of 3657mm (12 ft). This experiment was conducted to obtain the ultimate load behaviour and the crack pattern of reinforced concrete beams along with the tension stiffening along with bond-slip behaviour of reinforcements. The parameters related to geometry are $d'' = 40$mm, $\omega = 0.422$ ton/m-run, $E_{soft} = 5280$ MPa and $E_{crack} = 255$ MPa. Other parameters related to geometry and material properties are mentioned in Table 5.3.8-1.

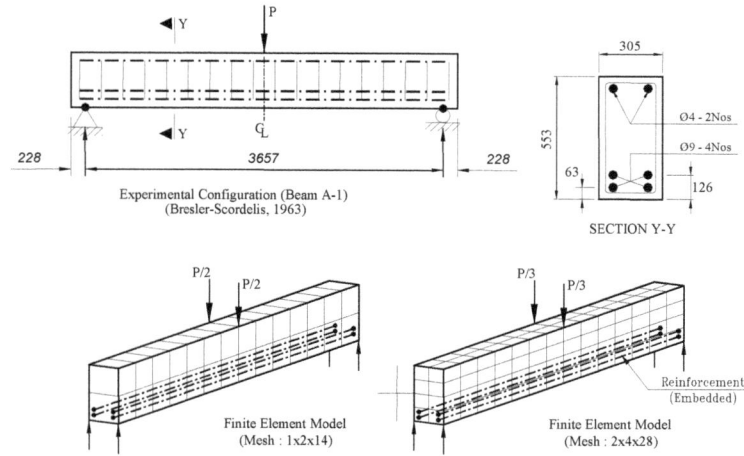

Fig. 5.3.8-1 : Details of RC beam (A-1)

Table 5.3.8-1 : Material Properties and load used for Beam # 8

f_{cu} (MPa)	E_0 (MPa)	μ_0	A_{st} (mm²)	f_y (MPa)	E_s (MPa)	P (ton)
24.5	23,674	0.17	2140	566	222,180	45

In order to study the effect of finite element mesh size on the numerical results of the proposed model, the following alternatives of were considered. In all cases the size of the element is maintained in such a way so that the aspect ratio of the dimensions of the side of the element remains close to unity.

Width(B) x Depth(D) x Length(L) = 305x553x3657				
Sl No.	Mesh designation	Mesh density $(N_B \times N_D \times N_L)$	Total number of elements.	Element Size.
1	Mesh-1	1x2x14	28	305x276.5x261.2
2	Mesh-2	2x4x28	224	152.5x138.3x130.6

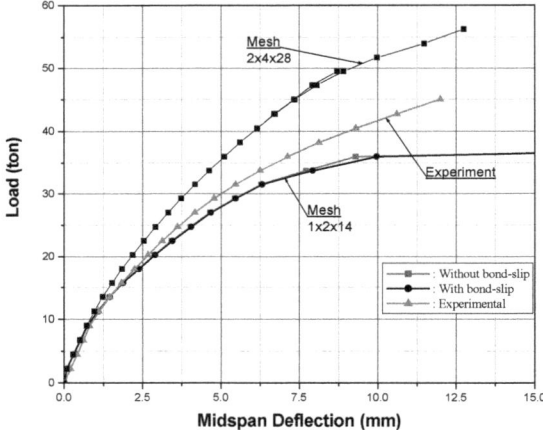

Fig. 5.3.8-2 : Load-deflection response (A-1)

Fig. 5.3.8-2 shows the correlation between the measured load-deflection response of the beam and the numerical results of the proposed model. To study the effect of finite element mesh size on the analytical results, two different mesh configurations were considered with 28 and 224 elements. In both the cases, the ratio of sides of the solid element has been consistently maintained close to 1.0 for better response. As Fig. 5.3.8-2 clearly indicates that the coarse mesh option in this case yields fairly better agreement with the experimental values along with the post yield predictions, whereas the finer mesh fails to predict the same being without yield plateau. The sensitivity of the second mesh is very high and it may be attributed to a large gap between the number of elements in those two cases, which is also obvious from Table 5.3.8-2.

In this particular example case, much difference in the response in regard to the contribution of bond-slip has been noted. The response of test data shows that the sudden failure of the beam took place, which may be attributed to higher percentage of reinforcements (highly over-reinforced) and it fails to pick up the definite yield plateau. It may be noted that the main longitudinal reinforcements in compression were not included in the present numerical study. In this perspective the proposed model produces a bit stiffer response even using coarse mesh.

Table 5.3.8-2 : Load vs Deflection of beam A-1(with & without bond-slip)

Sl No.	Load (ton)	Midspan Deflection (mm)				
		Experimental	Mesh 1x2x14		Mesh 2x4x28	
			Without bond-slip	With bond-slip	Without bond-slip	With bond-slip
1	0	0	0	0	0	0
2	2.25	0.2034	0.0907	0.0907	0.0859	0.0859
3	4.50	0.4068	0.3039	0.3039	0.2906	0.2906
4	6.75	0.6102	0.5175	0.5175	0.4958	0.4958
5	9.00	0.8136	0.7397	0.7397	0.7156	0.7156
6	11.25	1.1051	1.0742	1.0742	0.9628	0.9628
7	13.50	1.4447	1.4499	1.4532	1.2242	1.2242
8	15.75	1.8254	1.8713	1.8789	1.5167	1.5167
9	18.00	2.2373	2.3621	2.3783	1.8371	1.8371
10	20.25	2.6711	2.8757	2.8991	2.179	2.1791
11	22.50	3.1309	3.424	3.4566	2.5374	2.5375
12	24.75	3.626	4.0348	4.0493	2.9196	2.9196
13	27.00	4.1695	4.6514	4.6761	3.3184	3.3183
14	29.25	4.7775	5.4319	5.4616	3.7346	3.7346
15	31.50	5.4619	6.2676	6.3091	4.1726	4.1726
16	33.75	6.236	7.714	7.5698	4.6221	4.6221
17	36.00	7.1186	9.2927	9.2445	5.1005	5.0998
18	38.25	8.1343	34.8718	28.5897	5.6057	5.6048
19	40.50	9.2988	63.3161	56.2891	6.1426	6.141
20	42.75	10.604	175.6543	127.4326	6.7199	6.6928
21	45.00	12	--	--	7.3586	7.3311

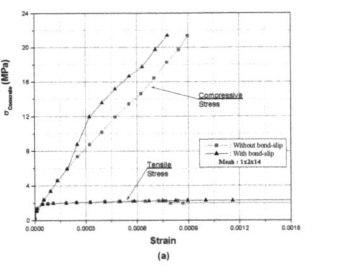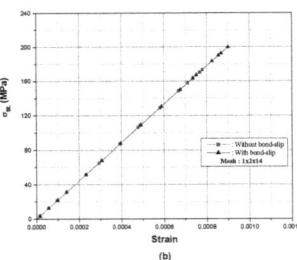

Fig. 5.3.8-3 : Stress-strain history (A-1)

(a) For concrete   (b) For bottom reinforcement

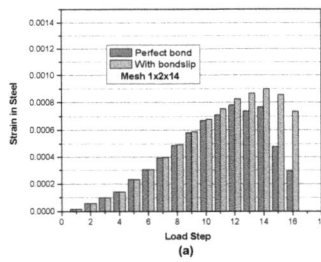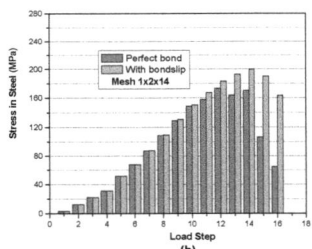

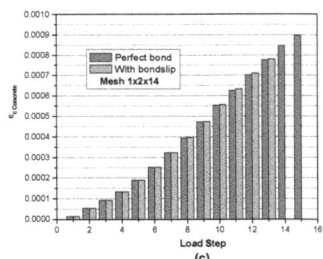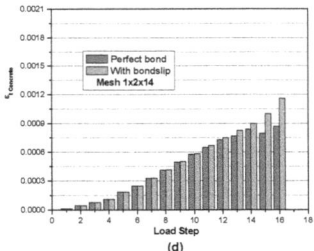

Fig. 5.3.8-4 : Effect of bond-slip (A-1)

(a) Strain in bottom reinforcement   (b) Stress in bottom reinforcement

(c) Compressive strain in concrete   (d) Tensile strain in concrete

Chapter 6

Conclusion & Outlook

In this chapter, some conclusions have been drawn based on the proposed model discussed so far and followed by comparison of results. Also the outlook as well as scope of future research have been highlighted.

6.1 Conclusion :

The objective of this work was to develop a reliable and computationally efficient three dimensional finite element tool to perform a comprehensive linear as well as nonlinear analysis of reinforced concrete beams under monotonic loading. A continuum mechanics based approach (considering the materials hypoelastic in nature) is implemented with various subroutines, which may generate mesh and calculate nodal loads on the system from the supplied external load as preprocessor. Once the basic geometrical and material properties are supplied in the form of input data (subroutine INDATAP and INDATAR), the parent concrete element domain can be prepared and also the reinforcement elements within the parent element can be prepared automatically using the subroutine MESGENPB and MESGENPF. The stiffness contribution of reinforcement within an element is calculated in a very consistent manner using the embedded approach, which may be determined independent of parent element mesh. The material model chosen for reinforcement is linearly elastic with strain hardening till the breaking point. This constitutive model is simple and appropriate as it evaluates the actual stiffness in the parent element domain with its spatial position and properties. Bond-slip has been accounted for using supplementary interface algorithm at the material level. An orthotropic hypoelasticity based formulation that uses five parameter Willam-Warnke failure criterion is utilized to model concrete both in linear as well as nonlinear regime including the cracking phenomenon following smeared crack concept.

The finite element formulation has been done using lower order solid hexahedral elements (HCiS18) with EAS approach for the sake of above purpose. The performance of this new enhanced strain element is found very similar to the higher order element (refer Fig, 5.2-13). In order to study the effect of finite element mesh size on the numerical results of the proposed model, a few alternatives were considered (refer Fig, 5.3.1-2, 5.3.3-2, 5.3.4-2). It has been found that the lower order elements HCiS18 modified with EAS variables are extremely efficient and effective in the analyzing three-dimensional problems, even with coarser meshes. This investigation work also establishes the utility and versatility of this element, in particular, in modeling concrete medium. The convergence of the iterative procedure has been considered on the accuracy of obtaining total displacements and the load steps were restricted to 5% of the failure load to avoid numerical instability or formation unrealistic numerical cracking, particularly in nonlinear regime.

This model also includes the discrete presence of the reinforcement in arbitrary direction without affecting the parent element mesh. It has been shown that the concept of this FE model (for incompressible situations) which includes the presence of the reinforcement in perfect bond condition and relaxed stress condition using bond-slip relation as per modelcode90 is very simple and economical in terms of time consumption in terms of analysis efforts compared to other generalized methods. The validity of the bond-slip formulation is tested by analyzing a few examples /case studies (refer Table 5.3.1-2, 5.3.7-2). It could be said that this model may work well for such reinforced concrete systems, where stiffness contribution of reinforcements are taken into account. The effect of variation of reinforcement ratio has also been studied((refer Fig, 5.3.1-5).

While considering the bond-slip phenomenon using continuous interface elements, it has been shown that the iterative scheme of the supplementary slip algorithm starts with the perfect bond predictions for reinforcement strains, which is obtained from the global solutions. In perfect bond situation, stresses are overestimated at the regions of the parent element domain, which experiences the highest strain. It has been noted that the continuous interface elements approach causes no problem as long as stress in the reinforcement does not exceed the elastic limit within the iterative scheme. Since within the embedded approach, reinforcements are not restricted to the parent element nodes, the computational effort is also reasonable. But when bond-slip is taken into account beyond the elastic limit of the reinforcement, it requires higher time (refer Table 5.3.2-2, 5.3.6-2, 5.3.8-2). However this seems to be irrelevant with the availability of high-speed computers. At the same time this model provides accurate representation of deformation and internal stress distribution (refer Fig. 5.3.1-3, 5.3.2-4, 5.3.4-4, 5.3.8-4).

Finally, with the existing experimental results, the proposed model demonstrates the general applicability and potentiality of the proposed model of reinforced concrete beams in the entire range of loading history (refer Fig. 5.3.3-2). The effective utility of the lower order EAS element HCiS18 in modeling the parent material i.e. concrete has been tested. It may be noted that the contribution of the reinforcement only in the tension zone has been given due attention in predicting the overall response /behaviour of reinforced concrete beams in three-dimension.

6.2 Outlook :

The developed model has a few segments. As far as the lower order solid elements are concerned, validity of the solid element HCiS18 could have been verified only. Although the literature suggests that HCiS12 performs better with even less no of extra variables, the same could not be verified in the proposed model. There are a variety other element types are available and hence the model could be extended for the same also.

In the proposed model, stiffness contribution of reinforcement has been accounted for only linear straight reinforcements and that too without automatic identification of intersection at the interfaces of parent elements. A parent element may include curved profile of reinforcement of tendons. Hence the inclusion of a generalized reinforcement or tendon profile, which may be extended to prestressed concrete structures also along with identification of intersection at the element boundary.

An advanced constitutive model may include both bond-slip as well anchorage loss model. Anchorage loss model is still not available with the program. As far as evaluation of slip is concerned, the proposed model fails to capture loss of stress in many a situation in spite of rigorous effort in this regard while developing the continuous interface element with the help of supplementary slip algorithm.

The constitutive law of concrete is very simple and straightforward. Implementing an advanced model for the sake of availability may be asked for. For such special applications, more sophisticated model are required to be incorporated in the program, e.g. fracture mechanics based, damage mechanics based models. The program has been initially designed for reinforcements in tension zone only. No provision and attempt has been made to incorporate effect of reinforcement in compressive zone as well as presence of shear reinforcements. The development of the stresses in the stirrups may contribute well in performing gross response of the system. As such the developed program is only suitable for under-reinforced sections only. Hence an opportunity remains open for development with deeper emphasis in this direction also.

For the implementation in nonlinear situation, an initial approach has been followed. The initial approach is robust but limited due to a very slow rate of convergence. Since this is an initial attempt to develop such a program in this direction, the same has been followed. At the same time it is important that the next step to implement an approach, which computes the stiffness terms with the tangential material stiffness and which may update the strains incrementally.

The hardened concrete is subjected to a process of complex interaction of temperature and shrinkage, also subjected to dynamic loads due to various reasons. A numerical tool, which is able to simulate all these influences and interactions, may provide valuable information about the reliability of hardened reinforced concrete structures. Such an advanced tool may be developed with an aim of to serve a practical guideline to the practicing engineers.

The major limitation of the work is that it could not be implemented with a very general sense to all categories of reinforced concrete structure with the span of the investigation work taken up for the purpose. Also, no experimental setup could be prepared during the work and as a result, the verification could not be done specifically for the proposed model.

The proposed model and the computer code developed during this programme needs more tests through case studies and necessary refinement has to be made, if necessary. A more detail and rigorous study of the same on frames may be extended in future to make the proposed model rational and practiacally acceptable in general. The author concludes after hard and earnest efforts on the development of the model and code that this may also verified from in-house experimental data.

Chapter 7

References

In this chapter, an exhaustive list of references has been presented, which has been referred by various chapter of this work.

1. [**Adey /Brebia** (1983)] **Adey R. A. and Brebia C. A.** (1983): '*Basic Computational Techniques for Engineers*', London : Plymouth, Pentech Press Ltd.

2. [**Amara** (1996)] **Amara K.B.** (1996): 'Griffith energy balance model for crack-growth prediction in reinforced cocncrete.' *Journal of Engineering mechanics ASCE*, Vol. 122, No. 7, pp 683-689.

3. [**Andelfinger /Ramm** (1993)] **Andelfinger U. and Ramm E.** (1993): 'EAS-elements for two-dimensional, three-dimensional, plate and shell structures and their equivalence to HR-elements.' *International Journal for Numerical Methods in Engineering*, Vol. 36, pp 1311-1337.

4. [**Arieas *et al.*** (2003)] **Arieas M. A. Pedro, Cesar de sa J. M. A., Antinio C. A. C. and Fernandes A. A.** (2003): 'Analysis of 3D problems using a new enhanced strain hexahedral element.' *International Journal for Numerical Methods in Engineering*, Vol. 58, pp 1637-1682.

5. [**Assan** (2002)] **Assan A. E.** (2002), '**Nonlinear** analysis of reinforced concrete cylindrical shells.', *Computers and Structures*, Vol. 80, pp. 2177-2184.

6. [**Avrum** *et al.* (1993)] **Avrum C., Bob C., Friedrich R. and Stoian V.** (1993): *'Numerical Analysis of Reinforced Concrete Structures'*, Bucharest, Eitura Academiei Romane.

7. [**Balan** *et al.* (1997)] **Balan T. A., Filippou F. C. and Popov E. P.** (1997), 'Constitutive model for 3D cyclic analysis of concrete structures.', *Journal of Engineering Mechanics*, Vol. 123, No. 2, pp. 143-153.

8. [**Balan** *et al.* (2001)] **Balan T. A., Spacone E. and Kwon M.** (2001), 'A 3D hypoelastic model for cyclic analysis of concrete structures', *Engineering Structures*, Vol. 23, pp. 333-342.

9. [**Barzegar /Maddipudi** (1994)] **Barzegar F. and Maddipudi S.** (1994): 'Generating reinforcements in FE modeling of concrete structures', *Journal of structural Engineering*, Vol. 120, No. 5, pp. 1656-1661.

10. [**Barzegar /Maddipudi** (1997):a] **Barzegar F. and Maddipudi S.** (1997): 'Three-dimensional modeling of concrete structures. I : Plain Concrete', *Journal of structural Engineering*, Vol. 123, No. 10, pp. 1339-1346.

11. [**Barzegar /Maddipudi** (1997):b] **Barzegar F. and Maddipudi S.** (1997): 'Three-dimensional modeling of concrete structures. II : Reinforced Concrete', *Journal of structural Engineering*, Vol. 123, No. 10, pp. 1347-1356.

12. [**Bathe /Wilson** (1978)] **Bathe K. J. and Wilson W.L.** (1978): *'Numerical methods in finite element analysis'*, Indian Reprint, New Delhi, Prentice-Hall of India (P) Ltd.

13. [**Bathe** (1997)] **Bathe K. J.** (1997): *'Finite Element Procedures'*, 4th Indian Reprint, New Delhi, Prentice-Hall of India (P) Ltd.

14. [**Bazant** (1997)] **Bazant Z.P.** (1997): 'Fracturing truss model : size effect in shear failure of reinforced concrete.' *Journal of Engineering mechanics ASCE*, Vol. 123, No. 12, pp 1276-1288.

15. [**Bazant /Canel** (2005)] **Bazant Z.P. and Canel F.C.** (2005): 'Microplane model M5 with kinematic and static constraints for concrete fracture an elasticity I

: Theory.' *Journal of Engineering mechanics ASCE*, Vol. 131, No. 1, pp 31-40.

16. [**Beer** (1985)] **Beer G**. (1985): 'An isoparametric joint/interface element for finite element analysis', *International Journal for Numerical Methods in Engineering'*, Vol. 21, pp. 585-600.

17. [**Bhatt /Kader** (1998)] **Bhatt P. and Kader M.A.** (1998): 'Prediction of shear strength of reinforced concrete beams by nonlinear finite element analysis.', *Computers & Structures'*, Vol. 68, pp. 139-155.

18. [**Bischoff /Ramm** (1997)] **Bischoff M and Ramm E.** (1997): 'Shear deformable shell elements for large strains and rotations.' *International Journal for Numerical Methods in Engineering*, Vol. 40, pp 4427-4449.

19. [**Bouzaiene /Massicotte** (1997)] **Bouzaiene A. and Massicotte B.** (1997), 'Hypoelastic tridimensional model for nonproportional loading of Plain concrete.', *Journal of Engineering Mechanics*, Vol. 123, No. 11, pp. 1111-1120.

20. [**Boresi /Sidebottom** (1985)] **Boresi A. P. and Sidebottom O. M.** (1985): '*Advanced Mechanics of Materials'*, New York, John Wiley & Sons Inc.

21. [**Brebbia /Connor** (1973)] **Brebbia C. A. and Connor J. J.** (1973): '*Fundamentals of Finite Element Techniques'*, London, England, Butterworth & Co. (Publishers) Ltd.

22. [**Buchter** *et al.* (1994)] **Buchter N., Ramm E and Roehl D.** (1994): 'Three-dimensional extension of non-linear shell formulation based on the enhanced strain assumed strain concept.' *International Journal for Numerical Methods in Engineering*, Vol. 37, pp 2551-2568.

23. [**Cesar /Natal Jorge** (1999)] **Cesar de sa J. M. A. and Natal Jorge R. M.** (1999): 'New enhanced strain elements for incompressible problems.' *International Journal for Numerical Methods in Engineering*, Vol. 44, pp 229-248.

24. [**Cesar** *et al.* (2002)] **Cesar de sa J. M. A., Natal Jorge R. M., Valente A. F. Robert and Arieas M. A. Pedro** (2002): 'Development of shear locking-

free shell elements using an enhanced assumed strain formulation.' *International Journal for Numerical Methods in Engineering*, Vol. 53, pp 1721-1750.

25. [**Chakraborty** (1987)] **Chakraborty J.** (1987): '*Theory of Plasticity*', Singapore, McGraw-Hill Book Co.

26. [**Channakeshava /Iyenger** (1988)] **Channakeshava C. and Iyenger K. T. S. R.** (1988): 'A computer software for nonlinear analysis of concrete structures.' *Journal of Structural Engineering*, Vol. 15, No. 1, pp 13-18.

27. [**Chen /Saleeb** (1982)] **Chen W. F. and Saleeb A. F.** (1982): '*Constitutive Equations for Engineering Materials, Volume-I : Elasticity and Modeling*', New York, John Wiley & Sons Inc.

28. [**Chen** (1982)] **Chen W. F.** (1982): '*Plasticity in Reinforced Concrete*', New York, McGraw Hill Inc.

29. [**Cheng /Fan** (1993)] **Cheng Y.M. and Fan Y.** (1993): 'Modeling of reinforcement in concrete and reinforcement coefficient', *Finite Element analysis and design*, Vol. 13, pp. 271-284.

30. [**Cho /Hotta** (2002)] **Cho C.G. and Hotta H.** (2002): 'A study on compressive strength of concrete in flexural regions of reinforced concrete beams using finite element analysis.', *Structural Engineering and Mechanics*', Vol. 13, No. 3 pp. 1-15

31. [**Cho /Park** (2003)] **Cho C. G. and Park M. H.** (2003), 'Finite element prediction of the influence of confinement on RC beam-columns under single or double curvature bending.', *Engineering Structures*, Vol. 25, pp. 1525-1536.

32. [**Cook** *et al.* (2003)] **Cook, R. D., Mulkus D. S., Plesha M. E. and Witt R. J.** (2003): '*Concepts and applications of finite element analysis*', 4th edition, Singapore, John Wiley & Sons (Asia) Pte Ltd.

33. [**Cook** (*1995*)] **Cook R. D.** (*1995*): '*Finite element modeling for stress analysis*', New York, John Wiley.

34. [**Crisfield** (1991)] **Crisfield M. A.** (1991): '*Non-Linear Finite Element Analysis of Solids and Structures : Volume-I(Essentials) & Volume-II(Advanced Topics)*', Chischester, UK, John Wiley & Sons Ltd.

35. [**Desai /Abel** (1972)] **Desai C. S. and Abel J. F.** (1972): '*Introduction to the finite element method*', New York, Van Nostrand Reinhold Ltd.

36. [**Desir** *et al.* (1999)] **Desir J.M., Romdhane M.R.B., Ulm F.J. and Fairburn E.M.R.** (1999): 'Steel-concrete interface : revisiting constitutive and numerical modeling.' *Computers & Structures*, Vol. 71, pp 489-503.

37. [**Elfgren /Shah** (1991)] **Elfgren L. and Shah S. P.** (1991): '*Analysis of Concrete Structures by Fracture Mechanics*', Proceedings No. 6 of the International RILEM Workshop, 1st edition, Madras, Chapman and Hall India.

38. [**El-Meaini /Citipitioglu** (1991)] **El-Meaini N. and Citipitioglu E.** (1991), 'Finite element analysis of prestressed and reinforced concrete structures.', *Journal of Structural Engineering,* ASCE, Vol. 117, No. 10, pp. 2851-2864.

39. [**Elwi /Hrudey** (1989)] **Elwi A.E. and Hrudey T. M.** (1989), 'Finite element model for curved embedded reinforcement.', *Journal of Engineering Mechanics*, Vol. 115, No. 4, pp. 740-754.

40. [**Elwi /Murray** (1979)] **Elwi A.E. and Murray D. W.** (1979), 'A 3d hypoelastic concrete constitutive relationship.', *Journal of Engineering Mechanics div.*, ASCE, Vol. 105, No. 4, pp. 623-641.

41. [**Fan** *et al.* (2001)] **Fan S.C., Yu M.H. and Yang S.Y.** (2001), 'On the unification of Yield Criteria.', *Journal of Applied Mechanics div.*, ASME, Vol. 68, pp. 341-343.

42. [**Ghandehari** *et al.* (2000)] **Ghandehari M., Krishnaswamy S. and Shah S** (2000): 'Bond-induced longitudinal fracture in reinforced concrete.', *Journal of Applied Mechanics ASME*', Vol. 67, pp. 740-748.

43. [**Gomes /Awruch** (2001)] **Gomes H. M. and Awruch** (2001): 'Some aspects of three-dimensional numerical modeling of reinforced concrete structures' *Advances in Engineering software*, Vol. 32, pp 257-277.

44. [**Goncalves** *et al.* (2000):] **Goncalves J. P. M., Moura de M. F. S. F., Castro de P. M. S. T. and Marques A. T.** (2000): 'Interface element including point-to-surface constraints for three-dimensional problems with damage propagation.' *Engineering Computations*, Vol. 17, No. 1, pp 28-47.

45. [**Gupta /Akbar** (1984)] **Gupta A.K. and Akbar H.** (1984): 'Cracking in reinforced concrete analysis.', *Journal of Structural Engineering'*, Vol. 110, No. 8, pp. 1735-1746.

46. [**Hartl** *et al.* (2000)] **Hartl H., Sparowitz L. and Elgamal A.** (2000): 'The 3D computational modeling of reinforced and prestressed structures', *Proceedings of the 3rd International PhD Symposium in Civil Engineering, Bergmeister K.(ed.)*, Vienna, , pp. 66-79.

47. [**Hartl /Elgamal** (2000)] **Hartl H. and Elgamal A.** (2000): 'Non linear modeling of prestressed structures based on a continuum mechanics approach', *Heft 45/Sept 2000, Osterreichische Vereinigung fur Beton-und Bautechnik*, Vienna, pp. 87-96.

48. [**Hartl /Beer** (2000)] **Hartl H. and Beer G.** (2000): 'Computational modeling of reinforced concrete structures', *Festschrift zum 60, Geburtstag von Lutz Sparowitz, TU-Graz*, pp. 105-114.

49. [**Hillerborg** *et al.* (1976)] **Hillerborg A., Modeer M. and Petersson P-E** (1976): 'Analysis of crack formation and crack growth in concrete by means of fracture mechanics and finite elements.' *Cement and Concrete Research*, Vol. 6, pp 773-782.

50. [**Hinton /Owen** (1977)] **Hinton E. and Owen D. R. J.** (1977): '*Finite element Programming'*, London, Academic Press.

51. [**Hinton /Owen** (1984)] **Hinton E. and Owen D. R. J.** (1984): '*Finite Element Software for Plates and Shell'*, Swansea, UK, Pineridge Press.

52. [**Irons /Sohrab** (1980)] **Irons B. and Sohrab A.** (1980): '*Techniques of Finite Element'*, Student edition, Chichester, Ellis Horwood Ltd.

53. **[Iyengar /Raviraj** (2001)] **Iyengar K.T.S.R. and Raviraj S.** (2001): 'Analytical study of fracture in concrete beams using Blunt crack model.' *Journal of Engineering mechanics ASCE*, Vol. 127, No. 8, pp 828-834.

54. **[Jendele /Cervenka** (2006)] **Jendele L. and Cervenka J.** (2006): 'Finite element modeling of reinforcement with bond.' *Computers & Structures*, Vol. 84, pp 1780-1791.

55. **[Kanchi** (1993)] **Kanchi B. Madhu** (1993): '*Matrix Method of Structural analysis*', 2nd and enlarged Edition, New Delhi, India, Wiley Eastern Ltd.

56. **[Klinkel /Wagner** (1997)] **Klinkel S. and Wagner W.** (1997): 'A geometrical non-linear brick element based on EAS-method.' *International Journal for Numerical Methods in Engineering*, Vol. 408, pp 4529-4545.

57. **[Kollegger /Mehlhorn** (1990)] **Kollegger J. and Mehlhorn G.** (1990), 'Material model for the analysis of reinforced concrete surface structures.', *Computational Mechanics*, Vol. 6, pp. 341-357.

58. **[Krishnamoorty /Paneerselvam** (1978)] **Krishnamoorty C. S. and Paneerselvam A.** (1978), 'FEPACS1- A finite element program for nonlinear of reinforced concrete framed structures.', *Computers & Structures*, Vol. 9, pp. 451-461.

59. **[Kwak /Filippou** (1997)] **Kwak H. G. and Filippou F. C.** (1997): 'Nonlinear FE analysis of R/C structures under monotonic loads.', *Computers & Structures'*, Vol. 65, No. 1, pp. 1-16

60. **[Kwak /Kim** (2001)] **Kwak H. G. and Kim S.P.** (2001), 'Bond-slip behavior under monotonic uniaxial loads.', *Engineering Structures*, Vol. 23, pp. 298-309.

61. **[Kwon /Spacone** (2002)] **Kwon M. and Spacone E.** (2002), 'Three dimensional finite element analyses of reinforced concrete columns.', *Computers and Structures*, Vol. 80, pp. 199-212.

62. **[Maekawa *et al.*** (2003)] **Maekawa K., Pimanmas A. and Okamura H.** (2003): '*Nonlinear Mechanics of Reinforced Concrete*', New York, USA, Spon Press.

63. [**Mijuca** (2004)] **Mijuca D.** (2004), 'On hexahedral finite element HC8/27 in elasticity.', _Computational Mechanics_, Vol. 33, No. 6, pp. 466-480.

64. [**Mukherjee /Som** (1985)] **Mukherjee A. K. and Som P. K.** (1985): '_Computer Methods of Structures_', 2nd Edition, New Delhi, Khanna Publishers.

65. [**Ngo /Scordelis** (1967)] **Ngo D. and Scordelis A.C.** (1967), 'Finite element analysis of reinforced concrete beams', _ACI Journal_, Vol. 64, pp. 152-163.

66. [**Nilson** (1968)] **Nilson A.H.** (1968), 'Nonlinear analysis of reinforced concrete by the finite element method.', _ACI Journal_, Vol. 65, No. 9, pp. 757-766.

67. [**Oliveira _et al_** (2008)] **Oliveira R.S., Ramalho M.A. and Correa M.R.S.** (2008), 'A layered finite element for reinforced concrete beams with bond-slip effects.', _Cement & Concrete composites_, **Vol. 30, No. 10, pp. 245-252**.

68. [**Ottosen** (1977)] **Ottosen N. S.** (1977): 'A failure criteria for concrete.' _Journal of Engineering Mechanics Division_, Vol. 103, pp 527-535.

69. [**Polak /Blackwell** (1998)] **Polak M. A. and Blackwell K. G.** (1998), 'Modeling tension in reinforced concrete members subjected to bending and axial load.', _Journal of Structural Engineering_, ASCE, Vol. 124, No. 9, pp. 1018-1024.

70. [**Press /Teukolsky** (1998)] **Press W. H.; Teukolsky S. A.** (1998): '_Numerical Recipes in FORTRAN : The art of scientific computing_', 2nd Indian edition, New Delhi, Replica Press for Cambrige University Press.

71. [**Rabczuk _et al_.** (2005)] **Rabczuk T., Akkermann J. and Eibl J.** (2005), 'A numerical model for reinforced concrete structures.', _International Journal of solids and Structures_, Vol. 42, pp. 1327-1354.

72. [**Raghuprasad /Iyenger** (1992)] **Raghuprasad B. K. and Iyenger K. T. S. R.** (1992): 'Fracture behaviour of reinforced concrete beams.' _Journal of Structural Engineering_, Vol. 19, No. 1, pp 27-36.

73. [**Raghuprasad _et al_.** (2005)] **Raghuprasad B.K., Bharatkumar B.H., Murthy D.S.R., Narayanan R and Gopalakrishnan S.** (2005): 'Fracture mechanics model for analysis of plain and reinforced high-performance

concret beams.' *Journal of Engineering mechanics ASCE*, Vol. 131, No. 8, pp 831-838.

74. **[Salari /Spacone (2001)] Salari M. R. and Spacone E.** (2001): 'Finite element formulations of one-dimensional element with bond-slip.' *Engineering Structures*, Vol. 23, pp 815-826.

75. **[Samanta /Ghosh (2008a)] Samanta Amiya Kr. and Ghosh Somnath.**(2008) : 'On Performance of EAS based Lower Order Element in 3D Computational Modeling of RC Beam in the Elastic Range.' *Proceedings of International Conference on Advances in Concrete and Construction (ICACC-2008), Hyderabad, India,* Feb 7-9, 2008, pp 1084-1093.

76. **[Samanta /Ghosh (2008b)] Samanta Amiya Kr. and Ghosh Somnath.**(2008) : 'A 3D Computational Model of RC Beam Using Lower Order Elements with Enhanced Strain Approach in the Elastic Range.', *Proceedings of International Conference on Computational & Experimental Engineering and Sciences (ICCES'08), Honolulu, Hawaii,* March 17-22, 2008, pp 113.

77. **[Samanta /Ghosh (2008c)] Samanta Amiya K. and Ghosh Somnath.**(2008) : 'A 3D Computational Model of RC Beam Using Lower Order Elements with Enhanced Strain Approach in the Elastic Range.', *Computers, Materials & Continua*, Vol. 8, No. 1, pp 43-52.

78. **[Samanta /Ghosh (2009a)] Samanta Amiya Kr. and Ghosh Somnath.**(2009) : 'A 3D Hypoelastic Computational Model of Reinforced Concrete Structure.', *Icfai Journal of Structural Engineering*, 2009, Vol. II, No. 1, pp 32-53.

79. **[Sankarasubramanian /Rajasekharan (1996)] Sankarasubramanian G. and Rajasekharan S.** (1996): 'Constitutive modeling of concrete using a new failure criterion.' *Computers & Structures*, Vol. 58, No. 5, pp 1003-1014.

80. **[Selby /Vecchio (1997)] Selby R. G. and Vecchio F. J.** (1997), 'A constitutive model for analysis of reinforced concrete structure.', *Canadian Journal of civil Engineering*, Vol. 24, pp. 460-470.

81. [**Shah** *et al.* (1993)] **Shah S.P., Swartz S. E. and Ouyang C.** (1993): '*Fracture Mechanics of Concrete : Applications of fracture mechanics to concrete, rock, and other quasi-brittle materials'*, Singapore, Wiley Interscience.

82. [**Simo /Armero** (1992)] **Simo J. C. and Armero F.** (1992): 'Geometrically non-linear enhanced strain mixed methods and the method of incompatible modes.' *International Journal for Numerical Methods in Engineering*, Vol. 33, pp 1413-1449.

83. [**Simo /Rifai** (1990)] **Simo J. C. and Rifai M. S.** (1990): 'A class of mixed assumed strain methods and the method of incompatible modes.', *International Journal for Numerical Methods in Engineering'*, Vol. 29, pp. 1595- 1638

84. [**Smith /Griffith** (2004)] **Smith I. M. and Griffith D. V.** (2004): '*Programming the finite element method'* 4th edition, 2004, West Sussex, John wiley

85. [**Sousa** *et al.* (2002)] **Sousa de R. J. A., Natal Jorge R. M., Valente A. F. Robert, Cesar de sa J. M. A., Arieas M. A. Pedro and Fernandes A. A.** (2002): 'Lower order elements for 3D analysis.' *5th world congress on Computational Mechanics WCCM-V*, July 7-12, Viena, Austria.

86. [**Sousa** *et al.* (2003):a] **Sousa de R. J. A., Natal Jorge R. M., Valente A. F. Robert and Cesar de sa J. M. A.** (2003): 'A new volumetric and shear locking-free 3D enhanced strain element.' *Engineering computations*, Vol. 20 No. 7, pp 896-925.

87. [**Sousa** *et al.* (2003):b] **Sousa de R. J. A., Natal Jorge R. M., Valente A. F. Robert and Cesar de sa J. M. A.** (2003): 'Formulation of EAS solid elements for incompressibility and thin shell application in Nonlinear range.' *VII International Conference on ComputationalPlasticity COMPLAS 2003*, Barcelona.

88. [**Souza** *et al.* (1996)] **Souza Neto de E. A., Peric D. Dutko M. and Owen D. R. J.** (1996): 'Design of simple low order finite elements for large strain analysis of nearly incompressible solids.' *International Journal of solids and structures*, Vol. 33, No. 20-22, pp 3277-3296.

89. **[Stevens *et al.* (1991)] Stevens N.J., Uzumeri S.M., Collins M.P. and Will G.T.** (1991): 'Constitutive model for reinforced cement concrete finite element analysis.' *ACI Structural Journal*, Vol. 88, No. 1, pp 49-59.

90. **[Timoshenko /Goodier (1970)] Timoshenko S.P. and Goodier J.N.** (1970): 'Theory of elasticity' *McGraw-Hill*, London.

91. **[Tzamtzis /Asteris (2004)] Tzamtzis A. D. and Asteris P.G.**(2004), 'FE analysis of complex discontinuous and jointed structural systems (Part 1 : Presenattion of the method – A state-of-the-art review).', *Electronic Journal of Structural Engineering*, Vol. 1, pp. 75-92.

92. **[Valente *et al.* (2002)] Valente A. F. Robert, Natal Jorge R. M., Cesar de sa J. M. A. and Arieas M. A. Pedro** (2002): 'Application of the enhanced assumed strain concept towards the development of shear locking-free shell elements.' *5th World Congress on Computational Mechanics (WCCM) July 7-12 2002*,Viena Austria, pp 1-20.

93. **[Valente *et al.* (2004)] Valente A. F. Robert, Sousa de R. J. A. and Natal Jorge R. M.,** (2004): 'An enhanced strain 3d element for large deformation elastoplastic thin-shell applications.' *Computational Mechanics*, Vol. 34, pp 38-52.

94. **[Vechhio (1992)] Vechhio F. J.** (1992), 'Finite element modeling of concrete expansion and confinement.', *Journal of Structural Engineering ASCE*, Vol. 118, N0. 9, pp. 2390-2406.

95. **[Vechhio /Collins (1993)] Vechhio F. J. and Collins M.P.** (1993), 'Compression response of cracked reinforced concrete.', *Journal of Structural Engineering ASCE*, Vol. 119, N0. 12, pp. 3590-3610.

96. **[Vechhio (1998)] Vechhio F. J.** (1998), 'Lesson from the analysis of a 3-D concrete shear wall.', *Structural Engineering and Mechanics*, Vol. 6, N0. 4, pp. 439-455.

97. **[Vechhio (2000):a] Vechhio F. J.** (2000), 'Analysis of shear-critical reinforced concrete beams.', *ACI Structural Journal* Vol. 97, N0. 1, pp. 102-110.

98. [**Vechhio** (2000):b] **Vechhio F. J.** (2000), 'Disturbed stress field model for reinforced concrete : Formulation.', *Journal of Structural Engineering ASCE*, Vol. 126, N0. 9, pp. 1070-1077.

99. [**Vechhio** (2001):a] **Vechhio F. J.** (2001), 'Disturbed stress field model for reinforced concrete : Implementation.', *Journal of Structural Engineering ASCE*, Vol. 127, N0. 1, pp. 12-19.

100. [**Vechhio** (2001):a] **Vechhio F. J.** (2001), 'Disturbed stress field model for reinforced concrete : Validation.', *Journal of Structural Engineering ASCE*, Vol. 127, N0. 4, pp. 350-358.

101. [**Vu-Quoc /Tan** (2003)] **Vu-Quoc L. and Tan X. G.** (2003): 'Optimal solid shells for non-linear analyses of multiplayer composites. I. Statics.' *Computer methods in applied mechanics and engineering*, Vol. 192, pp 975-1016.

102. [**Yon** *et al.* (1997)] **Yon J.H., Hawkins N.M. and Kobayashi A.S.** (1997): 'Comparisons of concrete fracture models.' *Journal of Engineering mechanics ASCE*, Vol. 123, No. 3, pp 196-203.

103. [**Yu** (2002)] **Yu M.H.** (2002), 'Advances in strength theories for materials under complex stress state in the 20th century.', *Applied Mechanics Div. ASME*, Vol. 55, No. 3, pp. 169-218.

104. [**Wang /Liu** (2003)] **Wang X. and Liu X.** (2003), 'A strain-softening model for steel-concrete bond.' *Cement and Concrete research*, Vol. 33, pp. 1669-1673.

105. [**Wilson** (2002)] **Wilson C.D.** (2002): 'A critical reexamination of classical metal plasticity.' *Journal of Applied Mechanics div.*, Vol. 69, pp 63-68.

106. [**Zienkiewicz** (1983)] **Zienkiewicz O. C.** (1983): '*The Finite Element Method*', 4th Indian Reprint, New Delhi, Tata McGraw-Hill Publishing Co. Ltd.

Chapter 8

Appendix

In this chapter, a brief list of matrices /vectors notations has been described, which are used in the proposed /employed model. Also a few derivations have been presented, which are not included in the main body of the proposed formulation.

8.1 Units

The basic equations and computer implementation are being developed, where we need to have a consistent dimension both for input as well as output.

- ➢ Length : mm
- ➢ Force : tonne
- ➢ Stress : MPa

8.2 Stress & Strain :

The following sign convention of continuum mechanics is used throughout the thesis and the developed computer program. Positive quantities are tensile stresses, tensile strains and increase in volume. A righted handed coordinate system is employed throughout.

Matrix notations are followed in this presentation. Hence for geometrically linear situation or for linear elastic analysis, the stress and strain tensor are written as proposed by *Timoshenko /Goodier (1970)*.

$$\sigma = \begin{Bmatrix} \sigma_x \\ \sigma_y \\ \sigma_z \\ \sigma_{xy} \\ \sigma_{yz} \\ \sigma_{zx} \end{Bmatrix} \quad \text{and} \quad \varepsilon = \begin{Bmatrix} \varepsilon_x \\ \varepsilon_y \\ \varepsilon_z \\ 2.\varepsilon_{xy} \\ 2.\varepsilon_{yz} \\ 2.\varepsilon_{zx} \end{Bmatrix} = \begin{Bmatrix} \varepsilon_x \\ \varepsilon_y \\ \varepsilon_z \\ \gamma_{xy} \\ \gamma_{yz} \\ \gamma_{zx} \end{Bmatrix} = \begin{Bmatrix} \dfrac{\partial u}{\partial x} \\ \dfrac{\partial v}{\partial y} \\ \dfrac{\partial w}{\partial z} \\ \dfrac{\partial u}{\partial y} + \dfrac{\partial v}{\partial x} \\ \dfrac{\partial v}{\partial z} + \dfrac{\partial w}{\partial y} \\ \dfrac{\partial u}{\partial z} + \dfrac{\partial w}{\partial x} \end{Bmatrix} \qquad \text{Eq. 8.2-1}$$

For geometrically non-linear situation, the Green-Lagrange strain tensor is written as [*Crisfield (1991)*].

$$\varepsilon = \begin{Bmatrix} \varepsilon_x \\ \varepsilon_y \\ \varepsilon_z \\ \gamma_{xy} \\ \gamma_{yz} \\ \gamma_{zx} \end{Bmatrix} = \varepsilon_0 + \varepsilon_L = \begin{Bmatrix} \dfrac{\partial u}{\partial x} \\ \dfrac{\partial v}{\partial y} \\ \dfrac{\partial w}{\partial z} \\ \dfrac{\partial u}{\partial y} + \dfrac{\partial v}{\partial x} \\ \dfrac{\partial v}{\partial z} + \dfrac{\partial w}{\partial y} \\ \dfrac{\partial u}{\partial z} + \dfrac{\partial w}{\partial x} \end{Bmatrix} + \begin{Bmatrix} \dfrac{1}{2}\left[\left(\dfrac{\partial u}{\partial x}\right)^2 + \left(\dfrac{\partial v}{\partial x}\right)^2 + \left(\dfrac{\partial w}{\partial x}\right)^2\right] \\ \dfrac{1}{2}\left[\left(\dfrac{\partial u}{\partial y}\right)^2 + \left(\dfrac{\partial v}{\partial y}\right)^2 + \left(\dfrac{\partial w}{\partial y}\right)^2\right] \\ \dfrac{1}{2}\left[\left(\dfrac{\partial u}{\partial z}\right)^2 + \left(\dfrac{\partial v}{\partial z}\right)^2 + \left(\dfrac{\partial w}{\partial z}\right)^2\right] \\ \left(\dfrac{\partial u}{\partial x}\cdot\dfrac{\partial u}{\partial y}\right) + \left(\dfrac{\partial v}{\partial x}\cdot\dfrac{\partial v}{\partial y}\right) + \left(\dfrac{\partial w}{\partial x}\cdot\dfrac{\partial w}{\partial y}\right) \\ \left(\dfrac{\partial u}{\partial y}\cdot\dfrac{\partial u}{\partial z}\right) + \left(\dfrac{\partial v}{\partial y}\cdot\dfrac{\partial v}{\partial z}\right) + \left(\dfrac{\partial w}{\partial y}\cdot\dfrac{\partial w}{\partial z}\right) \\ \left(\dfrac{\partial u}{\partial x}\cdot\dfrac{\partial u}{\partial z}\right) + \left(\dfrac{\partial v}{\partial x}\cdot\dfrac{\partial v}{\partial z}\right) + \left(\dfrac{\partial w}{\partial x}\cdot\dfrac{\partial w}{\partial z}\right) \end{Bmatrix}$$

Eq. 8.2-2

The second Piola-Kirchhoff stress tensor as ; $\qquad \sigma = \dfrac{\partial W}{\partial \varepsilon} = \begin{Bmatrix} \sigma_x \\ \sigma_y \\ \sigma_z \\ \sigma_{xy} \\ \sigma_{yz} \\ \sigma_{zx} \end{Bmatrix} \qquad$ Eq. 8.2-3

8.3 Matrices & Vectors :

The following matrices and vectors those have been used for the formulation purpose are well known and found in textbooks viz. *Boresi /Sidebottom (1985), Bathe (1997), Chen /Saleeb (1982) and Crisfield (1991).*

$B_{r,g}$ Strain displacement matrix for 3D reinforcement element in global coordinates,

$n_{linear} = 2$

$$B_{r,g} = \left[\frac{\partial N_{r1}}{\partial x} \quad \frac{\partial N_{r1}}{\partial y} \quad \frac{\partial N_{r1}}{\partial z} \quad : \quad \frac{\partial N_{r2}}{\partial x} \quad \frac{\partial N_{r2}}{\partial y} \quad \frac{\partial N_{r2}}{\partial z} \right] \qquad \text{Eq. 8.3-1}$$

$B_{r,l}$ Strain displacement matrix for 1D reinforcement element in global coordinates,

$n_{linear} = 2$

$$B_{r,l} = \left[\frac{\delta N_1}{\delta s} \quad \frac{\delta N_2}{\delta s} \right] = \frac{\left[\dfrac{\delta N_1}{\delta \xi} \quad \dfrac{\delta N_2}{\delta \xi} \right]}{|J|} \qquad \text{Eq. 8.3-2}$$

B_P Strain displacement matrix for 3D parent /concrete element, $n_{linear} = 8$

$$B_P = \begin{bmatrix} \dfrac{\partial N_1}{\partial x} & 0 & 0 & \dfrac{\partial N_2}{\partial x} & 0 & 0 & \cdots & \dfrac{\partial N_8}{\partial x} & 0 & 0 \\[2mm] 0 & \dfrac{\partial N_1}{\partial y} & 0 & 0 & \dfrac{\partial N_2}{\partial y} & 0 & \cdots & 0 & \dfrac{\partial N_8}{\partial y} & 0 \\[2mm] 0 & 0 & \dfrac{\partial N_1}{\partial z} & 0 & 0 & \dfrac{\partial N_2}{\partial z} & \cdots & 0 & 0 & \dfrac{\partial N_8}{\partial z} \\[2mm] \dfrac{\partial N_1}{\partial y} & \dfrac{\partial N_1}{\partial x} & 0 & \dfrac{\partial N_2}{\partial y} & \dfrac{\partial N_2}{\partial x} & 0 & \cdots & \dfrac{\partial N_8}{\partial y} & \dfrac{\partial N_8}{\partial x} & 0 \\[2mm] 0 & \dfrac{\partial N_1}{\partial z} & \dfrac{\partial N_1}{\partial y} & 0 & \dfrac{\partial N_2}{\partial z} & \dfrac{\partial N_2}{\partial z} & \cdots & 0 & \dfrac{\partial N_8}{\partial z} & \dfrac{\partial N_8}{\partial z} \\[2mm] \dfrac{\partial N_1}{\partial z} & 0 & \dfrac{\partial N_1}{\partial x} & \dfrac{\partial N_2}{\partial z} & 0 & \dfrac{\partial N_2}{\partial x} & \cdots & \dfrac{\partial N_8}{\partial z} & 0 & \dfrac{\partial N_8}{\partial x} \end{bmatrix}$$

$$\text{Eq. 8.3-3}$$

B_j Strain displacement matrix for reinforcement-concrete interface (joint) element,

---

$$n_{linear} = 2$$

$$B_j = \begin{bmatrix} N_1 & N_2 & \vdots & -N_1 & -N_2 \end{bmatrix}$$ Eq. 8.3-4

D_P Elasticity matrix for 3D stress state (isotropic continuum).

$$D_P = \frac{E_0}{(1+\mu).(1-\mu)} \begin{bmatrix} (1-\mu) & \mu & \mu & 0 & 0 & 0 \\ \mu & (1-\mu) & \mu & 0 & 0 & 0 \\ \mu & \mu & (1-\mu) & 0 & 0 & 0 \\ 0 & 0 & 0 & \frac{(1-2\mu)}{2} & 0 & 0 \\ 0 & 0 & 0 & 0 & \frac{(1-2\mu)}{2} & 0 \\ 0 & 0 & 0 & 0 & 0 & \frac{(1-2\mu)}{2} \end{bmatrix}$$

Eq. 8.3-5

D_r Elasticity matrix for 3D reinforcement (for uniaxial tension /compression).

$$D_R = \begin{bmatrix} E_s & 0 & 0 & 0 & 0 & 0 \\ 0 & 0 & 0 & 0 & 0 & 0 \\ 0 & 0 & 0 & 0 & 0 & 0 \\ 0 & 0 & 0 & 0 & 0 & 0 \\ 0 & 0 & 0 & 0 & 0 & 0 \\ 0 & 0 & 0 & 0 & 0 & 0 \end{bmatrix}$$ Eq. 8.3-6

F Force vector.

$$F^T = \begin{bmatrix} F_x & F_y & F_z \end{bmatrix}$$ Eq. 8.3-7

J Jacobian matrix for 3D parent element.

$$J = \begin{bmatrix} \frac{\partial x}{\partial \xi} & \frac{\partial y}{\partial \xi} & \frac{\partial z}{\partial \xi} \\ \frac{\partial x}{\partial \eta} & \frac{\partial y}{\partial \eta} & \frac{\partial z}{\partial \eta} \\ \frac{\partial x}{\partial \zeta} & \frac{\partial y}{\partial \zeta} & \frac{\partial z}{\partial \zeta} \end{bmatrix}$$ Eq. 8.3-8

N_P Shape function matrix for parent element, $n_{linear} = 8$

$$N_P = \begin{bmatrix} N_1 & \cdots & N_8 & 0 & \cdots & 0 & 0 & \cdots & 0 \\ 0 & \cdots & 0 & N_1 & \cdots & N_8 & 0 & \cdots & 0 \\ 0 & \cdots & 0 & 0 & \cdots & 0 & N_1 & \cdots & N_8 \end{bmatrix}$$ Eq. 8.3-9

$N_{r,g}$ Shape function matrix for reinforcement element in global system, $n_{linear} = 2$

$$N_{r,g} = \begin{bmatrix} N_1 & N_2 & 0 & 0 & 0 & 0 \\ 0 & 0 & N_1 & N_2 & 0 & 0 \\ 0 & 0 & 0 & 0 & N_1 & N_2 \end{bmatrix}$$ Eq. 8.3-10

$N_{r,l}$ Shape function matrix for reinforcement element in local system, $n_{linear} = 2$

$$N_{r,l} = \begin{bmatrix} N_1 & N_2 \end{bmatrix}$$ Eq. 8.3-11

N_j Shape function matrix for reinforcement-concrete interface (joint) element,

$$B_j = \begin{bmatrix} N_1 & -N_1 & \vdots & N_2 & -N_2 \end{bmatrix}$$ Eq. 8.3-12

R_P Residual nodal forces acting on a parent element,

$$R_P^T = \begin{bmatrix} R_{1,x} & R_{1,y} & R_{1,z} & R_{2,x} & R_{2,y} & R_{2,z} & \cdots & R_{8,x} & R_{8,y} & R_{8,z} \end{bmatrix}$$

Eq. 8.3-13

u Displacement vector.

$$u^T = \begin{bmatrix} u_x & u_y & z_z \end{bmatrix} = \begin{bmatrix} u & v & w \end{bmatrix}$$ Eq. 8.3-14

u_P Vector of nodal displacements for a parent element, $n_{linear} = 8$

$$u_P^T = \begin{bmatrix} u_{1,x} & \cdots & u_{8x} & u_{1,y} & \cdots & u_{8y} & u_{1,z} & \cdots & u_{8z} \end{bmatrix}$$

Eq. 8.3-15

$u_{r,g}$ Nodal displacements vector for 3D reinforcement element in global coordinates.

A 3D Hypoelastic Model of RC Structure using lower order EAS elements.

$$n_{linear} = 2$$

$$u^T_{r,g} = \left[u_{1,x} \quad u_{2,x} \quad u_{1,y} \quad u_{2,y} \quad u_{1,z} \quad u_{2,z} \right]$$ Eq. 8.3-16

$u_{r,l}$ Nodal displacements vector for 1D reinforcement element in local coordinates.

$$n_{linear} = 2$$

$$u^T_{r,l} = \left[u_{1,l} \quad u_{2,l} \right]$$ Eq. 8.3-17

u_j Nodal displacements vector for interface (joint) element.

$$n_{linear} = 2$$

$$u^T_j = \left[u_{1,r} \quad u_{1,r} \quad u_{1,p} \quad u_{2,p} \right]$$ Eq. 8.3-18

u_{slip} Vector of nodal slip displacements for interface (joint) element.

$$n_{linear} = 2$$

$$u^T_{slip} = \left[u_{1,slip} \quad u_{2,slip} \right]$$ Eq. 8.3-19

x Coordinates of a point.

$$x^T = \left[x \quad y \quad z \right]$$ Eq. 8.3-20

ξ Intrinsic Coordinates of a point.

$$\xi^T = \left[\xi \quad \eta \quad \zeta \right]$$ Eq. 8.3-21

x_P Coordinates of the parent /concrete element. $n_{linear} = 8$

$$x^T_P = \begin{bmatrix} x_1 & \cdots & x_8 & 0 & \cdots & 0 & 0 & \cdots & 0 \\ 0 & \cdots & 0 & y_1 & \cdots & y_8 & 0 & \cdots & 0 \\ 0 & \cdots & 0 & 0 & \cdots & 0 & z_1 & \cdots & z_8 \end{bmatrix}$$ Eq. 8.3-22

x_r Coordinates of the reinforcement element. $n_{linear} = 2$

$$x_r^T = \begin{bmatrix} x_1 & y_1 & z_1 & x_2 & y_2 & z_2 \end{bmatrix}$$ Eq. 8.3-23

8.4 Transformation of axis for Stresses & Strains :

The stresses and strains for the reinforcements are to be derived along its axis only as they are considered uniaxial element. Also for the stresses and strains at the crack planes are to be computed in the direction normal and parallel to crack plane. Hence transformation of axes in 3D situation is very much necessary. A novel and lucid derivation of the same is found in *Boresi /Sidebottom (1985)* and *Cook et al. (2003)*.

Let us consider x, y, z and ξ, η, ζ are the two right-hand Cartesian coordinate systems with the same origin. Using the directional cosines $l_1 = \cos\theta_{x\xi}, l_2 = \cos\theta_{x\eta}$ $l_3 = \cos\theta_{x\zeta}$, $m_1 = \cos\theta_{y\xi}, m_2 = \cos\theta_{y\eta}, 3_3 = \cos\theta_{y\zeta}$ and $n_1 = \cos\theta_{z\xi}, n_2 = \cos\theta_{z\eta}$ $n_3 = \cos\theta_{z\zeta}$ we may write the transformation matrix as

	x	y	z
ξ	l_1	m_1	n_1
η	l_2	m_2	n_2
ζ	l_3	m_3	n_3

$$T = \begin{bmatrix} l_1 & m_1 & n_1 \\ l_2 & m_2 & n_2 \\ l_3 & m_3 & n_3 \end{bmatrix}$$ Eq. 8.4-1

The transformation matrix T is orthogonal and hence $T^{-1} = T^T$. The local coordinates of a point, defined by global system may be computed by $x_l = T.x_g$.

$$\begin{Bmatrix} \xi \\ \eta \\ \zeta \end{Bmatrix} = \begin{bmatrix} l_1 & m_1 & n_1 \\ l_2 & m_2 & n_2 \\ l_3 & m_3 & n_3 \end{bmatrix} \begin{Bmatrix} x \\ y \\ z \end{Bmatrix}$$ Eq. 8.4-2

Similarly global coordinates of a point, defined by local coordinate system may be computed by $x_g = T^T.x_l$.   Eq. 8.4-3

The stress state σ defined in x, y, z system can be computed in ξ, η, ζ system by

$$\sigma_{\xi\eta\zeta} = T_{\sigma,gl}.\sigma_{xyz}$$

Eq. 8.4-4

$$
\begin{Bmatrix}
\sigma_{\xi\xi} \\
\sigma_{\eta\eta} \\
\sigma_{\zeta\zeta} \\
\sigma_{\xi\eta} \\
\sigma_{\eta\zeta} \\
\sigma_{\zeta\xi}
\end{Bmatrix}
=
\begin{bmatrix}
l_1^2 & m_1^2 & n_1^2 & 2l_1m_1 & 2m_1n_1 & 2n_1l_1 \\
l_2^2 & m_1^2 & n_2^2 & 2l_2m_2 & 2m_2n_2 & 2n_2l_2 \\
l_3^2 & m_1^2 & n_3^2 & 2l_3m_3 & 2m_3n_3 & 2n_3l_3 \\
l_1l_2 & m_1m_2 & n_1n_2 & l_1m_2+l_2m_1 & m_1n_2+m_2n_1 & l_1n_2+l_2n_1 \\
l_2l_3 & m_2m_3 & n_2n_3 & l_2m_3+l_3m_2 & m_2n_3+m_3n_2 & l_2n_3+l_3n_2 \\
l_3l_1 & m_3m_1 & n_3n_1 & l_3m_1+l_1m_3 & m_3n_1+m_1n_3 & l_3n_1+l_1n_3
\end{bmatrix}
\begin{Bmatrix}
\sigma_{xx} \\
\sigma_{yy} \\
\sigma_{zz} \\
\sigma_{xy} \\
\sigma_{yz} \\
\sigma_{zx}
\end{Bmatrix}
$$

Similarly the stress state ε defined in x, y, z system can be computed in ξ, η, ζ system by

$$\varepsilon_{\xi\eta\zeta} = T_{\xi,gl}.\varepsilon_{xyz}$$

Eq. 8.4-5

$$
\begin{Bmatrix}
\varepsilon_{\xi\xi} \\
\varepsilon_{\eta\eta} \\
\varepsilon_{\zeta\zeta} \\
\varepsilon_{\xi\eta} \\
\varepsilon_{\eta\zeta} \\
\varepsilon_{\zeta\xi}
\end{Bmatrix}
=
\begin{bmatrix}
l_1^2 & m_1^2 & n_1^2 & l_1m_1 & m_1n_1 & n_1l_1 \\
l_2^2 & m_1^2 & n_2^2 & l_2m_2 & m_2n_2 & n_2l_2 \\
l_3^2 & m_1^2 & n_3^2 & l_3m_3 & m_3n_3 & n_3l_3 \\
2l_1l_2 & 2m_1m_2 & 2n_1n_2 & l_1m_2+l_2m_1 & m_1n_2+m_2n_1 & l_1n_2+l_2n_1 \\
2l_2l_3 & 2m_2m_3 & 2n_2n_3 & l_2m_3+l_3m_2 & m_2n_3+m_3n_2 & l_2n_3+l_3n_2 \\
2l_3l_1 & 2m_3m_1 & 2n_3n_1 & l_3m_1+l_1m_3 & m_3n_1+m_1n_3 & l_3n_1+l_1n_3
\end{bmatrix}
\begin{Bmatrix}
\varepsilon_{xx} \\
\varepsilon_{yy} \\
\varepsilon_{zz} \\
\varepsilon_{xy} \\
\varepsilon_{yz} \\
\varepsilon_{zx}
\end{Bmatrix}
$$

The inverse relation may also be established by computing the transpose of the transformation matrix using $T^{-1} = T^T$ as defined above.

8.5 Calculation of Stresses :

Structural DOF (here Displacements $\{d\}$) at element nodes are calculated by solving equilibrium equations $[K]\{d\} = \{R\}$. Nodeless or internal DOF of elements do not appear as they are eliminated before assembly. Stresses are calculated element-wise using $\{\sigma\} = [C]\{\varepsilon\}$ with $\{\varepsilon\} = [B]\{d\}$. The matrix $[B]$ is a strain-displacement operator and is a function of the coordinates and is evaluated at the location where stresses are desired. Most commonly used type C^0 element does not display inter-element continuity of strain or curvature. Strain fields as well as stress field are likely to display error as they are obtained by differentiation of the displacement field. This variation of stress values is also an indicator that mess refinement. Also the element stresses do not satisfy the equilibrium condition for individual elements.

As the gradient fields are in general not continuous at the boundaries between elements, the adjacent elements display different states of stress at a node they share. As a result, the internal stresses and applied loads do not balance at any particular nodal point. Hence it is quite logical to use some average value of stress as representative for the element and considered more to be trusted than stress a node in any element attached to the node. A discontinuity of thickness or modulus also causes a discontinuity in stress. But for the problem in hand, this is not the case, rather its due to discontinuity in the gradient field at the common nodes the elements share and hence a nodal averaging scheme like the commercial software has been adopted, which may well be considered as continuous at the element boundaries.

8.6 Principal Stresses and Principal Directions :

Evaluation of principal stresses and principal directions are shown in various references such as *Boresi /Sidebottom (1985)* and *Chen /Saleeb (1982)*.

8.6.1 Principal Stresses

In the stress space, there are three orthogonal planes in which shear stresses vanish. These planes are called principal planes and the normal stresses on these planes are called principal stresses. Thus 'n' being the unit vector

$$\begin{bmatrix} \sigma_{xx} - \sigma & \sigma_{xy} & \sigma_{xz} \\ \sigma_{xy} & \sigma_{yy} - \sigma & \sigma_{yz} \\ \sigma_{xz} & \sigma_{yz} & \sigma_{zz} - \sigma \end{bmatrix} \begin{Bmatrix} n_x \\ n_y \\ n_z \end{Bmatrix} = \begin{Bmatrix} 0 \\ 0 \\ 0 \end{Bmatrix} \qquad \text{Eq. 8.6-1}$$

Since 'n' cannot be '0' the above equation holds true if the determinant of σ is '0'. Thus we have

$$\begin{vmatrix} \sigma_{xx} - \sigma & \sigma_{xy} & \sigma_{xz} \\ \sigma_{xy} & \sigma_{yy} - \sigma & \sigma_{yz} \\ \sigma_{xz} & \sigma_{yz} & \sigma_{zz} - \sigma \end{vmatrix} = 0 \qquad \text{Eq. 8.6-2}$$

Expanding the determinant, we have

$$\sigma^3 - I_1.\sigma^2 + I_2.\sigma - I_3 = 0 \qquad \text{Eq. 8.6-3}$$

The roots of the equation give rise to the values of principal stresses $\sigma_1, \sigma_2, \sigma_3$ where the stress invariants are given by

$$I_1 = \sigma_{xx} + \sigma_{yy} + \sigma_{zz} \qquad \text{Eq. 8.6-4a}$$

$$I_2 = \begin{vmatrix} \sigma_{xx} & \sigma_{xy} \\ \sigma_{xy} & \sigma_{yy} \end{vmatrix} + \begin{vmatrix} \sigma_{xx} & \sigma_{xz} \\ \sigma_{xz} & \sigma_{zz} \end{vmatrix} + \begin{vmatrix} \sigma_{yy} & \sigma_{yz} \\ \sigma_{yz} & \sigma_{zz} \end{vmatrix} \qquad \text{Eq. 8.6-4b}$$

$$= \sigma_{xx}.\sigma_{yy} + \sigma_{xx}.\sigma_{zz} + \sigma_{yy}.\sigma_{zz} - \sigma_{xy}^2 - \sigma_{xz}^2 - \sigma_{yz}^2$$

$$I_3 = \begin{vmatrix} \sigma_{xx} & \sigma_{xy} & \sigma_{xz} \\ \sigma_{xy} & \sigma_{yy} & \sigma_{yz} \\ \sigma_{xz} & \sigma_{yz} & \sigma_{zz} \end{vmatrix} \qquad \text{Eq. 8.6-4c}$$

$$= \sigma_{xx}\sigma_{yy}\sigma_{zz} + 2\sigma_{xy}\sigma_{yz}\sigma_{xz} - \sigma_{xx}\sigma_{yz}^2 - \sigma_{yy}\sigma_{xz}^2 - \sigma_{zz}\sigma_{xy}^2$$

Another way is to compute an additional sets of invariants; the deviator stress invariants J_2 and J_3, the octahedral stress σ_{oct} and the Lode angle θ (angle of similarity). If this set of invariants is visualized in the principal stress space (Haigh-Westergaar stress space), the principal stresses are the sections on the respective axes. Anyway both the method yields the same expression and the principal stresses are obtained as

$$\begin{Bmatrix} \sigma_1 \\ \sigma_2 \\ \sigma_3 \end{Bmatrix} = \begin{Bmatrix} \sigma_{oct} \\ \sigma_{oct} \\ \sigma_{oct} \end{Bmatrix} + \frac{2}{\sqrt{3}} J_2 \begin{Bmatrix} \cos\theta \\ \cos\left(\theta - \frac{2}{3}\pi\right) \\ \cos\left(\theta + \frac{2}{3}\pi\right) \end{Bmatrix} \qquad \text{Eq. 8.6-5}$$

Where

$$\sigma_m = \sigma_{oct} = \frac{1}{3}(\sigma_{xx} + \sigma_{yy} + \sigma_{zz})$$ Eq.8.6-6

$$J_1 = 0,$$ Eq.8.6-7a

$$J_2 = \frac{1}{6}\left[(\sigma_1 - \sigma_2)^2 + (\sigma_2 - \sigma_3)^2 + (\sigma_3 - \sigma_1)^2\right]$$ Eq.8.6-7b

$$J_3 = (\sigma_1 - \sigma_m)(\sigma_2 - \sigma_m)(\sigma_3 - \sigma_m)$$ Eq.8.6-7c

$$\cos(3\theta) = \frac{3\sqrt{3}}{2} \cdot \frac{J_3}{J_2^{3/2}}$$ Eq.8.6-8

8.6.2   Directions of Principal Stresses :

The principal stresses are interpreted mathematically as the eigenvalues of 'σ' and the directions of principal stresses are the associated eigenvectors. The principal directions (eigen vectors) can be computed in a conventional method (viz. following Jacobi's method) with the direction cosine condition /orthogonality condition $(n_1^2 + n_2^2 + n_3^2 = 1)$ as additional equation since the three equations given in Eq. 8.6-2 are linearly independent. However, for computational implementation it is more straightforward to follow *Chen /Saleeb (1982)* and *Adey /Brebia (1983)*.

$$M.x = \lambda.x$$ Eq.8.6-9

and from Eq. 8.6-1, we have $A.n = 0$ in which $A = \sigma - \sigma_p I$ Eq.8.6-10

The inverse of a matrix can be expressed by the adjoint matrix divided by the determinant of the matrix.

$$A^{-1} = \frac{A^a}{|A|}$$ Eq.8.6-11

Considering that $A.A^{-1} = I$ Eq.8.6-12

Eq.8.6-11 may be pre-multiplied by 'A', resulting in

$$A.A^{-1} = \frac{A.A^a}{|A|} = I$$ Eq.8.6-13

Eq.8.6-13 again may be multiplied with $|A|$ to have

$$A.A^a = I.|A|$$ Eq.8.6-14

In order to get the eigenvalue, $|A| = 0$ (comparing Eq. 8.6-1 and Eq.8.6-10)

$$I.|A| = 0$$ Eq.8.6-15

indicating thereby $A.A^a = 0$ Eq.8.6-16

Thus every row of adjoint matrix A^a may be observed as a vector for principal directions associated to the principal stress σ_P. In fact all three rows are linearly dependent and each is representing one of the three principal directions.

The adjoint matrix may be calculated forming the transpose matrix, whose elements are the cofactors of the given matrix.

$$A = \begin{bmatrix} A_{11} & A_{12} & A_{13} \\ A_{21} & A_{22} & A_{23} \\ A_{31} & A_{32} & A_{33} \end{bmatrix}$$

$$A = \begin{bmatrix} +\begin{vmatrix} a_{22} & a_{23} \\ a_{32} & a_{33} \end{vmatrix} & -\begin{vmatrix} a_{12} & a_{13} \\ a_{32} & a_{33} \end{vmatrix} & +\begin{vmatrix} a_{12} & a_{13} \\ a_{22} & a_{23} \end{vmatrix} \\ -\begin{vmatrix} a_{21} & a_{23} \\ a_{31} & a_{33} \end{vmatrix} & +\begin{vmatrix} a_{11} & a_{13} \\ a_{31} & a_{33} \end{vmatrix} & -\begin{vmatrix} a_{11} & a_{13} \\ a_{21} & a_{23} \end{vmatrix} \\ +\begin{vmatrix} a_{21} & a_{22} \\ a_{31} & a_{32} \end{vmatrix} & -\begin{vmatrix} a_{11} & a_{12} \\ a_{31} & a_{32} \end{vmatrix} & +\begin{vmatrix} a_{11} & a_{12} \\ a_{21} & a_{22} \end{vmatrix} \end{bmatrix}$$ Eq.8.6-17

As a further check, the three dot products of between elements of two of the three rows must be equal to zero, i.e.

$$\sum_{i=1}^{3} A_{1i}.A_{2i} = 0 \,,$$

Eq.8.6-18a

$$\sum_{i=1}^{3} A_{1i}.A_{3i} = 0 \,,$$

Eq.8.6-18b

$$\sum_{i=1}^{3} A_{2i}.A_{3i} = 0$$

Eq.8.6-18c

8.7 EAS based FE Formulation :

The formulation is covered in detail in various references, viz. *Sousa et al. (2002)*, *Sousa et al. (2003a)*, *Valente et al. (2004)*. Considering subspace analysis for volumetric locking of the incompressibility problem as a constrained minimization of a functional, the goal is set to obtain an admissible solution U for a displacement field u that minimizes the total energy of the system in the deformation field I, such that $I = \{u \in U : div(u) = 0\}$. Following FEM, the linear space of the admissible solutions U, and the respective subspace I are approximated by the spaces U^h and I^h respectively. A two-field finite element solution is expressed for linear elasticity according to *Cesar /Natal Jorge (1999)* as

$$\begin{bmatrix} K & Q \\ -Q & 0 \end{bmatrix} \begin{Bmatrix} u^h \\ p^h \end{Bmatrix} = \begin{Bmatrix} f_{ext}^h \\ 0 \end{Bmatrix}$$

Eq.8.7-1

where f_{ext}^h is the vector of applied external forces, p is the hydrostatic pressure and K is the stiffness matrix. The superscript h indicates finite element approximation.

Using the incompressibility condition $Q.u^h = 0$, the subspace of the incompressible deformations I^h may be defined as

$$I^h = \{u^h \in U^h : Q.u^h = 0\}$$

Eq.8.7-2

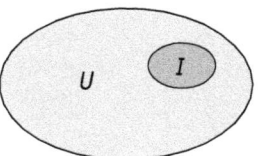

Fig. 8.7-1 : Space of admissible solution U and incompressible deformation I

To avoid trivial solution $u^h = 0$, the displacement field u^h should belong to nullspace of Q i.e. to the subspace of incompressible deformation I^h and hence the approximated displacements u^h are contained within I^h. If the subspace I^h is an approach to the original subspace I, it may be assumed that it can't reproduce all the possible solution contained in I. The volumetric locking phenomenon occurs when for a group of boundary conditions and external forces, the expected solution or few of its components do not appear properly in the subspace I^h.

For a standard isoparametric eight-node hexahedral element with domain Ω_e and $u \approx u^h = N(\xi,\eta,\zeta).d_e$, the incompressibility condition becomes

$$\int_{\Omega_e} div(u).d\Omega_e = 0 = \begin{bmatrix} N_\xi & N_\eta & N_\zeta \end{bmatrix}\{d_e\} \qquad \text{Eq.8.7-2}$$

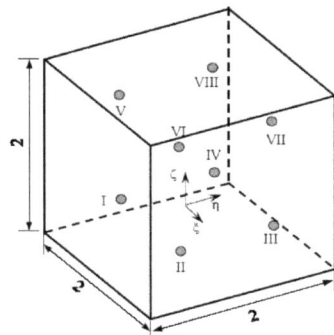

Fig. 8.7-2 : Standard 8-node hexahedral element with 8 Gauss points

A 3D Hypoelastic Model of RC Structure using lower order EAS elements.

Using a full integration scheme (2x2x2=8, Fig. 8.7-2), the left had side of the above equation yields rank(Q)=7 and nullity(Q)=24-7=17, 24 being total D.O.F. if order of integration is 1, it yields rank(Q)=1 and nullity(Q)=24-1=23. It may be noted that reduced integration produces six more incompressible displacement modes than the case of full integration and hence is preferred technique in volumetric locking problem. From Fig. 8.7-3, the six rigid body displacements may be obtained by linearly combining these elements.

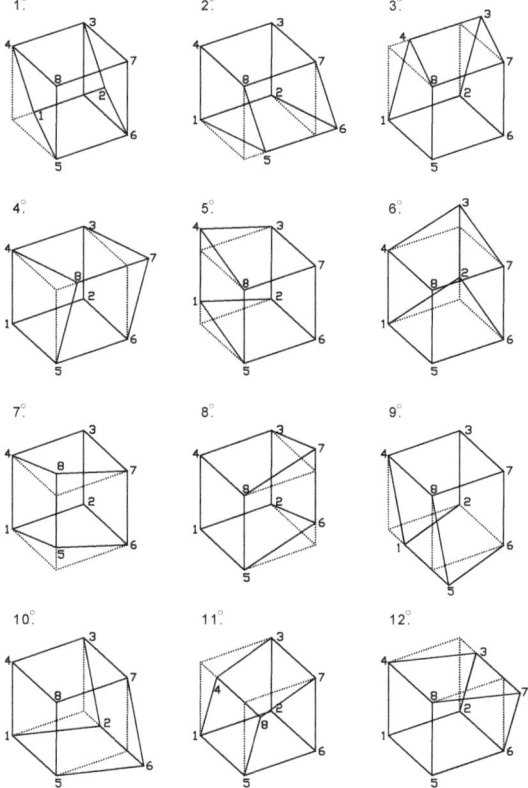

Fig. 8.7-3(a) : Basic components of incompressible deformation subspace

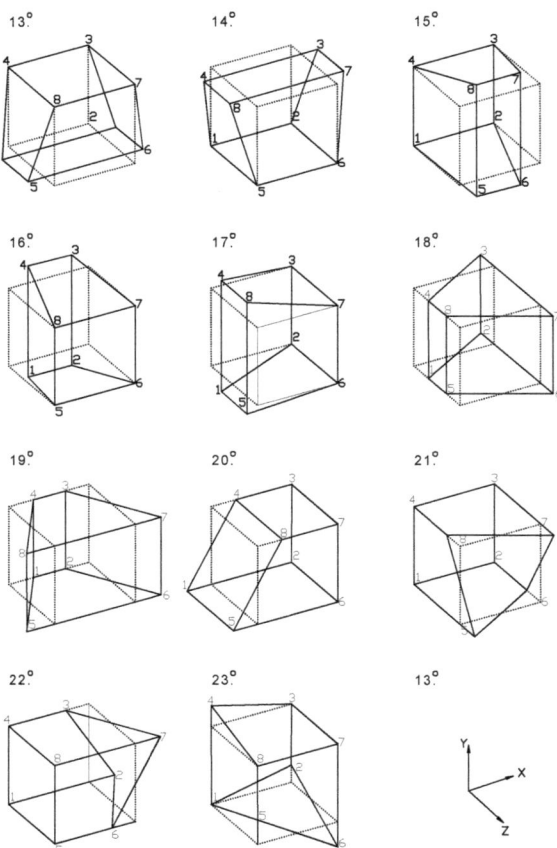

Fig. 8.7-3(b) : Basic components of incompressible deformation subspace

These deformations could be divided into four major groups

1) Edge translations in x,y,z directions, modes 1-12,

2) Expansion /contraction of one face, modes 13-17,

3) Hourglass modes modes 18-20 and

4) Warping modes 21-23

It is obvious that reduced integration scheme, or selective reduced integration(SRI) are the improved ones over full integration scheme for lower order element, but they not free of volumetric locking or transverse shear locking completely. Hence they could be eliminated by inclusion of additional variables for the enhanced strain field. Since these addition also leads to instabilities, numerical efficiency, number of additional variables in the enhanced field is a crucial matter. At the element level, the interpolation of the strain field follows the usual methodology of [**Simo /Rifai** (1990].

$$\{\varepsilon\} = \{\varepsilon_d\} + \{\varepsilon_\alpha\} = \begin{bmatrix} B_d^e & B_\alpha^e \end{bmatrix} \begin{Bmatrix} d^e \\ \alpha^e \end{Bmatrix}$$
Eq. 8.7-3

where B_d^e is the standard strain displacement matrix in FEM and B_α^e is the same for enhanced variables. At the element level, the operator B_α^e in the isoparametric space becomes M_α^e matrix and. Due to transition from isoparametric space to global reference frame for any arbitrary configuration, it has to satisfy patch test

$$\int_\Omega M_\alpha . d\Omega = 0$$
Eq. 8.7-4

which is nothing but a condition to satisfy orthogonality condition between the stress field and the enhanced strain field. The enhanced strain field B_α^e may be obtained by transforming M_α^e at the center of the element as proposed by *Simo /Rifai (1990)* and *Andelfinger /Ramm (1993)* as

$$B_\alpha^e = \frac{|J_0|}{|J|} . T_0 . M_\alpha^e$$
Eq. 8.7-5

where, J_0 and J is the Jacobian determinant evaluated respectively at $\xi = \eta = \varsigma = 0$ i.e. at the center of the element and at each Gauss points, T_o is the transformation matrix relating isoparametric space and global reference frame given by Eq. 8.4-5 with $T = J^{-1}$ again at the center of the element.

The crucial idea is to include an extra field of variables associated to the space derivatives of the displacement field (/the displacement gradient matrix) H, given by

$$
J = \begin{bmatrix} \dfrac{\partial u}{\partial x} & \dfrac{\partial u}{\partial y} & \dfrac{\partial u}{\partial z} \\[8pt] \dfrac{\partial v}{\partial x} & \dfrac{\partial v}{\partial y} & \dfrac{\partial v}{\partial z} \\[8pt] \dfrac{\partial w}{\partial x} & \dfrac{\partial w}{\partial y} & \dfrac{\partial w}{\partial z} \end{bmatrix} + \begin{bmatrix} \dfrac{\partial \tilde{u}}{\partial x} & \dfrac{\partial \tilde{u}}{\partial y} & \dfrac{\partial \tilde{u}}{\partial z} \\[8pt] \dfrac{\partial \tilde{v}}{\partial x} & \dfrac{\partial \tilde{v}}{\partial y} & \dfrac{\partial \tilde{v}}{\partial z} \\[8pt] \dfrac{\partial \tilde{w}}{\partial x} & \dfrac{\partial \tilde{w}}{\partial y} & \dfrac{\partial \tilde{w}}{\partial z} \end{bmatrix}
\qquad \text{Eq. 8.7-6}
$$

using the bubble function, $N_\alpha = \dfrac{1}{2}(1-\xi^2).(1-\eta^2).(1-\varsigma^2)$ extra compatible modes of deformations are added so that the dimension of the subspace I^h may become equal to 23. With this idea four nos. elements were proposed.

1. *Element HC9*

Nine nos. of extra compatible modes of deformation are considered which makes elementary D.O.F. equal to 24+9=33 from 24 and the matrix M_α^e designated as M_9^e for $\alpha = 9$

$$
M_9^e = \begin{bmatrix}
\dfrac{\partial N_\alpha}{\partial \xi} & 0 & 0 & 0 & 0 & 0 & 0 & 0 & 0 \\[8pt]
0 & \dfrac{\partial N_\alpha}{\partial \eta} & 0 & 0 & 0 & 0 & 0 & 0 & 0 \\[8pt]
0 & 0 & \dfrac{\partial N_\alpha}{\partial \zeta} & 0 & 0 & 0 & 0 & 0 & 0 \\[8pt]
0 & 0 & 0 & \dfrac{\partial N_\alpha}{\partial \xi} & \dfrac{\partial N_\alpha}{\partial \eta} & 0 & 0 & 0 & 0 \\[8pt]
0 & 0 & 0 & 0 & 0 & \dfrac{\partial N_\alpha}{\partial \xi} & \dfrac{\partial N_\alpha}{\partial \zeta} & 0 & 0 \\[8pt]
0 & 0 & 0 & 0 & 0 & 0 & 0 & \dfrac{\partial N_\alpha}{\partial \eta} & \dfrac{\partial N_\alpha}{\partial \zeta}
\end{bmatrix}
$$

Eq. 8.7-7

However, the number of null displacement modes associated equals to 20, which is still three less than the case of reduced integration scheme. Hence it may not remove the volumetric locking problem completely. With this idea, three more new variables are added so as to reproduce all modes of Fig. 8.7-3 arriving at the next element.

2. *Element HCi12*

Twelve nos. of extra compatible modes of deformation are considered which makes elementary D.O.F. equal to 24+12=36 from 24 and the matrix M_α^e designated as M_{12}^e for $\alpha = 12$

$$M_{12} = \begin{bmatrix} M_9^e \end{bmatrix} \begin{bmatrix} \dfrac{\partial^2 N_\alpha}{\partial \xi \partial \eta} & \dfrac{\partial^2 N_\alpha}{\partial \xi \partial \zeta} & \dfrac{\partial^2 N_\alpha}{\partial \eta \partial \zeta} \\ \dfrac{\partial^2 N_\alpha}{\partial \xi \partial \eta} & \dfrac{\partial^2 N_\alpha}{\partial \xi \partial \zeta} & \dfrac{\partial^2 N_\alpha}{\partial \eta \partial \zeta} \\ \dfrac{\partial^2 N_\alpha}{\partial \xi \partial \eta} & \dfrac{\partial^2 N_\alpha}{\partial \xi \partial \zeta} & \dfrac{\partial^2 N_\alpha}{\partial \eta \partial \zeta} \\ 0 & 0 & 0 \\ 0 & 0 & 0 \\ 0 & 0 & 0 \end{bmatrix} \qquad \text{Eq. 8.7-8}$$

It considers all modes related volumetric locking. Hence it improves performance of thin plates and shells, where bending is present but it can't handle transverse shear locking which also tends to appear at the same time. In fact last two elements HC9 and HCi12 show strong sensitivity to the shear locking phenomenon in problems if thin plates and shells. Thus to enforce nullity of transverse shear strain energy by including enhanced strain field over transverse shear strain terms becomes an aim resulting in the next element.

3. *Element HCiS18*

Eighteen nos. of extra compatible modes of deformation are considered which makes elementary D.O.F. equal to 24+18=42 from 24 and the matrix M_α^e designated as M_{18}^e for $\alpha = 18$

$$
M_{18}^e = M_{12}^e
\begin{bmatrix}
0 & 0 & 0 & 0 & 0 & 0 \\
0 & 0 & 0 & 0 & 0 & 0 \\
0 & 0 & 0 & 0 & 0 & 0 \\
\dfrac{\partial^2 N_\alpha}{\partial \xi \partial \eta} & \dfrac{\partial^2 N_\alpha}{\partial \eta \partial \zeta} & 0 & 0 & 0 & 0 \\
0 & 0 & \dfrac{\partial^2 N_\alpha}{\partial \xi \partial \eta} & \dfrac{\partial^2 N_\alpha}{\partial \eta \partial \zeta} & 0 & 0 \\
0 & 0 & 0 & 0 & \dfrac{\partial^2 N_\alpha}{\partial \xi \partial \eta} & \dfrac{\partial^2 N_\alpha}{\partial \xi \partial \zeta}
\end{bmatrix}
\qquad \text{Eq. 8.7-9}
$$

This element satisfies patch test and performs well in situations of volumetric and transverse shear locking problems, even with distorted or coarse meshes. In an alternative approach, M_{18}^e may be considered as consists of two groups of enhanced modes; one being related to volumetric part (M_{VL}^e) and the other one related to transverse shear part (M_{TSL}^e). This results in a new class of element as follows

4. *Element HCi12*

As described $\left[M_{18}^e \right] = \left[M_{VL}^e \quad M_{TSL}^e \right]$ such that

$$
M_{VL}^e =
\begin{bmatrix}
\dfrac{\partial N_\alpha}{\partial \xi} & 0 & 0 & \dfrac{\partial^2 N_\alpha}{\partial \xi \partial \eta} & \dfrac{\partial^2 N_\alpha}{\partial \xi \partial \zeta} & \dfrac{\partial^2 N_\alpha}{\partial \eta \partial \zeta} \\
0 & \dfrac{\partial N_\alpha}{\partial \eta} & 0 & \dfrac{\partial^2 N_\alpha}{\partial \xi \partial \eta} & \dfrac{\partial^2 N_\alpha}{\partial \xi \partial \zeta} & \dfrac{\partial^2 N_\alpha}{\partial \eta \partial \zeta} \\
0 & 0 & \dfrac{\partial N_\alpha}{\partial \zeta} & \dfrac{\partial^2 N_\alpha}{\partial \xi \partial \eta} & \dfrac{\partial^2 N_\alpha}{\partial \xi \partial \zeta} & \dfrac{\partial^2 N_\alpha}{\partial \eta \partial \zeta} \\
0 & 0 & 0 & 0 & 0 & 0 \\
0 & 0 & 0 & 0 & 0 & 0 \\
0 & 0 & 0 & 0 & 0 & 0
\end{bmatrix}
\qquad \text{Eq. 8.7-10}
$$

$$
M_{TSL}^e = \begin{bmatrix}
0 & 0 & 0 & 0 & 0 & 0 & 0 & 0 & 0 & 0 & 0 & 0 \\
0 & 0 & 0 & 0 & 0 & 0 & 0 & 0 & 0 & 0 & 0 & 0 \\
0 & 0 & 0 & 0 & 0 & 0 & 0 & 0 & 0 & 0 & 0 & 0 \\
\dfrac{\partial N_\alpha}{\partial \xi} & \dfrac{\partial N_\alpha}{\partial \eta} & 0 & 0 & 0 & 0 & \dfrac{\partial^2 N_\alpha}{\partial \xi \partial \eta} & \dfrac{\partial^2 N_\alpha}{\partial \eta \partial \zeta} & 0 & 0 & 0 & 0 \\
0 & 0 & \dfrac{\partial N_\alpha}{\partial \xi} & \dfrac{\partial N_\alpha}{\partial \zeta} & 0 & 0 & 0 & 0 & \dfrac{\partial^2 N_\alpha}{\partial \xi \partial \eta} & \dfrac{\partial^2 N_\alpha}{\partial \eta \partial \zeta} & 0 & 0 \\
0 & 0 & 0 & 0 & \dfrac{\partial N_\alpha}{\partial \eta} & \dfrac{\partial N_\alpha}{\partial \zeta} & 0 & 0 & 0 & 0 & \dfrac{\partial^2 N_\alpha}{\partial \xi \partial \eta} & \dfrac{\partial^2 N_\alpha}{\partial \xi \partial \zeta}
\end{bmatrix}
$$

Eq. 8.7-11

The use of (M_{VL}^e) matrix is sufficient to arrive at incompressible deformation subspace in volumetric locking free element. To enforce nullity of transverse shear strain energy, only six additional variables are adequate. Thus M_{TSL}^e is modified to get M_{TSL*}^e such that $\left[M_{HCiS12}^e \right] = \left[M_{VL}^e \quad M_{TSL*}^e \right]$ and

$$
M_{TSL*}^e = \begin{bmatrix}
0 & 0 & 0 & 0 & 0 & 0 \\
0 & 0 & 0 & 0 & 0 & 0 \\
0 & 0 & 0 & 0 & 0 & 0 \\
0 & 0 & 0 & 0 & 0 & 0 \\
\dfrac{\partial N_\alpha}{\partial \xi} & \dfrac{\partial N_\alpha}{\partial \eta} & \dfrac{\partial^2 N_\alpha}{\partial \xi \partial \eta} & 0 & 0 & 0 \\
0 & 0 & 0 & \dfrac{\partial N_\alpha}{\partial \xi} & \dfrac{\partial N_\alpha}{\partial \eta} & \dfrac{\partial^2 N_\alpha}{\partial \xi \partial \eta}
\end{bmatrix}
$$

Eq. 8.7-10

It is proposed that HCiS12 is an improvement over HCiS18, whose performance is good and has the clear advantage of six less variables in its enhanced strain field. As a result total D.O.F. reduces to 24+12=36 and accordingly the size of element stiffness matrix, which indicates more numerical stability and CPU costs.

8.8   Geometric nonlinearity in three-dimension :

There are two different formulations that may be employed for the description of large deformation problems. *Total Lagrangian Approach* in which the current stress (2nd Piola-Kichhoff) and strain (Green's strain) are referred to the original geometric configuration and the displacement field gives the current configuration of the system with respect to its initial position. *Updated Lagrangian Approach* in which the current configuration of the system is used to define current stress and strain. The geometry of the system is continuously updated during the incremental process and stress/strain fields are referred to the last evaluated configuration.

The most appropriate formulation for numerical solution depends on nature of analysis being carried out. For the work considered here, a total Lagrangian formulation is adopted in which large deflection and moderate rotation could be accounted for. Reference of the problem variables to the original configuration is advantageous, since computationally expensive transfer of quantities between local and global axes need to be performed only once. The strain displacement matrix is calculated only once during nonlinear process and its nonlinear part is updated using current displacements by a simple matrix product. The constitutive relations defined previously in terms of engineering stresses and strains are considered valid for the new stress /strain quantities measured in original configuration.

For an incremental /iterative solution of a finite element nonlinear problem, a residual Ψ_i^n exist in i-th iteration cycle of n-th load step such that

$$\Psi_i^n = f^n - p_i^n = f^n - \int_v B^T \sigma_i dv \neq 0 \qquad\qquad \text{Eq. 8.8-1}$$

Taking a variation of the above with respect to displacement, we have

$$K.du = dp = \int_v B^T .d\sigma.dv + \int_v dB^T .\sigma.dv \qquad\qquad \text{Eq. 8.8-2}$$

The strain-displacement matrix B may be considered consisting of the usual infinitesimal linear part B_0 along with nonlinear contribution B_L such that $B = B_0 + B_L$. Consequently $dB^T = dB_L^T$ and geometric stiffness matrix becomes

$$K_\sigma.du = \int_v dB_L^T.\sigma.dv$$ Eq. 8.8-3

On substitution $\sigma = D.\varepsilon$, the first term in Eq. 8.8-2 reduces to usual element stiffness $\overline{K} = \int_v B^T.D.B.dv$ and we have $K = \overline{K} + K_\sigma$.

Using the Green's strain(Eq. 8.2-2) for three-dimensional problem and considering the variation of the same we get additional stiffness (K_σ) due to large deformation as

$$K_\sigma = \int G^T.\sigma.G.dv,$$ Eq. 8.8-4

where,

$$\sigma = \begin{bmatrix} S & 0 & 0 \\ 0 & S & 0 \\ 0 & 0 & S \end{bmatrix} \text{ with } S = \begin{bmatrix} \sigma_x & \tau_{xy} & \tau_{xz} \\ \tau_{xy} & \sigma_y & \tau_{yz} \\ \tau_{xz} & \tau_{yz} & \sigma_z \end{bmatrix}$$

and $B_L = A.G$ with $[A]$ as the matrix of displacement derivatives as below and $[G]$ may be referred to **Crisfield** (1991).

$$[A] = \begin{bmatrix}
\dfrac{\partial u}{\partial x} & 0 & 0 & \dfrac{\partial v}{\partial x} & 0 & 0 & \dfrac{\partial w}{\partial x} & 0 & 0 \\[2mm]
0 & \dfrac{\partial u}{\partial y} & 0 & 0 & \dfrac{\partial v}{\partial y} & 0 & 0 & \dfrac{\partial w}{\partial y} & 0 \\[2mm]
0 & 0 & \dfrac{\partial u}{\partial z} & 0 & 0 & \dfrac{\partial v}{\partial z} & 0 & 0 & \dfrac{\partial w}{\partial z} \\[2mm]
\dfrac{\partial u}{\partial y} & \dfrac{\partial u}{\partial x} & 0 & \dfrac{\partial v}{\partial y} & \dfrac{\partial v}{\partial x} & 0 & \dfrac{\partial w}{\partial y} & \dfrac{\partial w}{\partial x} & 0 \\[2mm]
\dfrac{\partial u}{\partial z} & 0 & \dfrac{\partial u}{\partial x} & \dfrac{\partial v}{\partial z} & 0 & \dfrac{\partial v}{\partial x} & \dfrac{\partial w}{\partial z} & 0 & \dfrac{\partial w}{\partial x} \\[2mm]
0 & \dfrac{\partial u}{\partial z} & \dfrac{\partial u}{\partial y} & 0 & \dfrac{\partial v}{\partial z} & \dfrac{\partial v}{\partial y} & 0 & \dfrac{\partial w}{\partial z} & \dfrac{\partial u}{\partial y}
\end{bmatrix}$$ Eq. 8.8-5

and

$$[G] = \begin{bmatrix} \dfrac{\partial N_1}{\partial x} & 0 & 0 & \dfrac{\partial N_2}{\partial x} & 0 & 0 & \cdots & \dfrac{\partial N_8}{\partial x} & 0 & 0 \\[2mm] 0 & \dfrac{\partial N_1}{\partial x} & 0 & 0 & \dfrac{\partial N_2}{\partial x} & 0 & \cdots & 0 & \dfrac{\partial N_8}{\partial x} & 0 \\[2mm] 0 & 0 & \dfrac{\partial N_1}{\partial x} & 0 & 0 & \dfrac{\partial N_2}{\partial x} & \cdots & 0 & 0 & \dfrac{\partial N_8}{\partial x} \\[2mm] \dfrac{\partial N_1}{\partial y} & 0 & 0 & \dfrac{\partial N_2}{\partial y} & 0 & 0 & \cdots & \dfrac{\partial N_8}{\partial y} & 0 & 0 \\[2mm] 0 & \dfrac{\partial N_1}{\partial y} & 0 & 0 & \dfrac{\partial N_2}{\partial y} & 0 & \cdots & 0 & \dfrac{\partial N_8}{\partial y} & 0 \\[2mm] 0 & 0 & \dfrac{\partial N_1}{\partial y} & 0 & 0 & \dfrac{\partial N_2}{\partial y} & \cdots & 0 & 0 & \dfrac{\partial N_8}{\partial y} \\[2mm] \dfrac{\partial N_1}{\partial z} & 0 & 0 & \dfrac{\partial N_2}{\partial z} & 0 & 0 & \cdots & \dfrac{\partial N_8}{\partial z} & 0 & 0 \\[2mm] 0 & \dfrac{\partial N_1}{\partial z} & 0 & 0 & \dfrac{\partial N_2}{\partial z} & 0 & \cdots & 0 & \dfrac{\partial N_8}{\partial z} & 0 \\[2mm] 0 & 0 & \dfrac{\partial N_1}{\partial z} & 0 & 0 & \dfrac{\partial N_2}{\partial z} & \cdots & 0 & 0 & \dfrac{\partial N_8}{\partial z} \end{bmatrix}$$

Eq. 8.8-6

8.9 Program listing (Selected) :

```
* * * * * * * * * * * * * * * * * * * * * * * * * * * * * * * * * * * *
*
*     ...............................................................
*     .                                                             .
*     .                                                             .
*     .                                                             .
*     .                          N A C O N                          .
*     .                                                             .
*     .               (Non-linear Analysis of CONcrete)            .
*     .              Both Material & Geometric Nonlinearity         .
*     .         A 3D FEM Program using low order solid brick elements. .
*     .                                                             .
*     .                                                             .
*     .     THIS IS A 3D LINEAR /NON-LINEAR STATIC ANALYSIS PACKAGE  .
*     .                                                             .
*     .                DEVELOPED BY  : AMIYA KR. SAMANTA.           .
*     .                                                             .
*     .                                                             .
*     ...............................................................
*     .                                                             .
*     .                                                             .
*     .     THIS IS THE MAIN PROGRAMME  ::                          .
*     .                                                             .
*     . (a) IT OPENS THE FOLLOWING DATABASES :                      .
*     .                                                             .
*     .    UNIT NO.   FILE NAME  ACCESS   STATUS   REMARKS          .
*     .    --------   ---------  -------  -------  --------         .
*     .       1       INB-PARENT  READ.   SEQUEN.  THIS IS THE INPUT .
*     .               INF-PARENT                   DATABASE FOR CONC/.
*     .                                            PARENT ELEMENT.   .
*     .               B=BEAM; F=FRAME                               .
*     .       2       INB-REINF   READ.   SEQUEN.  THIS IS THE INPUT .
*     .               INF-REINF                    DATABASE FOR 1D   .
*     .                                            REINF. ELEMENT.   .
*     .       3       OUT-BEAM    Write.   SEQUEN.  WriteS THE OUTPUT .
*     .               OUT-FRAME                    OF THE RUN ONTO   .
*     .                                            THIS FILE.        .
*     .       4       GRDAT       Write.   SEQUEN   AIDS IN LOAD VS.  .
*     .                                            DEFLECTION GRAPH  .
*     .                                            FOR A PARTICULAR  .
*     .                                            DEGREE OF FREEDOM..
*     .       5 *     E-STIF      READ /   SEQUEN.  WriteS THE ELEMENT.
*     .                           Write.            STIFFNESS MATRICES.
*     .       6 *     E-LOAD      READ /   SEQUEN.  WriteS THE LOAD   .
*     .                           Write.            STIFFNESS MATRICES.
*     .       7 *     E-STRES     READ /   SEQUEN.  WriteS THE STRESS .
*     .                           Write.            OF AN ELEMENT     .
*     .     8,9 *     G-STIF/     Write.   SEQUEN   STORES GLOBAL     .
*     .               G-LOAD                        STIFFNESS MATRICES.
*     .    10,11      CHECK_1/    Write.   SEQUEN   CHECKS VALUES OF  .
*     .               CHECK_2                       INTERMEDIATE STEPS.
*     .      12 *     RCORD       Write.   SEQUEN   CHECKS CALCULATION.
*     .                                            RELATED TO REINF  .
*     .      13 *     BSLIP       Write.   SEQUEN   CHECKS CALCULATION.
*     .                                            RELATED TO BONDSLIP.
*     .                                                             .
*     . (b)  THE MAIN PROGRAMME CALLS THE FOLLOWING SUBROUTINES :    .
*     .               1.   MESSGENPB /MESSGENPF                      .
*     .               2.   GRAPHFRM                                 .
*     .                      1 GRAPH                                .
*     .               3.   INDATAP                                  .
*     .                      1 CHECKP                               .
```

A 3D Hypoelastic Model of RC Structure using lower order EAS elements.

```
*   .                  -----------------------------------           .
*   .                  -: F O R   L I N E A R   A N A L Y S I S :-    .
*   .                  -----------------------------------           .
*   .                  4.   STIFL.                                    .
*   .                             1 DPMAT   (TRANFMS /MULT /INVERT)   .
*   .                             2.DPHYPO.(TRANFMS /MODULII)         .
*   .                             3 INDATAR                           .
*   .                             4 DRMAT   (TRANFME /MULT /INVERT)   .
*   .                             5 GAUSS                             .
*   .                             6 SHAP                              .
*   .                             7 ESHAP                             .
*   .                             8 JACOBP                            .
*   .                             9 BPMAT                             .
*   .                            10 EBPMAT                            .
*   .                            11 DBMATP                            .
*   .                            12 MESSGENR                          .
*   .                            13 SHAPR                             .
*   .                            14 NEWTRAPH                          .
*   .                  5.   LOAD                                      .
*   .                  6.   SOLVBND                                   .
*   .                             1. SOLV1 /ABELSOLV                  .
*   .                             2. RESERROR                         .
*   .                             3. MAXDIS                           .
*   .                  7.   PRNDISP.                                  .
*   .                  8.   STRES.                                    .
*   .                  9.   BONDSLIP.                                 .
*   .                             1. SLIP                             .
*   .                             2. ELOAD                            .
*   .                             3. SOLVBND                          .
*   .                             4. NEWTRAP                          .
*   .                             5. MESSGENR                         .
*   .                             6. SHAPR                            .
*   .                  -------------------------------------          .
*   .                  -: F O R   N O N-L I N E A R   A N A L Y S I S :-  .
*   .                  -------------------------------------          .
*   .                  4.   PARAMTR                                   .
*   .                  5.   INCREM                                    .
*   .                             1. ELOAD                            .
*   .                  6.   SOLVBND                                   .
*   .                  7.   PRINTDISP.                                .
*   .                  8.   STIFNL.                                   .
*   .                             1. AS IN STIFL +                    .
*   .                             2. HYPODPMT                         .
*   .                                   a. PRINSTR                    .
*   .                                   b. ARGYRIS                    .
*   .                                   c. MODULII                    .
*   .                                   d. DPHYPO                     .
*   .                  9.   RESTRES.                                  .
*   .                  10.  CONVDISP                                  .
*   .                                                                 .
*   . (c)   IT USES THE FOLLOWING MAJOR VARIABLES OF IMPORTANCE :     .
*   .                                                                 .
*   .       NDF   = MAXIMUM NUMBER OF DEGREE-OF-FREEDOM'S PER NODE.   .
*   .       NSL   = MAXIMUM NUMBER OF SLIP D.O.F.S PER ELEMENT.       .
*   .       NSTR  = MAXIMUM NUMBER OF STRESS/STRAIN COMPONENTS        .
*   .       NCN   = MAXIMUM NUMBER OF NODES PER ELEMENT(PARENT)       .
*   .       NC    = MAXIMUM NUMBER OF NODES PER ELEMENT(REINF.)       .
*   .       NNSM  = ADDITIONAL DOF FOR EAS MODES)                     .
*   .       NCORD = MAXIMUM NUMBER OF CO-ORDINATE AXES                .
*   .       NGP   = MAXIMUM NUMBER OF GAUSS POINTS                    .
*   .       NSZF  = TOTAL NO OF D.O.F.s IN ENTIRE CONTINUUM           .
*   .       NSM   = TOTAL NO OF D.O.F.s PER ELEMENT                   .
*   .       NSMM  = NSM MODIFIED, INCLUDING INCOMPATIBLE D.O.F.s      .
*   .               PER ELEMENT                                       .
*   .       NP    = TOTAL NO OF NODAL POINTS IN THE ENTIRE CONTINUUM .
*   .       NE    = TOTAL NO OF ELEMENTS IN THE ENTIRE CONTINUUM      .
```

A 3D Hypoelastic Model of RC Structure using lower order EAS elements.

```
*   .      NB      = TOTAL NO OF NODAL POINTS AT THE BOUNDARY OF THE  .
*   .              ENTIRE CONTINUUM                                    .
*   .      NLD     = TOTAL NO OF LOAD CASES                            .
*   .      NOP     = NODAL CONNECTIVITY VECTOR PER ELEMENT OF THE      .
*   .              ENTIRE CONTINUUM                                    .
*   .      CORD    = NODAL POINT CO-ORDINATE VECTOR OF THE CONTINUUM   .
*   .      NBC     = BOUNDARY CONDITION CODE FOR NODES AT BOUNDARY     .
*   .      BFIX    = MAXIMUM NUMBER OF NODES FOR WHICH D.O.F.'S        .
*   .              ARE FIXED OR SPECIFIED.                             .
*   .      NBST    = NODAL VECTOR FOR WHICH D.O.F.'S ARE FIXED OR      .
*   .              SPECIFIED.                                          .
*   .      Econc   = YOUNG'S MODULUS OF THE PARENT MATERIAL/ELEMENT    .
*   .      ANUconc = POISSOIN'S RATIO OF THE PARENT MATERIAL/ELEMENT   .
*   .      TRANFMS = STRESS TRASFORMATION VECTOR                       .
*   .      TRANFME = STRAIN TRASFORMATION VECTOR                       .
*   .      QBK     = ELASTICITY MATRIX/VECTOR W.R.T. LOCAL AXES        .
*   .      DFMT    = TRANSFORMED ELASTICITY MATRIX IN GLOBAL AXES SYS..
*   .      KGP     = NO OF GAUSS POINTS FOR NUMERIAL INTEGRATION       .
*   .      ZX      = NORMALISED CO-ORDINATES ALONG GAUSSIAN X-DIR.     .
*   .      ZY      = NORMALISED CO-ORDINATES ALONG GAUSSIAN Y-DIR.     .
*   .      ZZ      = NORMALISED CO-ORDINATES ALONG GAUSSIAN Z-DIR.     .
*   .      SFN     = VECTOR OF SHAPE FUNCTIONS IN NORMALISED CO-ORD    .
*   .      XJAC    = JACOBIAN MATRIX <IST ORDER TRANSFORMATION>        .
*   .      XJACI   = INVERSE OF JACOBIAN MATRIX <XJAC>                 .
*   .      CARTDC  = FIRST ORDER CARTESIAN DERIVATIVE OF SHAPE FUNCTION
*   .      SM      = STIFFNESS MATRIX OF THE ELEMENT                   .
*   .      SMM     = SM MODIFIED, INCLUDING INCOMPATIBLE MODES         .
*   .      GSM     = GLOBAL STIFFNESS MATRIX OF THE ENTIRE CONTINUUM   .
*   .      ELOAD   = ELEMENT LOAD VECTOR                               .
*   .      GLOAD   = GLOBAL LOAD VECTOR OF THE ENTIRE CONTINUUM        .
*   .      DISP    = GLOBAL DISPLACEMENT VECTOR                        .
*   .      EDISP   = ELEMENT DISPLACEMENT VECTOR                       .
*   .      GPCOD   = CARTESIAN CO-ORDINATES FOR EACH GAUSS-POINT       .
*   .      IPLD    = LOAD INDEX for POINT LOAD    = 0 - NO             .
*   .                                             = 1 - YES            .
*   .      IGLD    = LOAD INDEX for GRAVITY LOAD  = 0 - NO             .
*   .                                             = 1 - YES            .
*   .      NINCS   = TOTAL NO OF LOAD INCREMENTS PER ANALYSIS          .
*   .      TFAC    = CUMULATIVE LOAD FACTOR UPTO AND INCLUDING THE     .
*   .                PRESENT INCREMENT.                                .
*   .                                                                  .
*   . (d) CALLED BY :                                                  .
*   .                    NONE.                                         .
*   .                                                                  .
*   . (e) INPUT VARIABLES IN SEQUENCE :                                .
*   .      Ntype = BASIC TYPE OF THE PROBLEM ,    0 - BEAM             .
*   .                                             1 - FRAME            .
*   .      NEtype= NATURE OF ELEMENT USED         0 - HCiS18           .
*   .                                             1 - HCiS12           .
*   .      NRF   = REBAR EFFECT INCORPORATED,     0 - NO               .
*   .                                             Nos- YES             .
*   .      ISLIP = BONDSLIP EFFECT INCORPORATED, 0 - NO                .
*   .                                             1 - YES              .
*   .      NATR  = BASIC NATURE OF THE PROBLEM , 0 - LINEAR            .
*   .                                             1 - NON LINEAR       .
*   .      LARGE = GEOMETRIC NONLINEARITY,        0 - NOT INCLUDE      .
*   .                                             1 - INCLUDE          .
*   .      NREST = RESTART FACILITY PARAMETER ,   0 - NO               .
*   .                                             1 - YES              .
*   .      NALGO = NONLINEAR SOLUTION PROCESS INDICATOR                .
*   .                    = 0 - INITIAL STIFFNESS METHOD                .
*   .                    = 1 - TANGENTIAL STIFFNESS METHOD             .
*   . (f) PURPOSE :                                                    .
*   .          THE MAIN PROGRAMME TAKES THE INPUT-VALUES OF THE        .
*   .      PROBLEM UNDER CONSIDERATION,SOLVES IT & PRINTS THE OUTPUT. .
*   .      THE STATIC(LINEAR /NON-LINEAR) RESPONSE OF THE STRUCTURE    .
```

A 3D Hypoelastic Model of RC Structure using lower order EAS elements.

```
*        .      IS OBTAINED.                                          .
*        .                                                           .
*        ..............................................................
*
C************************************************************************
c
c                    M A S T E R    P R O G R A M
c
      Implicit Real *8(a-h,o-z)
      Common/CONC/Fck,Econc,ANUconc/BND/mband,NB/EAS/NEAS,NSMM
      Common/NBeam/Dbeamx,Dbeamy,Dbeamz,Nbeamx,Nbeamy,Nbeamz
      Common/JT/CORD(5000,3)/MC/NOP(2000,8)/PAR/NP,NE/GPAR/NSZF
      Common/BC/BFIX(100,3),NBST(100,3),NBC(100)/TH/Theta(3,3)
      Common/FACT/FACTO,NINCS,MITER,NALGO
      Common/ULTSTR/Fcu,Ft,Fcb,Ecu,Ecm,Et,Em,Ecb
      Common/RFSE/RCORDS(10,3),RCORDE(10,3)/CONCRACK/Ecrack,Esoft
      Common/ULTST/A0,A1,A2,B0,B1,B2/ULTSR/EA0,EA1,EA2,EB0,EB1,EB2
      Common/ARF/RFDIA(9),AREINF(9),NNELRF(99)
      Common/RF/Esteel,Esh,NELRF,Fy,Eyp,Eyf
      Parameter(NDF=3,NSM=24,NSTR=6)
      Dimension RSLOD(2000,24),ELOAD(2000,24),TLOAD(2000,24),DISP(5000),
     *          DISPINC(5000),TDISP(5000),STRSG(NSTR,5000),TREAC(100,3),
     *          EQLOAD(2000,24),STRSR(NSTR,5000),DLOAD(2000,24),
     *          RLOAD(2000,24),DISPIN(5000),STRG(NSTR,5000),
     *          STRNG(NSTR,5000),STRNR(NSTR,5000)
      Character(9) TODAY
      Character(8) TIM
      Real(4) IT,TA(2)
c
c*** Read the basic NATURE of the problem
c
      Write(*,101)
      Write(*,201)
      Write(*,300)
        Read(*,*)NATR
          If (NATR.EQ.1) Then
             Write(*,301)
          Read(*,*)LARGE
           Endif
      Write(*,305)
          Read(*,*) Ntype
c
c*** Read input data for MESS generation of PARENT ELEMENTS of Beam
c
      If (Ntype.EQ.0) Then
      Open(unit=1,file='1_INB-PARENT')
      Open(unit=2,file='2_INB-REINF')
      Open(unit=3,file='3_OUT-BEAM')
      Open(unit=4,file='4_GRDAT')
      Write(3,100)
       If (NATR.EQ.0) Then
        Write(3,105)
         Elseif (NATR.EQ.1) Then
           Write(3,106)
       If (LARGE.EQ.0) Write (3,302)
       If (LARGE.EQ.0) Write (4,302)
       If (LARGE.EQ.1) Write (3,303)
       If (LARGE.EQ.1) Write (4,303)
        Endif
***  Get the clock time/date at the time of run/execution
      Call Date(TODAY)
         Write(3,*) 'LAST DATE OF RUN/EXECUTION  ::  ', TODAY
         Write(4,*) 'LAST DATE OF RUN/EXECUTION  ::  ', TODAY
           Call Clock (TIM)
           Write(3,*) 'LAST TIME OF RUN/EXECUTION  ::  ',TIM
           Write(4,*) 'LAST TIME OF RUN/EXECUTION  ::  ',TIM
```

A 3D Hypoelastic Model of RC Structure using lower order EAS elements.

```
      Call MESGENPB()
*     Call GRAPHFRM()
c
c*** Read input data for MESS generation of PARENT ELEMENTS of Frame
c
      Elseif (Ntype.EQ.1) Then
      Open(unit=1,file='1_INF-PARENT')
      Open(unit=2,file='2_INF-REINF')
      Open(unit=3,file='3_OUT-FRAME')
      Open(unit=4,file='4_GRDAT')
      Write(3,104)
       If (NATR.EQ.0) Then
       Write(3,105)
         Elseif (NATR.EQ.1) Then
           Write(3,106)
         If (LARGE.EQ.0) Write (3,302)
         If (LARGE.EQ.1) Write (3,303)
         Endif
*
c*** Get the clock time/date at the time of run/execution
      Call Date(TODAY)
         Write(3,*) 'LAST DATE OF RUN/EXECUTION  ::  ', TODAY
             Call Clock (TIM)
             Write(3,*) 'LAST TIME OF RUN/EXECUTION  ::  ',TIM
      Call MESGENPF()
*     Call GRAPHFRM()
      Endif
c
c*** Open the various other files to be used later....
c
      Open(unit=5,file='5_E-STIF')
      Open(unit=6,file='6_E-LOAD')
      Open(unit=7,file='7_E-STRES')
      Open(unit=8,file='8_E-STIF_NL')
      Open(unit=9,file='9_G-LOAD')
      Open(unit=10,file='10_CHECK_1')
      Open(unit=11,file='11_CHECK_2')
      Open(unit=12,file='12_RCORD')
      Open(unit=13,file='13_BSLIP')
      Open(unit=14,file='14_NLR-Fail')
      Open(unit=15,file='15_NLR-Rc-E')
      Open(unit=16,file='16_NLR-Moduli')
      Open(unit=17,file='17_NLR-EpsU-C')
      Open(unit=18,file='18_NLR-Hist')
      Open(unit=19,file='19_NLR-SEincrm')
      Open(unit=20,file='20_NLR-Gmatx')
      Open(unit=21,file='21_NLR-SMii')
      Open(unit=22,file='22_NLINR')
      Open(unit=23,file='23_NLSTRAIN')
      Open(unit=24,file='24_NLSTRESS')
         Write(23,*) 'LAST DATE OF RUN/EXECUTION  ::  ', TODAY
         Write(24,*) 'LAST DATE OF RUN/EXECUTION  ::  ', TODAY
           Write(23,*) 'LAST TIME OF RUN/EXECUTION  ::  ',TIM
           Write(24,*) 'LAST TIME OF RUN/EXECUTION  ::  ',TIM
c
c*** Read input data (supt data and property) of PARENT ELEMENTS
c
      Call INDATAP(NRF,ISLIP,NEtype,NATR)
      Call DPMAT ()
      If (NRF.NE.0) Then
      Call INDATAR (NRF,NATR)
      Call DRMAT ()
      Endif
c
c*** Read loading parameters /Form element load vector /Initialise arrays
c
```

A 3D Hypoelastic Model of RC Structure using lower order EAS elements.

```
      Call LOAD (RSLOD,RLOAD,DLOAD,Ntype)
      Call ZERO (ELOAD,TLOAD,DISP,DISPINC,DISPIN,TDISP,STRSG,STRG,STRSR,
     *           TREAC,STRNG,STRNR)
*=============================================================================
c*** Perform Linear elastic analysis, if required.
c
      If (NATR.EQ.0) Then
      incs=0;MITER=0;TFAC=0
          Call STIFL (NEtype,NRF)
           Call SOLVBND(RSLOD,DISP,TREAC)
         Call MAXDIS (DISP,MND,DISMAX)
        Write(3,910) MND,DISMAX
  910 Format(/,3x,'Global Nodal DOF=',I5,3x,'Max Displacement =',F10.4)
      If (ISLIP.EQ.1) Call BONDSLIP (NRF,RSLOD,DISP)
      Call PRNOUT(incs,MITER,TFAC,NATR,DISP,DISPINC,TDISP,TREAC,kdefln)
      Call STRES (DISP,NRF)
*=============================================================================
c*** Perform NON-LINEAR ANALYSIS, if required.
c
      Elseif (NATR.EQ.1) Then
      Write(4,595)
c
c*** Compute parameters of Argyris Eqn for both Ult stress Surface &
c    Equivalent Uniaxial Strain Surface
c
      Call PARAMTR ()
*     Call PARAKHR ()
c
c*** Start the load increment loop as specified load factor<FACTO>
c
      TFAC=0.0
      Do 155 incs=1,NINCS
       KITER=0
      Call INCREM(incs,TFAC,DLOAD,RLOAD,ELOAD,TLOAD)
      Call STIFNL(incs,NEtype,LARGE,NRF,KSYSFAIL,STRSG,STRG,STRSR,
     *            DISPINC,DISPIN,TDISP)
       If (KSYSFAIL.EQ.1) Goto 156
  265  KITER=KITER+1
       Write(*,695) KITER
       Call SOLVBND(ELOAD,DISP,TREAC)
        If (ISLIP.EQ.1.AND.incs.GT.5) Call BONDSLIP(NRF,ELOAD,DISP)
       Call TLDISP(DISP,DISPINC,TDISP)
        Call PRNOUT(incs,KITER,TFAC,NATR,DISP,DISPINC,TDISP,TREAC,kdefln)
       Call RESTRES (incs,KITER,LARGE,NRF,DISP,DISPIN,TDISP,STRSG,STRG,
     *              STRSR,EQLOAD)
       If (kdefln.EQ.1) Goto 156
        Call CONVDISP (incs,KITER,DISP,DISPINC,ELOAD,EQLOAD,KCHECK)
        If (KITER.EQ.MITER) Goto 155
        If (KCHECK.EQ.1) Goto 265
  155 Continue
      Endif
  156  Continue
C*=============================================================================
c*** Check /delete intermediate files prepared for the analysis
c
      Close(unit=5,status='delete')
      Close(unit=6,status='delete')
      Close(unit=7,status='delete')
      Close(unit=8,status='delete')
      Close(unit=9,status='delete')
      Close(unit=10,status='delete')
      Close(unit=11,status='delete')
      Close(unit=12,status='delete')
      Close(unit=13,status='delete')
      Close(unit=14,status='delete')
      Close(unit=15,status='delete')
```

```
          Close(unit=16,status='delete')
          Close(unit=17,status='delete')
          Close(unit=18,status='delete')
          Close(unit=19,status='delete')
          Close(unit=20,status='delete')
          Close(unit=21,status='delete')
          Close(unit=22,status='delete')
c
c***  Print CPU time of run
c
          IT=DTIME(TA)
          Write(*,190) IT
          Write(3,190) IT
          Write(4,190) IT
          Write(23,190) IT
          Write(24,190) IT
c
   101 Format(/,'....................................................
      c.......',
      c//,24x,'W E L C O M E',//29x,'T O',//18x,'-: N   A   C   O   N :-'
      c,//14x,'(Non-linear Analysis of CONcrete)',/6x,
      c'A 3D FEM LINEAR /NON-LINEAR STATIC ANALYSIS PACKAGE',//6x,
      c'GUIDED BY : PROF. S. N. GHOSH. Jadavpur University.'/8x,
      c'DEVELOPED BY : AMIYA K. SAMANTA. NIT-Durgapur.',/,'.............
      c..................................................',///)
   201 Format('*=*=*=*=*=*  M A S T E R   P R O G R A M   P A R A M E T',
      *'E R S  *=*=*=*=*=*',/)
   190 Format(/,2X,'C.P.U. : RUN TIME REQD. :',1X,F10.2,1X,'Seconds.')
   300 Format(x,'ENTER OPTION <NATR> FOR NATURE OF ANALYSIS ?',/,
      *        5x,'<0>. Linear',/,5x,'<1>. Non-Linear')
   301 Format(x,'ENTER OPTION <LARGE> TO INCLUDE GEOMETRIC NON-LINEARITY
      *  ?',/,5x,'<0>. No',/,5x,'<1>. Yes')
   302 Format(4x,'*** GEOMETRIC NON-LINEARITY NOT INCLUDED ***',/)
   303 Format(6x,'***** GEOMETRIC NON-LINEARITY INCLUDED *****',/)
   305 Format(x,'ENTER OPTION <Ntype> FOR ANALYSIS OF ?',/,
      *        5x,'<0>. Beam',/,5x,'<1>. Frame')
   100 Format(/,x,'Output of Simply-Supported BEAM Analysis :')
   105 Format(x,'***** NATURE OF ANALYSIS : LINEAR *****')
   106 Format(x,'***** NATURE OF ANALYSIS : NON-LINEAR <MATERIAL> *****')
   104  Format(/,x,'Output of Single-Bay FRAME Analysis :',/)
*  595 Format(/,5x,'LOAD INCREMENT',5x,'ITER',5x,'TOTAL LOAD',5x,
*      *'CENTRAL',7x,'CUM CENTRAL',//,11x,'NO',12x,'No.',7x,'FACTOR',6x,
*      *'DEFLN:(mm)',6x,'DEFLN:(mm)',//,5X,'----------'
*      *'-----------------------------------------------------------')
   595 Format(/,5x,'LOAD INCREMENT',5x,'ITER',5x,'TOTAL LOAD',5x,
      *'CENTRAL',7x,'DISPINC',7x,'CUM CENTRAL',//,11x,'NO',12x,'No.',7x,
      *'FACTOR',6x,'DEFLN:(mm)',20x,'DEFLN:(mm)',//,5x,'----------'
      *'-----------------------------------------------------------'
      *'--------------')
   695 Format(/,5x,'CURRENT ITERATION No <KITER>=',I3,/,5x,
      *'*=*=*=*=*=*=*=*=*=*=*=*=*=*',/)
          Write(*,*)'*=*=*  S U C C E S S F U L L Y   E X E C U T E D *=*=*'
          Stop
          End
c ********************************************************************************
c
          Subroutine ESHAP (ZX,ZY,ZZ,SDR9)
c
c***  This subroutine computes the BUBBLE SHAPE functions and it's
c     normalised derivatives at the centre of the element under considn.
c ----------------------------------------------------------------------
          Implicit real *8(a-h,o-z)
          Parameter (NCORD=3)
          Dimension SDR9(NCORD,2)
c ----------------------------------------------------------------------
          Do 360 i=1,NCORD
```

A 3D Hypoelastic Model of RC Structure using lower order EAS elements.

```
      Do 360 j=1,2
      SDR9(i,j)=0.0
 360 Continue
c
c *** BUBBLE SHAPE functions for 8-noded 3D brick element
c
      SFN9=(1-ZX*ZX)*(1-ZY*ZY)*(1-ZZ*ZZ)/2
c
c ----To calculate its' 1st order derivative
c
      SDR9(1,1)=-ZX*(1-ZY*ZY)*(1-ZZ*ZZ)
      SDR9(2,1)=-(1-ZX*ZX)*ZY*(1-ZZ*ZZ)
      SDR9(3,1)=-(1-ZX*ZX)*(1-ZY*ZY)*ZZ
c
c ----To calculate its' MIXED 2nd order derivative
c
      SDR9(1,2)=2*ZX*ZY*(1-ZZ*ZZ)
      SDR9(2,2)=2*ZX*(1-ZY*ZY)*ZZ
      SDR9(3,2)=2*(1-ZX*ZX)*ZY*ZZ
c     Write(*,*)'++++ Exit ESHAP :--------------------'
      Return
      End
c ****************************************************************************
c
          Subroutine SHAPR (ZX,kgpr,SFNR,SDRR,ECORDR,DTJACR,GPCODR)
c
c***  This subroutine computes Det of Jacobian Matrix for 1-D line Element
c     (to calculate the length of Reinforcement within an element)
c ---------------------------------------------------------------------
      Implicit real *8(a-h,o-z)
      Parameter (NC=2,NCORDR=1,NCORD=3)
      Dimension SDRR(NCORDR,NC),XJACR(NCORDR,NCORDR),ECORDR(NCORD,NC),
     *          SFNR(NC),GPCODR(NCORD,NC)
c ---------------------------------------------------------------------
      Do 360 i=1,NC
 360 SFNR(i)=0.0
      Do 361 i=1,NCORDR
      Do 361 j=1,NC
 361 SDRR(i,j)=0.0
c
c *** SHAPE functions for 2-noded uniaxial line element
c
      SFNR(1)=(1-ZX)/2
      SFNR(2)=(1+ZX)/2
c
      SDRR(1,1)=-0.5
      SDRR(1,2)=0.5
c
      XJACR(1,1)=0.0
      XJACR(1,1)=SDRR(1,1)*ECORDR(1,1)+SDRR(1,2)*ECORDR(1,2)
      If (abs(XJACR(1,1)).LT.0.1E-05) XJACR(1,1)=0.0
      DTJACR= XJACR(1,1)
c
c *** Evaluate the global co-cord of gauss point of rebar
c
      Do 210 ic=1,NCORD
      GPCODR(ic,kgpr)=0.0
      Do 210 inode=1,NC
 210 GPCODR(ic,kgpr)=GPCODR(ic,kgpr)+ECORDR(ic,inode)*SFNR(inode)
      Return
      End
c ****************************************************************************
c
          Subroutine EBPMAT (NEtype,ECORD,DTJAC,iel,SDR9,BPMT,EBPMT)
c
c***  This subroutine calculates various components of strain matrix
```

```
c      of the parent material
c  -------------------------------------------------------------------
       Implicit real *8(a-h,o-z)
       Common/EAS/NEAS,NSMM
       Parameter (NCN=8,NCORD=3,NSM=24,NSTR=6)
       Dimension ECORD(NCORD,NCN),SDR9(NCORD,2),TRNF(NSTR,NSTR),
     *           XJAC9(NCORD,NCORD),XJACI9(NCORD,NCORD),BPMT(NSTR,NSM),
     *           ADBPMT(NSTR,NEAS),BPMTT(NSTR,NEAS),EBPMT(NSTR,NSMM)
c  -------------------------------------------------------------------
c
c***   Calculate determinant & inverse of Jacbian matrix(XJACI9)at the
c      centre of the element
c
*      Write(*,*)'NEAS=',NEAS,'NSMM=',NSMM
       Do 510 i=1,NCORD
       XJAC9(1,i)=0.0
       XJAC9(1,i)=(-ECORD(i,1)-ECORD(i,2)-ECORD(i,3)-ECORD(i,4)
     *            +ECORD(i,5)+ECORD(i,6)+ECORD(i,7)+ECORD(i,8))/8
       XJAC9(2,i)=0.0
       XJAC9(2,i)=(-ECORD(i,1)-ECORD(i,2)+ECORD(i,3)+ECORD(i,4)
     *            -ECORD(i,5)-ECORD(i,6)+ECORD(i,7)+ECORD(i,8))/8
       XJAC9(3,i)=0.0
       XJAC9(3,i)=(+ECORD(i,1)-ECORD(i,2)-ECORD(i,3)+ECORD(i,4)
     *            +ECORD(i,5)-ECORD(i,6)-ECORD(i,7)+ECORD(i,8))/8
  510 Continue
c
       DTJAC9= XJAC9(1,1)*(XJAC9(2,2)*XJAC9(3,3)-XJAC9(2,3)*XJAC9(3,2))
     *        -XJAC9(1,2)*(XJAC9(2,1)*XJAC9(3,3)-XJAC9(2,3)*XJAC9(3,1))
     *        +XJAC9(1,3)*(XJAC9(2,1)*XJAC9(3,2)-XJAC9(2,2)*XJAC9(3,1))
c      Write(3,*) 'DTJAC9 =',DTJAC9
       If (DTJAC.LE.0) Write(*,455) iel,DTJAC
  455 Format (/,3X'Program halted in EBPMAT :',/,10x,'Zero/Negative '
     *       ,'Volm :',//,10x,'Element no=',I3,3x,'DTJAC=',E15.3)
c
       Call INVERT (XJAC9,XJACI9,NCORD)
c      Write(3,219) ((XJACI9(i,j),j=1,NCORD),i=1,NCORD)
c 219 Format(/,3x, 'XJACI9 :',//,3(E10.3))
c
c *** Form the additional components of BPMT to include modes of EAS
c     (6x12 matrix for HCiS12 element as per Ceser) in natural co-ord
c
       Do 515 i=1,NSTR
       Do 515 j=1,NEAS
  515 ADBPMT(i,j)=0.0
c
       If (NEtype.EQ.1) Goto 731
       mg=1
       ADBPMT(mg,1)=SDR9(1,1);ADBPMT(mg,10)=SDR9(1,2)
       ADBPMT(mg,11)=SDR9(2,2);ADBPMT(mg,12)=SDR9(3,2)
       mg=mg+1
       ADBPMT(mg,2)=SDR9(2,1);ADBPMT(mg,10)=SDR9(1,2)
       ADBPMT(mg,11)=SDR9(2,2);ADBPMT(mg,12)=SDR9(3,2)
       mg=mg+1
       ADBPMT(mg,3)=SDR9(3,1);ADBPMT(mg,10)=SDR9(1,2)
       ADBPMT(mg,11)=SDR9(2,2);ADBPMT(mg,12)=SDR9(3,2)
       mg=mg+1
       ADBPMT(mg,4)=SDR9(1,1);ADBPMT(mg,5)=SDR9(2,1)
       ADBPMT(mg,13)=SDR9(2,2);ADBPMT(mg,14)=SDR9(3,2)
       mg=mg+1
       ADBPMT(mg,6)=SDR9(1,1);ADBPMT(mg,7)=SDR9(3,1)
       ADBPMT(mg,15)=SDR9(1,2);ADBPMT(mg,16)=SDR9(3,2)
       mg=mg+1
       ADBPMT(mg,8)=SDR9(2,1);ADBPMT(mg,9)=SDR9(3,1)
       ADBPMT(mg,17)=SDR9(1,2);ADBPMT(mg,18)=SDR9(2,2)
       Goto 732
c
```

A 3D Hypoelastic Model of RC Structure using lower order EAS elements.

```
  731  mg=1
       ADBPMT(mg,1)=SDR9(1,1);ADBPMT(mg,4)=SDR9(1,2)
       ADBPMT(mg,5)=SDR9(2,2);ADBPMT(mg,6)=SDR9(3,2)
       mg=mg+1
       ADBPMT(mg,2)=SDR9(2,1);ADBPMT(mg,4)=SDR9(1,2)
       ADBPMT(mg,5)=SDR9(2,2);ADBPMT(mg,6)=SDR9(3,2)
       mg=mg+1
       ADBPMT(mg,3)=SDR9(3,1);ADBPMT(mg,4)=SDR9(1,2)
       ADBPMT(mg,5)=SDR9(2,2);ADBPMT(mg,6)=SDR9(3,2)
       mg=mg+2
       ADBPMT(mg,7)=SDR9(1,1);ADBPMT(mg,8)=SDR9(2,1)
       ADBPMT(mg,9)=SDR9(1,2)
       mg=mg+1
       ADBPMT(mg,10)=SDR9(1,1);ADBPMT(mg,11)=SDR9(2,1)
       ADBPMT(mg,12)=SDR9(1,2)
  732  Continue
c
c *** Form the TRANSFORMATION matrix to modify ADBPMT from natural co-ord
c      system to global reference frame
c
       Call TRANFME (XJACI9,TRNF)
c
c *** Form the additional components of BPMT to include modes of EAS
c      (6x18 matrix for HCiS18 element as per Ceser) in global frame or
c      (6x12 matrix for HCiS12 element as per Ceser) in global frame
c
       Const=DTJAC9/DTJAC
*        Write(*,*)  'Const=',Const
       Do 525 i=1,NSTR
       Do 525 j=1,NSTR
  525  TRNF(i,j)=TRNF(i,j)*Const
       Call DBMATP (NSTR,NEAS,TRNF,ADBPMT,BPMTT)
c
c *** Form enhanced strain matrix i.e. add extra incompatible modes
c
       Do 530 i=1,NSTR
       Do 530 l=1,NSMM
  530  EBPMT(i,l)=0.0
c
       Do 535 i=1,NSTR
       Do 535 j=1,NSM
  535  EBPMT(i,j)=BPMT(i,j)
       N1=NSM+1
       Do 540 i=1,NSTR
       Do 540 k=N1,NSMM
       l=k-NSM
  540  EBPMT(i,k)=BPMTT(i,l)
c        Write(*,*)'++++ Exit EBPMAT :--------------------'
       Return
       End
c *****************************************************************************
c
       Subroutine SLIP (DISP,NRF,SIG)
c
c*** This subr calculates bond slip(dispt) contribution of reinf.at material
c    level following approach of G. BEER.(Continuous Interface Element)
c
c *** NSL=No of slip DOF for INTERFACE ELEMENT
c ----------------------------------------------------------------------
       Implicit real *8(a-h,o-z)
       Common/JT/CORD(5000,3)/MC/NOP(2000,8)/PAR/NP,NE/GPAR/NSZF
       Common/CONC/Fck,Econc,ANUconc/CONCRACK/Ecrack,Esoft
       Common/ARF/RFDIA(9),AREINF(9),NNELRF(99)
       Common/RF/Esteel,Esh,NELRF,Fy,Eyp,Eyf
       Common/RFSE/RCORDS(10,3),RCORDE(10,3)
       Parameter (NDF=3,NCN=8,NC=2,NSL=4,NSM=24,NCORD=3,NSTR=6,NGR=2)
```

```
      Dimension ECORD(NCORD,NCN),SFN(NCN),SDR(NCORD,NCN),DISP(5000),
     *          ECORDR(NCORD,NC),EDISP(NSM),EDISR(NC,NDF),GPRF(NCORD),
     *          A(NCORD),H(NCORD),GPCORD(NCORD,NC),SFNR(NC),SDRR(1,NC),
     *          BRMAT(1,NSL),DBR(1,NSL),BSM(NSL,NSL),BIMAT(1,NSL),
     *          CARTD(NCORD,NCN),EDISB(NSL),ESLIP(NC),GSLIP(250,10),
     *          BPMT(NSTR,NSM),STRSRES(NSTR),SIGRESP(NSM),STRNR(NC,NSTR)
     *          ,STR(NSTR),RCORDST(99,3),RCORDEND(99,3),SIG(2000,24)
c  -----------------------------------------------------------------------
*        Write(*,*) '-------: ENTERED SUBROUTINE-SLIP :-------'
c        Write(13,957)
         Write(13,960)
         ireinf=0
         Do 900 iel=1,NE
         Do 905 iy=1,NSM
  905    SIG(iel,iy)=0.0
         Write(13,60)iel
   60 Format('---------------------- iel=',I2,'--------------------')
c
c*** Form Element co-ordinate vector
c
         Do 915 inode=1,NCN
         l=NOP(iel,inode)
         Do 915 j=1,NCORD
  915    ECORD(j,inode)=CORD(l,j)
c
c*** Form Parent Element displacement vector(EDISP)
c
*        Write(12,920)
         Do 925 inode=1,NCN
         m=NOP(iel,inode)
         Do 930 j=1,NDF
         kr=(m-1)*NDF
         k=(inode-1)*NDF
         ij=k+j
         kj=kr+j
         EDISP(ij)=DISP(kj)
  930    Continue
  925    Continue
c
c*** Calculate displ at REINF. nodes(EDISR) on the parent domain
c
         Do 752 na=1,NELRF
         ia=NNELRF(na)
         If (iel.NE.ia) Goto 752
c
         Do 753 irf=1,NRF
         Call MESSGENR(irf,RCORDST,RCORDEND)
         Do 754 j=1,NCORD
         ECORDR(j,1)=RCORDST(na,j)
         ECORDR(j,2)=RCORDEND(na,j)
  754    Continue
c
         Do 755 inode=1,NC
         Call NEWTRAPH (ECORDR,ECORD,inode,GPRF)
         Zx=GPRF(1)
         Zy=GPRF(2)
         Zz=GPRF(3)
         Call SHAP (Zx,Zy,Zz,SFN,SDR)
         Do 982 i=1,NDF
         EDISR(inode,i)=0.0
         Do 983 k=1,NCN
         kk=(k-1)*NDF+i
  983    EDISR(inode,i)=EDISR(inode,i)+SFN(k)*EDISP(kk)
  982    Continue
  755    Continue
         Write(13,*)'EDISR:'
```

A 3D Hypoelastic Model of RC Structure using lower order EAS elements.

```
       Write(13,555) iel,((EDISR(inode,i),i=1,NDF),inode=1,NC)
   555 Format(I9,3x,3(2x,F12.4),/,12x,3(2x,F12.4))
c
c*** Calculate total Strain/ELONGATION of the Rebar
c
       Do 756 inode=1,NC
       Call NEWTRAPH (ECORDR,ECORD,inode,GPRF)
       Zx=GPRF(1)
       Zy=GPRF(2)
       Zz=GPRF(3)
       Call SHAP (Zx,Zy,Zz,SFN,SDR)
       Call JACOBP (iel,inode,SFN,SDR,ECORD,DTJAC,CARTD)
       Call BPMAT (CARTD,BPMT)
       Call GAUSS (NGR,A,H)
       Call SHAPR (Zx,inode,SFNR,SDRR,ECORDR,DTJACR,GPCORD)
       Dleng=DTJACR*H(inode)
c
       Do 984 i=1,NSTR
       STRNR(inode,i)=0.0
       Do 984 kdf=1,NSM
       STRNR(inode,i)=STRNR(inode,i)+BPMT(i,kdf)*EDISP(kdf)
   984 Continue
   756 Continue
c
       STRAIN=STRNR(1,1)+STRNR(2,1)
       ELONGR=STRAIN*Dleng
       If (STRAIN.LE.0.002) Then
       Es=Esteel
       Elseif (STRAIN.GT.0.002) Then
       Es=Esteel/50.0
       Endif
       Write(13,131) ELONGR,Es
   131 Format(3x,'ELONGATION OF REINF=',F10.4,3x,'Es=',E10.4)
c
c *** calculate stiffness of Reinf element at G Points(as truss element)=BSM
c
       Do 305 ip=1,NSL
       Do 305 jp=1,NSL
   305 BSM(ip,jp)=0.0
c
       Call GAUSS (NGR,A,H)
       kgpr=0
       Do 100 igr=1,NGR
       kgpr=kgpr+1
       Zxx=A(igr)
       Call SHAPR (Zxx,kgpr,SFNR,SDRR,ECORDR,DTJACR,GPCORD)
       Dleng=DTJACR*H(igr)
c
       Do 105 id=1,NSL
       BRMAT(1,id)=0.0
       If (id.GE.3) Goto 105
       BRMAT(1,id)=SDRR(1,id)/DTJACR
   105 Continue
       Do 110 ie=1,NSL
       DBR(1,ie)=0.0
       DBR(1,ie)=BRMAT(1,ie)*Es
   110 Continue
       Write(13,*) 'DBR============='
       Write(13,318) (DBR(1,i1),i1=1,NSL)
c
       Do 115 ia=1,NSL
       Do 115 ja=1,NSL
       Do 115 ka=1,1
   115 BSM(ia,ja)=BSM(ia,ja)+BRMAT(ka,ia)*DBR(ka,ja)*AREINF(irf)*Dleng
   100 Continue
       Write(13,316) irf,((BSM(i,j),j=1,NSL),i=1,NSL)
```

A 3D Hypoelastic Model of RC Structure using lower order EAS elements.

```
 316    Format(3x,'BSM(i,j) for irf= :',I5,//,4(3x,E9.3))
c
c *** Calculate Interface Element stiffness at Gauss Points for each Reinf
c     element(as Supplementary Interface Model)
c
        Call DISPSLIP(iel,irf,ELONGR,ECORDR,BSM,EDISB)
        Write(13,*) 'EDISB============='
        Write(13,318) (EDISB(i1),i1=1,NSL)
 492  Format(3x,I3,9x,I2,4x,2(2x,E12.4))
c
c***   Calculate SLIP /relative displacement at rebar nodes <ESLIP> for
c      individual element.
c
        Do 320 inode=1,NC
        Call NEWTRAPH (ECORDR,ECORD,inode,GPRF)
        If (ABS(GPRF(1)).GT.1.0) GPRF(1)=-1.0
        If (ABS(GPRF(1)).LT.1.0) GPRF(1)=1.0
        Zx1=GPRF(1)
        Call SHAPR (Zx1,inode,SFNR,SDRR,ECORDR,DTJACR,GPCORD)
c
        Do 420 ik=1,NSL
 420    BIMAT(1,ik)=0.0
        BIMAT(1,1)=SFNR(1);BIMAT(1,2)=-SFNR(1)
        BIMAT(1,3)=SFNR(2);BIMAT(1,4)=-SFNR(2)
c
        ESLIP(inode)=0.0
        Do 421 id=1,NSL
 421    ESLIP(inode)=ESLIP(inode)+BIMAT(1,id)*EDISB(id)
        ESLIP(inode)=ABS(ESLIP(inode))
 320  Continue
c
c *** Form global SLIP vector for reinf No.-1 present in all elements
c
        If (irf.GT.1) Goto 325
        Write(13,*) 'ESLIP=========================='
        Write(13,940) iel,irf,(ESLIP(inod),inod=1,NC)
        ireinf=ireinf+irf
        Do 330 inode=1,NC
        GSLIP(ireinf,inode)=ESLIP(inode)
 330  Continue
 325  Continue
c
c *** Compute correction stress due to slip at Gauss Points <SIGRESP>
c
        Call GAUSS (NGR,A,H)
        kgpr=0
        Do 530 igr=1,NGR
        kgpr=kgpr+1
        Zxx=A(igr)
        Call SHAPR (Zxx,kgpr,SFNR,SDRR,ECORDR,DTJACR,GPCORD)
        Dleng=DTJACR*H(igr)
        Dvolm=AREINF(irf)*Dleng
c
        Do 535 id=1,NSL
        BRMAT(1,id)=0.0
        BRMAT(1,id)=SDRR(1,id)/DTJACR
 535  Continue
        STRNSL=(BRMAT(1,1)*ESLIP(1)+BRMAT(1,2)*ESLIP(2))*1E+8
        SIGSL=STRNSL*Es*1E-8
c
        Call NEWTRAPH (GPCORD,ECORD,kgpr,GPRF)
        Zx=GPRF(1)
        Zy=GPRF(2)
        Zz=GPRF(3)
        Call SHAP (Zx,Zy,Zz,SFN,SDR)
        Call JACOBP (iel,kgpr,SFN,SDR,ECORD,DTJAC,CARTD)
```

A 3D Hypoelastic Model of RC Structure using lower order EAS elements.

```
      Call BPMAT (CARTD,BPMT)
      Do 870 ia=1,NSTR
      STR(ia)=0.0
      Do 870 kdf=1,NSM
      STR(ia)=STR(ia)+BPMT(ia,kdf)*EDISP(kdf)*1E+8
  870 Continue
      SIGRB=STR(1)*Es*1E-8
c
      Do 540 ii=1,NSTR
  540 STRSRES(ii)=0.0
      STRSRES(1)=SIGSL
c
      Do 545 ip=1,NSM
      SIGRESP(ip)=0.0
      Do 545 kdf=1,NSTR
      SIGRESP(ip)=SIGRESP(ip)+BPMT(kdf,ip)*STRSRES(kdf)*Dvolm
  545 Continue
  530 Continue
c
c *** Completes reinf(irf) loop
c
      Do 550 ij=1,NSM
  550 SIG(iel,ij)=SIG(iel,ij)+SIGRESP(ij)
  753 Continue
  752 Continue
      Write(13,*) 'Residual stress due to slip :=================='
      Write(13,546) iel,(SIG(iel,ip),ip=1,NSM)
c
  900 Continue
c
  318  Format(4(3x,E9.3))
  937  Format(3I10,4x,F12.4)
  940  Format(2I10,4x,2F12.4)
  546  Format(I6,/,3(2x,F12.1))
  547  Format(3(2x,F12.4))
  566  Format(2I6,/,3(2x,E12.4))
  957  Format(/,3x,'Element no',4x,'Reinf No',3x,'Slip(Node#1)',2x,'Slip'
      *,'(Node#2)'

      *, /,2x,'-------------------------------------------------')
  960  Format(//,3x,'Element No',3x,'Reinf No',3x,'Gauss Point',3x,
      *'SLIP-Stress',/,3x,'-------------------------------------------')
c
      Write(*,*) '++++ Exit SLIP :--------------------'
      Return
      End
c ****************************************************************************
c
      Subroutine LDISP (CARTD,ETDISP,GMATX,BPMT)
c
c*** This subroutine calculates strain matrix due to LARGE DISPLACEMENT
c    & evaluates BPMT(final)=BPMT(initial)+BLMT
c -------------------------------------------------------------------
      Implicit real *8 (a-h,o-z)
      Parameter (NCN=8,NCORD=3,NSTR=6,NSM=24)
      Dimension BPMT(NSTR,NSM),CARTD(NCORD,NCN),ETDISP(NSM),
      *         GMATX(9,NSM),RMATX(9),SMATX(6,9),BLMT(NSTR,NSM)
c -------------------------------------------------------------------
      Do 470 i=1,NSTR
      Do 470 j=1,NSM
  470 GMATX(i,j)=0.0
      Write(20,*)'=================================================='
c
c *** Compute G-matrix
c
      ng=0
```

```
      Do 475 i=1,NCN
      mg=ng+1
      GMATX(1,mg)=CARTD(1,i)
      GMATX(2,mg)=CARTD(2,i)
      GMATX(3,mg)=CARTD(3,i)
      ng=mg+1
      GMATX(4,ng)=CARTD(1,i)
      GMATX(5,ng)=CARTD(2,i)
      GMATX(6,ng)=CARTD(3,i)
      mg=ng+1
      GMATX(7,mg)=CARTD(1,i)
      GMATX(8,mg)=CARTD(2,i)
      GMATX(9,mg)=CARTD(3,i)
      ng=mg
  475 Continue
c ------------------------------------------------------------------
      Write(20,111)((GMATX(i,j),j=1,NSM),i=1,9)
  111 Format(/,3x,'GMATX :',//,3(E10.3))
c ------------------------------------------------------------------
c
c *** Compute x, y. z-derivatives<RMATX> of u,v,w-displacments
c
      Do 480 ia=1,9
      RMATX(ia)=0.0
      Do 480 kdf=1,NSM
      RMATX(ia)=RMATX(ia)+GMATX(ia,kdf)*ETDISP(kdf)
      If (abs(RMATX(ia)).LT.0.1E-8) RMATX(ia)=0.0
  480 Continue
c ------------------------------------------------------------------
      Write(20,112)(RMATX(i),i=1,9)
  112 Format(/,3x,'RMATX :',//,3(E10.3))
c ------------------------------------------------------------------
c
c *** Set up SMATX
c
      Do 485 ia=1,NSTR
      Do 485 ja=1,9
  485 SMATX(ia,ja)=0.0
      SMATX(1,1)=RMATX(1);SMATX(1,4)=RMATX(4);SMATX(1,7)=RMATX(7)
      SMATX(2,2)=RMATX(2);SMATX(2,5)=RMATX(5);SMATX(2,8)=RMATX(8)
      SMATX(3,3)=RMATX(3);SMATX(3,6)=RMATX(6);SMATX(3,9)=RMATX(9)
      SMATX(4,1)=RMATX(2);SMATX(4,2)=RMATX(1);SMATX(4,4)=RMATX(5)
      SMATX(4,5)=RMATX(4);SMATX(4,7)=RMATX(8);SMATX(4,8)=RMATX(7)
      SMATX(5,1)=RMATX(3);SMATX(5,3)=RMATX(1);SMATX(5,4)=RMATX(6)
      SMATX(5,6)=RMATX(4);SMATX(5,7)=RMATX(9);SMATX(5,9)=RMATX(7)
      SMATX(6,2)=RMATX(3);SMATX(6,3)=RMATX(2);SMATX(6,5)=RMATX(6)
      SMATX(6,6)=RMATX(5);SMATX(6,8)=RMATX(9);SMATX(6,9)=RMATX(8)
c ------------------------------------------------------------------
      Write(20,113)((SMATX(i,j),j=1,9),i=1,NSTR)
  113 Format(/,3x,'SMATX :',//,3(E10.3))
c ------------------------------------------------------------------
c
c *** Now calculate (BLMT)=(SMATX)x(GMATX)
c
      Do 490 ia=1,NSTR
      Do 490 ja=1,NSM
      BLMT(ia,ja)=0.0
      Do 490 kdf=1,9
      BLMT(ia,ja)=BLMT(ia,ja)+SMATX(ia,kdf)*GMATX(kdf,ja)
  490 Continue
c ------------------------------------------------------------------
      Write(20,114)((BLMT(i,j),j=1,NSM),i=1,NSTR)
  114 Format(/,3x,'BLMT ---- Nonlinear :',//,3(E10.3))
c ------------------------------------------------------------------
c
c *** Now [updated (BPMT)] = [old (BPMT) + New (BLMT)]
```

```
c
      Do 495 ia=1,NSTR
      Do 495 ja=1,NSM
      BPMT(ia,ja)=BPMT(ia,ja)+BLMT(ia,ja)
  495 Continue
c -----------------------------------------------------------------
      Write(20,115)((BPMT(i,j),j=1,NSM),i=1,NSTR)
  115 Format(/,3x,'BPMT-(Lin+Nonlin) :',//,3(E10.3))
c -----------------------------------------------------------------
      Return
      End
c ***************************************************************************
c
      Subroutine STIFNL(incs,NEtype,LARGE,NRF,KSYSFAIL,STRSG,STRG,
     *                  STRSR,DISPINC,DISPIN,TDISP)
c
c***  This subroutine computes the updated element stiffness matrix based
c     on hypoelastic analysis /current total stress.
c -----------------------------------------------------------------
      Implicit real *8(a-h,o-z)
      Common/JT/CORD(5000,3)/MC/NOP(2000,8)/PAR/NP,NE/GPAR/NSZF
      Common/EAS/NEAS,NSMM/ULTSTR/Fcu,Ft,Fcb,Ecu,Ecm,Et,Em,Ecb
      Common/ULTST/A0,A1,A2,B0,B1,B2/ULTSR/EA0,EA1,EA2,EB0,EB1,EB2
      Common/ARF/RFDIA(9),AREINF(9),NNELRF(99)/DRM/DRMT(6,6)
      Common/RF/Esteel,Esh,NELRF,Fy,Eyp,Eyf
      Common/RFSE/RCORDS(10,3),RCORDE(10,3)
      Parameter (NDF=3,NCN=8,NC=2,NCORD=3,NGP=2,NGR=2,NSTR=6,NSM=24)
      Dimension DPH(6,6),ECORD(NCORD,NCN),SM(NSM,NSM),
     *          A(NCORD),H(NCORD),SFN(NCN),SDR(NCORD,NCN),SDR9(NCORD,2),
     *          CARTD(NCORD,NCN),BPMT(NSTR,NSM),EBPMT(NSMM,NSMM),
     *          EDBMTP(NSTR,NSMM),AKP(NSMM,NSMM),SMM(NSMM,NSMM),
     *          SFNR(NC),DBMTR(NSTR,NSM),AKR(NSM,NSM),ECORDR(NCORD,NC),
     *          GPCODR(NCORD,NC),GPRP(NCORD),DRH(NSTR,NSTR),SDRR(1,NC),
     *          EDISP(NSM),ETDISP(NSM),TDISP(5000),STRES(NSTR),STRN(6),
     *          STRNR(NSTR),GMATX(9,NSM),STRSG(NSTR,5000),STRNP(NSTR),
     *          RCORDST(99,3),RCORDEND(99,3),STRS(NSTR),STRSR(NSTR,5000)
     *          ,DISPINC(5000),DISPIN(5000),STRG(NSTR,5000)
c -----------------------------------------------------------------
*     Write(*,*)'*---------------: Entered STIFNL :---------------*'
      Rewind 5
      kgaus=0
      kgasr=0
c
      Do 700 iel=1,NE
c
c***  Initialise the components /elements of stiffness matrix
c
      Do 710 j=1,NSMM
      Do 710 k=1,NSMM
      AKP(j,k)=0.0; SMM(j,k)=0.0
  710 Continue
      Do 715 j=1,NSM
      Do 715 k=1,NSM
      AKR(j,k)=0.0; SM(j,k)=0.0
  715 Continue
c
c***  Form Element co-ordinate vector
c
      Do 720 inode=1,NCN
      l=NOP(iel,inode)
      Do 720 j=1,NCORD
  720 ECORD(j,inode)=CORD(l,j)
c
c***  Form Element displacement vector<EDISP> at present INCREMENT level
c
      Do 925 inode=1,NCN
```

```
      m=NOP(iel,inode)
      Do 930 j=1,NDF
      kr=(m-1)*NDF
      k=(inode-1)*NDF
      ij=k+j
      kj=kr+j
      EDISP(ij)=0.0; EDISP(ij)=DISPIN(kj)
      ETDISP(ij)=0.0; ETDISP(ij)=TDISP(kj)
  930 Continue
  925 Continue
c
c***  Start loop over numerical integration
c
      Call GAUSS (NGP,A,H)
      kgp=0
      Do 730 i=1,NGP
      Do 730 j=1,NGP
      Do 730 k=1,NGP
      kgp=kgp+1
      kgaus=kgaus+1
      ZX=A(i)
      ZY=A(j)
      ZZ=A(k)
      Write(10,731)iel,kgp
      Write(14,731)iel,kgp
      Write(16,731)iel,kgp
      Write(18,731)iel,kgp
c
c***  Compute STRAIN INCREMENT :-
c
      Call SHAP (ZX,ZY,ZZ,SFN,SDR)
      Call ESHAP (ZX,ZY,ZZ,SDR9)
      Call JACOBP (iel,kgp,SFN,SDR,ECORD,DTJAC,CARTD)
      Call BPMAT (CARTD,BPMT)
      Dvolm=DTJAC*H(i)*H(j)*H(k)
      If (LARGE.EQ.1.AND.incs.GT.3) Then
      Call LDISP (CARTD,ETDISP,GMATX,BPMT)
      Endif
c
      Do 735 ia=1,NSTR
      STRNP(ia)=0.0
      Do 735 kdf=1,NSM
      STRNP(ia)=STRNP(ia)+BPMT(ia,kdf)*EDISP(kdf)
  735 Continue
      Do 736 ia=1,NSTR
      STRN(ia)=0.0
      STRN(ia)=STRNP(ia)
  736 Continue
      Write(14,*) 'kgp          STRNP'
      Write(14,880) kgp,(STRNP(ii),ii=1,NSTR)
      Write(18,1000) kgp
c
c***  Compute constitutive matrix <DPH> at current total stress level.
c
      Do 130 istr=1,NSTR
      STRES(istr)=0.0
  130 STRES(istr)=STRG(istr,kgaus)
      Call HYPODPMT (incs,iel,kgp,STRNP,STRES,DPH)
      Write(18,65)((DPH(iy,jy),jy=1,NSTR),iy=1,NSTR)
c
c***  Calculate enhanced strain matrix(EBPMT)
c
      Call EBPMAT (NEtype,ECORD,DTJAC,iel,SDR9,BPMT,EBPMT)
      Call DBMATP (NSTR,NSMM,DPH,EBPMT,EDBMTP)
c
c***  Form the matrix for the stiffness contribution from the PARENT MAT.
```

A 3D Hypoelastic Model of RC Structure using lower order EAS elements.

```
c
      Do 750 i1=1,NSMM
      Do 750 j1=1,i1
      Do 750 k1=1,NSTR
  750 AKP(i1,j1)=AKP(i1,j1)+EBPMT(k1,i1)*EDBMTP(k1,j1)*Dvolm
c
c*** Calculate Geometric Matrix=(G)x(Sigma)x(G)
c
      If (LARGE.EQ.1.AND.incs.GT.3) Then
      Call GEOMETK (Dvolm,AKP,GMATX,STRN,DPH)
      Endif
  730 Continue
      Dvol=Dvolm*NGP*NGP*NGP
      Do 760 is=1,NSMM
      Do 760 js=1,is
  760 SMM(is,js)=AKP(is,js)
c
c*** Form the upper triangle of the OVERALL stiffness matrix
c
      n1=NSMM-1
      Do 770 k=1,n1
      k1=k+1
      Do 770 l=k1,NSMM
  770 SMM(k,l)=SMM(l,k)
      Do 771 i=1,NSMM
      Do 771 j=1,NSMM
  771 If (ABS(SMM(i,j)).LT.10E-05) SMM(i,j)=0.0
      Do 784 jk=1,NSMM
  784 If (SMM(jk,jk).LE.1.) SMM(jk,jk)=1.0
c --------------------------------------------------------------------
      Write(8,796) iel,((SMM(i,j),j=1,NSMM),i=1,NSMM)
  796 Format(I6,4x,21F11.1,/,(10x,21F11.1))
c --------------------------------------------------------------------
  901 Format(/,3x,'Element No.=',I3,2x,'== LOAD incs:',I2)
  701 Format(/,3x,'kgp:',2x,'ITER:',2x,'S(1):',2x,'S(2):',2x,'S(3):',3x,
     *'Rc(1):',2x,'Rc(2):',2x,'Rc(3):',3x,'E(1):',2x,'E(2):',2x,'E(3):',
     *4x,'Anu:',/,2x,'--------------------------------------------------'
     *'---------------------------')
  702 Format(/,3x,'kgp:',2x,'ITER:',2x,'EpslnU(1):',x,'EpslnU(2):',x,
     *'EpslnU(3)',2x,'EpslnC(1):',x,'EpslnC(2):',x,'EpslnC(3):'
     *,/,2x,'----------------------------------------------------------',
     *'--------------------')
  731 Format(/,3x,'iel=======',I4,'kgp=',I4)
  880  Format(/,I9,4x,6E10.2)
 1000 Format(/,4x,'Gauss Point no.=',I2,x,/,4x,'******************')
   65 Format(10x,'Final(DPH)',//,6(2x,E9.3))
  199 Format(x,'iel===',I4,3x,'Element Volume=',F12.2)
c
c*** Check for negative/zero value of diagonal elements of the stiffness
c    matrix <PARENT>
c
      If (NRF.NE.0) Goto 980
      Do 775 i=1,NSMM
      If (SMM(i,i).EQ.0.) Then
      Write(*,780) i,SMM(i,i),incs,iel
      Pause
      KSYSFAIL=1
      Goto 1001
      Endif
  775 Continue
  780 Format(3x,'SMM(i,i):Zero/negative value for i=',I4,3x,'SMM=',F4.1,
     *          /,3x,'<Load Increment No.=',I2,4x,'Element no.=',I3,'>')
  980 Continue
c
c*** Condense stiffnesses associated with incompatible/EAS modes
c
```

```
      Do 785 j=1,NEAS
      ij=NSMM-j
      ik=ij+1
      Pivot=SMM(ik,ik)
      Do 790 k=1,ij
      F=SMM(ik,k)/Pivot
      SMM(ik,k)=F
      Do 795 i=k,ij
      SMM(i,k)=SMM(i,k)-F*SMM(i,ik)
  795 SMM(k,i)=SMM(i,k)
  790 Continue
  785 Continue
      Do 800 is=1,NSM
      Do 800 js=1,is
  800 SM(is,js)=SMM(is,js)
c  ------------------------------------------------------------------
      Write(10,325) iel,(SM(i,i),i=1,NSM)
      Write(21,325) iel,(SM(i,i),i=1,NSM)
  325 Format(3x,'SM(i,i)-without AKR for iel= :',I5,//,3(3x,E11.5))
c  ------------------------------------------------------------------
c
c*** Identify elements with reinf. and calculate contribution of REINF.
c
      If (NRF.NE.0) Then
      Do 752 na=1,NELRF
      iaa=NNELRF(na)
      If (iel.NE.iaa) Goto 752
c
      Do 761 irf=1,NRF
      Write(18,1110) irf
 1110 Format(/,4x,'Reinforcement No. =',I2,x,/,4x,'=================')
      Call MESSGENR(irf,RCORDST,RCORDEND)
      Do 762 j=1,NCORD
      ECORDR(j,1)=RCORDST(na,j)
      ECORDR(j,2)=RCORDEND(na,j)
  762 Continue
      Write(12,219) ((ECORDR(i,j),j=1,NC),i=1,NCORD)
  219 Format(/,3x, 'ECORDR in SM :',//,2(E10.3))
c
      Call GAUSS (NGR,A,H)
      kgpr=0
      Do 763 i=1,NGR
      kgpr=kgpr+1
      kgasr=kgasr+1
      Zxx=A(i)
      Call SHAPR (Zxx,kgpr,SFNR,SDRR,ECORDR,DTJACR,GPCODR)
      Dleng=DTJACR*H(i)
c
c *** GPRP=Gauss Point co-ord of Rebar in Parent element domain reqd for
c     rebar stiffness evaluation
c
      Call NEWTRAPH (GPCODR,ECORD,kgpr,GPRP)
      Zx=GPRP(1)
      Zy=GPRP(2)
      Zz=GPRP(3)
      Call SHAP (Zx,Zy,Zz,SFN,SDR)
      Call JACOBP (iel,kgpr,SFN,SDR,ECORD,DTJAC,CARTD)
      Call BPMAT (CARTD,BPMT)
      If (LARGE.EQ.1.AND.incs.GT.3) Then
      Call LDISP (CARTD,ETDISP,GMATX,BPMT)
      Endif
c
      Do 835 ia=1,NSTR
      STRNR(ia)=0.0
      Do 835 kdf=1,NSM
      STRNR(ia)=STRNR(ia)+BPMT(ia,kdf)*EDISP(kdf)
```

```
          If (abs(STRNR(ia)).LT.0.1E-8) STRNR(ia)=0.0
   835 Continue
          Write(14,*) 'kgpr          STRNR'
          Write(14,880) kgpr,(STRNR(ii),ii=1,NSTR)
          Write(18,1100) kgpr
  1100 Format(/,4x,'Rebar Gauss Point =',I2,x,/,4x,'*****************')
c
c*** Compute constitutive matrix <DPH> at current total stress level.
c
          Do 131 istr=1,NSTR
          STRS(istr)=0.0
   131 STRS(istr)=STRSR(istr,kgasr)
          Call HYPODRMT (incs,kgpr,STRNR,STRS,DRH)
          Write(18,865) ((DRH(iy,jy),jy=1,NSTR),iy=1,NSTR)
   865 Format(10x,'Final(DRH)',//,6(2x,E9.3))
c
          Call DBMATP (NSTR,NSM,DRH,BPMT,DBMTR)
          Do 764 i1=1,NSM
          Do 764 j1=1,i1
          Do 764 k1=1,NSTR
   764 AKR(i1,j1)=AKR(i1,j1)+BPMT(k1,i1)*DBMTR(k1,j1)*AREINF(irf)*Dleng
   763 Continue
   761 Continue
   752 Continue
          Endif
c
c*** Form the overall stiffness matrix of an ELEMENT <PARENT+REINF.>
c
          Do 271 i=1,NSM
          Do 271 j=1,NSM
   271 If (ABS(AKR(i,j)).LT.10E-05) AKR(i,j)=0.0
          Do 171 i=1,NSM
   171 If (ABS(AKR(i,i)).LT.1.0) AKR(i,i)=0.0
c -----------------------------------------------------------------
          Write(10,315) iel,(AKR(i,i),i=1,NSM)
          Write(21,315) iel,(AKR(i,i),i=1,NSM)
   315 Format(3x,'AKR(i,i) for iel= :',I5,//,3(3x,E11.5))
c -----------------------------------------------------------------
          Do 801 is=1,NSM
          Do 801 js=1,is
   801 SM(is,js)=SM(is,js)+AKR(is,js)
c
c*** Check for diagonal elements=0, of the stiffness matrix <TOTAL>
c
          Do 175 i=1,NSM
          If (SM(i,i).EQ.0.) Then
          Write(*,180) i,SM(i,i),incs,iel
          Pause
          KSYSFAIL=1
          Goto 1001
          Endif
   175 Continue
   180 Format(3x,'SM(i,i):Zero value for i=',I4,3x,'SM<Conc+Rebar>=',F4.1,
      *         /,3x,'<Load Increment No.='I2,4x,'Element no.=',I3,'>')
c
          nn=NSM-1
          Do 810 k=1,nn
          kn=k+1
          Do 810 l=kn,NSM
   810 SM(k,l)=SM(l,k)
          Write(5,797) iel,((SM(i,j),j=1,NSM),i=1,NSM)
   797 Format(I6,4x,24F11.1,/,(10x,24F11.1))
c
          If (NRF.NE.0) Then
          Write(10,326) iel,(SM(i,i),i=1,NSM)
          Write(21,326) iel,(SM(i,i),i=1,NSM)
```

A 3D Hypoelastic Model of RC Structure using lower order EAS elements.

```
 326  Format(3x,'SM(i,i)-with AKR for iel= :',I5,//,3(3x,E11.5))
      Endif
 700  Continue
      Do 501 id=1,NSZF
      DISPIN(id)=0.0
      DISPIN(id)=DISPINC(id)
 501  DISPINC(id)=0.0
      Do 502 ir=1,NSTR
      Do 502 jr=1,5000
      STRG(ir,jr)=0.0
 502  STRG(ir,jr)=STRSG(ir,jr)
c
      If (NRF.NE.0) Then
      Write(*,*)'++++ Added Stiffness of REBARs :-------------------'
      Endif
      Write(*,*)'++++ Exit STIFNL :--------------------'
      Goto 1003
1001  Write(*,1002)
1002  Format(5x,'STIFFNESS REDUCES TO zero -> SYSTEM COLLAPSES:',/,
     *         31x,'-> EXIT STIFNL :')
1003  Return
      End
c ****************************************************************************
c
      Subroutine HYPODRMT (incs,kgp,STRNR,STRS,DRH)
c
c*** To calculate current updated elasticity matrix for REBARS
c
c -------------------------------------------------------------------------
      Implicit real *8(a-h,o-z)
      Common/TH/Theta(3,3)/CONC/Fck,Econc,ANUconc/CONCRACK/Ecrack,Esoft
      Common/ULTSTR/Fcu,Ft,Fcb,Ecu,Ecm,Et,Em,Ecb
      Common/ARF/RFDIA(9),AREINF(9),NNELRF(99)
      Common/RF/Esteel,Esh,NELRF,Fy,Eyp,Eyf
      Parameter(NDF=3,NCORD=3,NSTR=6,NIM=1,TOLER=1.0E-02)
      Dimension STRNR(NSTR),TSIGR(NSTR),DELSIGR(NSTR),STRS(NSTR),
     *          EpslnU(3),KRebar(3),DRH(6,6),
     *          Theta1(3,3),Theta2(3,3)
     *
c -------------------------------------------------------------------------
      Write(18,200)
 200  Format(5X,'++++ Entered HYPO  D R M T...................... ')
c
c***  Formulate DRH with "INITIAL Esteel"
c
      Do 205 j=1,NSTR
      Do 205 k=1,NSTR
 205  DRH(j,k)=0.0
      Do 210 ip=1,NCORD
      Do 210 jp=1,NCORD
      Theta1(ip,jp)=0.0
      Theta1(ip,jp)=Theta(ip,jp)
 210  Continue
      Esec=Esteel
      Call DRHYPO (Esec,Theta1,DRH)
      If (incs.LE.3) Goto 199
c
c***  Compute Initial Stress Increment with DRH<assumed>
c
      Do 215 ja=1,NSTR
      DELSIGR(ja)=0.0
      Do 215 kk=1,NSTR
      DELSIGR(ja)=DELSIGR(ja)+DRH(ja,kk)*STRNR(kk)
 215  Continue
c
c***  Define Current total Stress
```

A 3D Hypoelastic Model of RC Structure using lower order EAS elements.

```
c
      Do 220 jb=1,NSTR
      TSIGR(jb)=0.0
  220 TSIGR(jb)=STRS(jb)+DELSIGR(jb)
      Write(14,221) kgp,(TSIGR(ii),ii=1,NSTR)
  221 Format(I9,4x,6F10.4)
      Write(18,222)
  222 Format(5X,'++++ Calculated TOTAL STRESS INCREMENT(Rebar)')
c
c*** Compute Equivalent Uniaxial Strain
c
      Do 225 ic=1,NCORD
      EpslnU(ic)=0.0
  225 EpslnU(ic)=EpslnU(ic)+TSIGR(ic)/Esec
      Write(18,226) (EpslnU(i),i=1,NCORD)
  226 Format(10x,'EpslnU=',3(F9.5,3x))
c
c*** Check for STRESS level at GP and calculate FAILURE INDEX <KRebar>
c
      Do 705 ik=1,NCORD
  705 KRebar(ik)=0.0
      If (STRNR(1).LT.Eyp) Then
      KRebar(1)=1
      Elseif (STRNR(1).GE.Eyp.AND.STRNR(1).LT.Eyf) Then
      KRebar(2)=1
      Elseif (STRNR(1).GT.Eyf) Then
      KRebar(3)=1
      Endif
      Write(18,1008) (KRebar(i),i=1,NCORD)
 1008 Format(5X,'++++ Rebar Stress lev INDEX<KRebar> =',3(I2))
      Do 710 ip=1,NCORD
      Do 710 jp=1,NCORD
       Theta2(ip,jp)=0.0
        Theta2(ip,jp)=Theta(ip,jp)
  710 Continue
c
c*** For ICASE=1<Tension> determine Econ, ANU & appropriate DPH
c    If within Yield Point/Proof Strain, E=Const=Esteel
c    If beyond Yield Point but upto EpslnF, E=??
c    If beyond EpslnF, E=0.0
c
      If (KRebar(1).EQ.1) Then
        Esec=Esteel
         Call DRHYPO (Esec,Theta2,DRH)
      Elseif (KRebar(2).EQ.1) Then
      ITER=0
      SIGMA=0.0
  265 EsecI=1.0/Esec
      ITER=ITER+1
       DSTRNR=0.0
         DSTRNR=DSTRNR+EsecI*SIGMA
        If (abs(DSTRNR).LT.0.1E-8) DSTRNR=0.0
       STRNR=STRNR+DSTRNR
       Esec=((EpslnU(1)-Eyp)*Esh+Fy)/EpslnU(1)
       EpslnU(1)=EpslnU(1)+SIGMA/Esec
       Call DRHYPO (Esec,Theta2,DRH)
        SIGR=0.0
         SIGR=Esec*EpslnU(1)
       SIGMA=0.0
       SIGMA=TSIGR(1)-SIGR
       If (ITER.EQ.NIM) Goto 260
       If (SIGMA-TOLER) 260,260,265
  260 Continue
       Call DRHYPO (Esec,Theta2,DRH)
       Write(18,270)ITER
  270 Format(5X,'++++ Calculated "UPDATED Esec<REBAR>" in ITER=',I3)
```

A 3D Hypoelastic Model of RC Structure using lower order EAS elements.

```
c
      Elseif (KRebar(3).EQ.1) Then
      Esec=1.0
      Call DRHYPO (Esec,Theta2,DRH)
      Endif
      Write(18,276) Esec
  276 Format(5x,'Esec=',F9.1)
      Write(18,277)
  277 Format(5X,'++++ Calculated DRH <REBAR> in corresponding Regime')
c
  199 Continue
      Write(18,278)
  278 Format(5X,'++++ Exit HYPO  D R M T  +++++++++++++++++++++++++++')
      Return
      End
c ******************************************************************************
c
      Subroutine DRHYPO (Es,Theta,DRH)
c
c*** This subroutine calculates DRH for the Reinforcements
c ---------------------------------------------------------------------------
      Implicit real *8(a-h,o-z)
      Parameter (NCORD=3,NSTR=6)
      Dimension DRMT1(NSTR,NSTR),DRH(NSTR,NSTR),Theta(3,3),
     *          TFMG(NSTR,NSTR),TFMGI(NSTR,NSTR),TFM(NCORD,NCORD)
c ---------------------------------------------------------------------------
      Do 220 i=1,NSTR
      Do 220 j=1,NSTR
      DRH(i,j)=0.0; DRMT1(i,j)=0.0
  220 Continue
      DRMT1(1,1)=Es
       Do 230 ip=1,NCORD
       Do 230 icord =1,NCORD
  230  TFM(ip,icord)=0.0
c
      Do 235 ip=1,NCORD
       Do 235 icord =1,NCORD
        TFM(ip,icord)=COSD(Theta(ip,icord))
      If (abs(TFM(ip,icord)).LE.1.0E-4) TFM(ip,icord)=0.0
  235 Continue
      Call TRANFME (TFM,TFMG)
      Call INVERT (TFMG,TFMGI,NSTR)
      Call MULT (TFMGI,DRMT1,TFMG,DRH,NSTR)
c
      nn1=NSTR-1
       Do 240 kk=1,nn1
       kk1=kk+1
        Do 240 ll=kk1,NSTR
        DRH(kk,ll)=DRH(ll,kk)
  240 Continue
      Return
      end
c ******************************************************************************
c
      Subroutine HYPODPMT (incs,iel,kgp,STRNP,STRES,DPH)
c
c*** To calculate current updated elasticity matrix for CONCRETE
c
c ---------------------------------------------------------------------------
      Implicit real *8(a-h,o-z)
      Common/TH/Theta(3,3)/CONC/Fck,Econc,ANUconc/CONCRACK/Ecrack,Esoft
      Common/ULTSTR/Fcu,Ft,Fcb,Ecu,Ecm,Et,Em,Ecb
      Parameter(NDF=3,NCORD=3,NSTR=6,NIM=1,tgp=8,TOLER=1.0E-02)
      Dimension STRNP(NSTR),SIGP(NSTR),TSIGP(NSTR),SIG(3),
     *          SIGDR(3,3),Rc(3),EpslnU(3),EpslnC(3),Econ(3),ANU(6),
     *          TOFOR(6),DPH(6,6),DPHI(NSTR,NSTR),DSTRNP(NSTR),
```

A 3D Hypoelastic Model of RC Structure using lower order EAS elements.

```
        *              SIGMA(NSTR),RATIO(6),Theta1(3,3),Theta2(3,3),
        *              Alfa(3),beta(3),KTstr(3,4),KCstr(4),STRES(NSTR),
        *              DELSIGP(NSTR)
c ---------------------------------------------------------------------
        Write(18,200)
  200 Format(5X,'++++ Entered H Y P O D P M T...................... ')
c
c*** Formulate DPH with "INITIAL Econc & ANUconc"
c       Alfa(ip)=Correction Factor for 'G' for cracked concrete
c
        Do 205 j=1,NSTR
        ANU(j)=0.0; ANU(j)=ANUconc
        Do 205 k=1,NSTR
  205 DPH(j,k)=0.0
        Do 210 ip=1,NCORD
         Econ(ip)=0.0; Alfa(ip)=0.0
         Econ(ip)=Econc; Alfa(ip)=1.0
        Do 210 jp=1,NCORD
         Theta1(ip,jp)=0.0
          Theta1(ip,jp)=Theta(ip,jp)
  210 Continue
        Call DPHYPO (Alfa,Econ,ANU,Theta1,DPH)
        If (incs.LE.3) Goto 199
c
c*** Compute Initial Stress Increment with DPH<assumed>
c
        Do 215 ja=1,NSTR
         DELSIGP(ja)=0.0
          Do 215 kk=1,NSTR
           DELSIGP(ja)=DELSIGP(ja)+DPH(ja,kk)*STRNP(kk)
            If (abs(SIGP(ja)).LT.1.0E-4) SIGP(ja)=0.0
  215 Continue
c
c*** Define Current total Stress
c
        Do 220 jb=1,NSTR
         TSIGP(jb)=0.0
  220 TSIGP(jb)=STRES(jb)+DELSIGP(jb)
        Write(14,221) kgp,(TSIGP(ii),ii=1,NSTR)
  221 Format(I9,4x,6F10.4)
        Write(18,222)
  222 Format(5X,'++++ Calculated TOTAL STRESS INCREMENT ')
        Write(18,955)
  955 Format(/2x,'Gauss Point',6x,'Sx :',6x,'Sy :',6x,'Sz :',5x,'Sxy :',
        *          5x,'Syz :',5x,'Szx :',/,2x,'--------------------',
        * '-------------------------------------------------')
        Write(18,221) kgp,(TSIGP(ii),ii=1,NSTR)
c
c*** Compute Corresponding PRINCIPAL STRESSES & its DIRECTION
c
        Call PRINSTR (TSIGP,SIG,SIGDR)
        Write(18,900) (SIG(i),i=1,NCORD)
  900 Format(/,3x,'SIG(1)=',F7.3,2x,'SIG(2)=',F7.3,2x,'SIG(3)=',F7.3,/)
c
c*** Check Loading ID <Compr or Tension> for the GAUSS POINT
c
        Call LOADID (SIG,ICASE)
        Write(18,223) ICASE
  223 Format(5X,'++++ Loading Type <ICASE:Compn=0,Tension=1>=',I2)
c
c*** Compute Equivalent Uniaxial Strain
c
        Do 225 ic=1,NCORD
         EpslnU(ic)=0.0
  225 EpslnU(ic)=EpslnU(ic)+SIG(ic)/Econ(ic)
        Write(18,226) (EpslnU(i),i=1,NCORD)
```

A 3D Hypoelastic Model of RC Structure using lower order EAS elements.

```
  226 Format(10x,'EpslnU=',3(F9.5,3x))
c
c***  Check whether PRINCIPAL STRESS at GP outside FAILURE SURFACE or not
c     and calculate FAILURE INDEX <KTstr,KCstr>
c
      Do 705 ik=1,NCORD
      Do 705 jk=1,4
      KCstr(jk)=0.0
  705 KTstr(ik,jk)=0.0
      Call FAILURE (incs,iel,kgp,ICASE,SIG,EpslnU,beta,KTstr,KCstr)
      Do 710 ip=1,NCORD
      Do 710 jp=1,NCORD
       Theta2(ip,jp)=0.0
        Theta2(ip,jp)=Theta(ip,jp)
  710 Continue
c
c***  For ICASE=1<Tension> determine Econ, ANU & appropriate DPH
c     If within Ult Surface<for uncracked concrete> E=Const=Econc
c     If beyond Ult Surface but upto Epsln0<for cracked conc> E=Rc/EpslnU
c     If beyond Epsln0 <for Tensile Failure> E=0.0(1.0 to avoid SINGULARITY)
c
      If (ICASE.EQ.1) Then
      Do 715 iz=1,NCORD
      idir=NCORD+1-iz
      If (idir.EQ.1) id=3
      If (idir.EQ.2) id=1
      If (idir.EQ.3) id=2
          ip=NCORD+idir
         iq=NCORD+id
      If (KTstr(idir,1).EQ.1) Then
         Econ(idir)=Econc ;
          ip=NCORD+idir
        ANU(idir)=ANUconc;ANU(ip)=ANU(idir)
      Elseif (KTstr(idir,2).EQ.1) Then
         Econ(idir)=Econc
          ip=NCORD+idir
        ANU(idir)=0.0;ANU(ip)=0.0
      ANU(idir)=0.36-(0.36-ANUconc)*SQRT(1-(beta(idir)-0.8)*5.0)
        If (ANU(idir).GE.0.36) Then
        ANU(idir)=0.36; ANU(ip)=ANU(idir)
        Endif
      Elseif (KTstr(idir,3).EQ.1) Then
         Econ(idir)=(-Ecrack)*(Em-EpslnU(idir))/EpslnU(idir)
         Alfa(idir)=0.5*(1-EpslnU(idir)/Em)
        ANU(idir)=0.0;ANU(ip)=0.0;ANU(id)=0.0;ANU(iq)=0.0
      Elseif (KTstr(idir,4).EQ.1) Then
         Econ(idir)=1.0
         Alfa(idir)=0.0
        ANU(idir)=0.0;ANU(ip)=0.0;ANU(id)=0.0;ANU(iq)=0.0
      Endif
  715 Continue
      Write(18,231) (Econ(i),ANU(i),alfa(i),i=1,NCORD)
  231 Format(10x,'Econ=',F9.1,3x,'ANU=',F5.3,3x,'alfa(i)=',F5.3)
      Call DPHYPO (Alfa,Econ,ANU,Theta2,DPH)
      Write(18,241)
  241 Format(5X,'++++ Calculated DPH <Tension> in corresponding Regime')
*
c***  For ICASE=1<Compression> determine Econ, ANU & appropriate DPH
c     If within Ult Surface<upto Rc> E=Popovics equation
c     If beyond Ult Surface <but upto Epslnf> E=Rc/EpslnU
c     If beyond Epsln0 <for comprn crushing> E=0.0
c
      Elseif (ICASE.EQ.0) Then
      Call ARGYRIS (SIG,Rc,EpslnU,EpslnC)
      Write(17,801) kgp,ITER,(EpslnU(i),i=1,3),(EpslnC(i),i=1,3)
      Write(18,242)
```

```
 242 Format(5X,'++++ Calculated Rc & EpslnC')
*
     If (KCstr(1).EQ.1.OR.KCstr(2).EQ.1.) Then
     ITER=0
     Do 230 i=1,NSTR
 230 SIGMA(i)=0.0
 265 Call INVERT (DPH,DPHI,NSTR)
     ITER=ITER+1
     Do 235 ja=1,NSTR
      DSTRNP(ja)=0.0
       Do 235 kk=1,NSTR
        DSTRNP(ja)=DSTRNP(ja)+DPHI(ja,kk)*SIGMA(kk)
        If (abs(DSTRNP(ja)).LT.0.1E-8) DSTRNP(ja)=0.0
 235 Continue
     Do 240 jb=1,NSTR
 240 STRNP(jb)=STRNP(jb)+DSTRNP(jb)
     Do 245 ic=1,NCORD
 245 EpslnU(ic)=EpslnU(ic)+SIGMA(ic)/Econ(ic)
     Call MODULII (KCstr,EpslnU,EpslnC,Rc,Econ,ANU)
     Call DPHYPO (ALFA,Econ,ANU,SIGDR,DPH)
     Do 250 jc=1,NCORD
      SIGP(jc)=0.0
      SIGP(jc)=Econ(jc)*EpslnU(jc)
 250 Continue
     Do 255 ig=1,NCORD
      TOFOR(ig)=0.0
      TOFOR(ig)=TOFOR(ig)+TSIGP(ig)
      SIGMA(ig)=0.0
      SIGMA(ig)=SIG(ig)-SIGP(ig)
      RATIO(ig)=0.0
      If (ITER.EQ.NIM) Goto 260
      If (SIGMA(ig)-TOLER) 260,260,265
 255 Continue
 260 Continue
     Write(18,270)ITER
 270 Format(5X,'++++ Calculated "UPDATED Econc & Anu" in ITER=',I3)
     Write(15,800) kgp,ITER,(SIG(i),i=1,NCORD),(Rc(i),i=1,NCORD),
     *            (Econ(i),i=1,NCORD),Anu(1)
 800 Format(2I4,6(F8.3),2x,3(F8.0),2x,F5.3)
 801 Format(5x,2I4,6(2x,E9.3))
c
     Elseif (KCstr(3).EQ.1) Then
        Do 925 iv=1,NCORD
           id=NCORD+1-iv
     If (iv.EQ.1) id=3
     If (iv.EQ.2) id=1
     If (iv.EQ.3) id=2
           ip=NCORD+iv
        iq=NCORD+id
        EpslnU(iv)=abs(EpslnU(iv))+0.002
        Econ(iv)=(Esoft*(0.004-ABS(EpslnU(iv)))+0.85*Fcu)/EpslnU(iv)
        ANU(iv)=0.0;ANU(id)=0.0
        ANU(ip)=0.0;ANU(iq)=0.0
 925 Continue
c
     Elseif (KCstr(4).EQ.1) Then
        Do 930 iv=1,NCORD
     If (iv.EQ.1) id=3
     If (iv.EQ.2) id=1
     If (iv.EQ.3) id=2
           ip=NCORD+iv
        iq=NCORD+id
        Econ(iv)=1.0
        ANU(iv)=0.0;ANU(id)=0.0
        ANU(ip)=0.0;ANU(iq)=0.0
 930 Continue
```

A 3D Hypoelastic Model of RC Structure using lower order EAS elements.

```
        Endif
        Write(18,276) (Econ(i),ANU(i),i=1,NCORD)
    276 Format(5x,'Econ=',F9.1,3x,'ANU=',F5.3)
        Call DPHYPO (Alfa,Econ,ANU,Theta2,DPH)
        Write(18,277)
    277 Format(5X,'++++ Calculated DPH <Comprn> in corresponding Regime')
        Endif
C
    199 Continue
        Write(18,278)
    278 Format(5X,'++++ Exit H Y P O D P M T +++++++++++++++++++++++++')
        Return
        End
C ********************************************************************************
C
        Subroutine DPHYPO (Alfa,Econ,ANU,Thett,DPH)
C
C***   This subroutine formulates transformed incremental constitutive
C      matrix, i.e.<DPH> for the parent material in COMPRESSION
C      Ref:Balan et al, (1997,2002)          =====: CHECKED : OKAY   :=====
C ----------------------------------------------------------------------
        Implicit real *8(a-h,o-z)
        Parameter (NCORD=3,NSTR=6)
        Dimension DPH1(NSTR,NSTR),DPH(6,6),TFMG(NSTR,NSTR),DT(NSTR,NSTR),
       *          TFM(NCORD,NCORD),Econ(3),ANU(6),Thett(NCORD,NCORD),
       *          Alfa(3)
C ----------------------------------------------------------------------
C
C***   Calculate elasticity matrix of the parent/concrete material
C
        Do 210 i=1,NSTR
        Do 210 j=1,NSTR
    210 DPH1(i,j)=0.0;DPH(i,j)=0.0
        If (Econ(1).EQ.0.AND.Econ(2).EQ.0.AND.Econ(3).EQ.0.) Goto 555
C
        ANU12=ANU(1); ANU23=ANU(2); ANU31=ANU(3)
        ANU21=ANU(4); ANU32=ANU(5); ANU13=ANU(6)
*
        G12=Econ(1)*Econ(2)/(Econ(1)*(1+ANU12)+Econ(2)*(1+ANU21))
        G23=Econ(2)*Econ(3)/(Econ(2)*(1+ANU23)+Econ(3)*(1+ANU32))
        G31=Econ(3)*Econ(1)/(Econ(3)*(1+ANU31)+Econ(1)*(1+ANU13))
        phi=(1-ANU12*ANU21-ANU23*ANU32-ANU31*ANU13-ANU12*ANU23*ANU31
       *    -ANU21*ANU32*ANU13)
        If (phi.LE.0.) Write(*,780) phi
    780 Format(/,4x,'phi<DPH> ???..... : Zero/negative value =',E11.4)
C
        DPH1(1,1)=Econ(1)*(1-ANU32*ANU23)
        DPH1(1,2)=Econ(1)*(ANU21+ANU23*ANU31)
        DPH1(1,3)=Econ(1)*(ANU31+ANU21*ANU32)
        DPH1(2,1)=Econ(2)*(ANU12+ANU32*ANU13)
        DPH1(2,2)=Econ(2)*(1-ANU13*ANU31)
        DPH1(2,3)=Econ(2)*(ANU32+ANU12*ANU31)
        DPH1(3,1)=Econ(3)*(ANU13+ANU12*ANU23)
        DPH1(3,2)=Econ(3)*(ANU23+ANU13*ANU21)
        DPH1(3,3)=Econ(3)*(1-ANU12*ANU21)
        DPH1(4,4)=G12*phi*Alfa(1)
        DPH1(5,5)=G23*phi*Alfa(2)
        DPH1(6,6)=G31*phi*Alfa(3)
*
        Do 221 i=1,NSTR
        Do 221 j=1,NSTR
    221 DPH1(i,j)=DPH1(i,j)/phi
        Do 222 i=4,NSTR
        If (DPH1(i,i).EQ.0.0) DPH1(i,i)=1.0
    222 Continue
C ----------------------------------------------------------------------
```

```
      Write(10,300)((DPH1(i,j),j=1,NSTR),i=1,NSTR)
  300 Format(10x,'DPH1-MATX',//,6(2x,E9.3))
c -------------------------------------------------------------------
c*** Calculate transformed elasticity matrix of the parent material
c
      Do 235 ip=1,NCORD
      Do 235 icord =1,NCORD
      TFM(ip,icord)=0.0
      TFM(ip,icord)=COSD(Thett(ip,icord))
      If (abs(TFM(ip,icord)).LE.1.0E-4) TFM(ip,icord)=0.0
  235 Continue
      Call TRANFMS (TFM,TFMG)
      Do 250 i=1,NSTR
      Do 250 j=1,NSTR
      DT(i,j)=0.0
      Do 250 k=1,NSTR
      DT(i,j)=DT(i,j)+DPH1(i,k)*TFMG(k,j)
  250 Continue
      Do 260 i1=1,NSTR
      Do 260 j1=1,i1
      DPH(i1,j1)=0.0
      Do 260 k1=1,NSTR
  260 DPH(i1,j1)=DPH(i1,j1)+TFMG(k1,i1)*DT(k1,j1)
c
      n1=NSTR-1
      Do 270 k=1,n1
      k1=k+1
      Do 270 l=k1,NSTR
      DPH(k,l)=DPH(l,k)
  270 Continue
c -------------------------------------------------------------------
      Write(10,65 )((DPH(i,j),j=1,NSTR),i=1,NSTR)
   65 Format(10x,'TRANSFORMED INCREMENTAL MODULLI(DPH)',//,6(2x,E9.3))
c -------------------------------------------------------------------
*     Write(*,*)'*-------------: E X I T    DPHYPO :---------------*'
  555 Return
      End
c ********************************************************************************
c
      Subroutine MODULII  (KCstr,EpslnU,EpslnC,Rc,Econ,ANU)
c
c*** This subroutine INCREMENTAL ELASTICITY MODULUS & POISSONS' RATIO
c    Ref; Kwon /Spacone (2002)      =====: CHECKED : OKAY :=====
c            (*) INPUT : KCFAIL,EpslnU(i),EpslnC(i) & Rc(i)
c            (*) OUTPUT: Econ(i) & Anu(i)
c -------------------------------------------------------------------
      Implicit real *8 (a-h,o-z)
      Common/CONC/Fck,Econc,ANUconc/ULTSTR/Fcu,Ft,Fcb,Ecu,Ecm,Et,Em,Ecb
      Parameter (NCORD=3)
      Dimension EpslnF(3),EpslnC(3),Rf(3),Rc(3),EpslnU(3),
     *          gK(3),gKe(3),gKs(3),gKv(3),A(3),B(3),C(3),D(3),r(3),
     *          Cons(3),Const(3),ANUu(3),ANU(6),Esec(3),Econ(3),KCstr(3)
c -------------------------------------------------------------------
*     Write(*,*)'*************************: E N T E R E D   MODULII :-'
      Write(16,665)
      Write(16,666)
c
c*** Calculate VARIABLE /INCREMENTAL Modulus of Elasticity
c
      Do 200 i=1,NCORD
      EpslnF(i)=0.0;Rf(i)=0.0;r(i)=0.0;;ANUu(i)=0.0;
      gK(i)=0.0;gKe(i)=0.0;gKs(i)=0.0;gKv(i)=0.0;
      A(i)=0.0;B(i)=0.0;C(i)=0.0;D(i)=0.0;
      Cons(i)=0.0;Const(i)=0.0;Esec(i)=0.0;Econ(i)=0.0;
      EpslnF(i)=1.41*EpslnC(i)
      Rf(i)=0.85*Rc(i)
```

A 3D Hypoelastic Model of RC Structure using lower order EAS elements.

```
      Esec(i)=Rc(i)/EpslnC(i)
       gK(i)=Econc/Esec(i)
         gKe(i)=EpslnF(i)/EpslnC(i)
           gKs(i)=Rc(i)/Rf(i)
           gKv(i)=2.0*Rc(i)/(EpslnC(i)*Econc)
             C(i)=gK(i)*(gKs(i)-1)/((gKe(i)-1)**2)-1.0/gKe(i)
             B(i)=1.0-2.0*C(i)
            A(i)=C(i)+gK(i)-2.0
       Cons(i)=EpslnU(i)/EpslnC(i)
c
c***  If fc<Fck use Sanaz curve to estimate Econ - Ref.:Balan(2001)
c
      XDEN=1.0+A(i)*Cons(i)+B(i)*Cons(i)**2+C(i)*Cons(i)**3
         Const(i)=1.0/XDEN
       If (Const(i).GT.1.0) Const(i)=1.0
         Econ(i)=Econc*Const(i)
       Write(16,667) Esec(i),gK(i),gKe(i),gKs(i),A(i),B(i),C(i),Cons(i),
      *              Const(i),Econ(i)
c
      If (KCstr(1).EQ.1) Then
      ip=NCORD+I
      ANU(i)=ANUconc;ANU(ip)=ANUconc
c
      Elseif (KCstr(2).EQ.1) Then
      gK(i)=0.0;A(i)=0.0;B(i)=0.0;C(i)=0.0;Const(i)=0.0;ANUu(i)=0.0;
      gK(i)=1/(2*ANUconc)
         C(i)=gK(i)*(gKs(i)-1)/((gKe(i)-1)**2)-1/gKe(i)
         B(i)=1-2*C(i)
         A(i)=C(i)+gK(i)-2
      Const(i)=(1+(A(i)*Cons(i)+B(i)*Cons(i)**2+C(i)*Cons(i)**3)/gKv(i))
      ANUu(i)=ANUconc*Const(i)
      If (ANUu(i).GT.0.36) ANUu(i)=0.36
      Endif
  200 Continue
c
c***  Calculate Final Poisson Ratio Ref.: Balan(2001)
c     ANU12=ANU(1); ANU23=ANU(2); ANU31=ANU(3)
c     ANU21=ANU(4); ANU32=ANU(5); ANU13=ANU(6)
c
      If (KCstr(2).EQ.1) Then
      Do 210 j=1,6
  210 ANU(j)=0.0
      ANU(1)=SQRT(ANUu(1)*ANUu(2)*Econ(1)/Econ(2))
      ANU(2)=SQRT(ANUu(2)*ANUu(3)*Econ(2)/Econ(3))
      ANU(3)=SQRT(ANUu(3)*ANUu(1)*Econ(3)/Econ(1))
      ANU(4)=SQRT(ANUu(2)*ANUu(1)*Econ(2)/Econ(1))
      ANU(5)=SQRT(ANUu(3)*ANUu(2)*Econ(3)/Econ(2))
      ANU(6)=SQRT(ANUu(1)*ANUu(3)*Econ(1)/Econ(3))
      Endif
c
  665 Format('Esec(i)',2x'gK(i)',2x,'gKe(i)',2x,'gKs(i)',4x,'A(i)',3x,
      *'B(i)',3x,'C(i)',2x,'Cons(i)',2x,'Const(i)',5x,'Econ/ANUu')
  666 Format('----------------------------------------------------'
      *'-------------------------------')
  667 Format(F9.3,2x,8(F8.3),2x,F9.3)
      Return
      End
c ******************************************************************************
c
      Subroutine FAILURE(incs,iel,kgp,ICASE,SIG,EpslnU,beta,KTstr,KCstr)
c
c***  This subroutine FAILURE level/Stress Level for
c     a given Principal Stress Ratio /Eqiv. Uniax Strain Ratio.
c     ICASE = 0 ===>COMPRESSION
c     ICASE = 1 ===>TENSION
```

```
c
c                 (*) INPUT : SIG(i) & EpslnU(i)
c                 (*) OUTPUT: KTstr(i),KCstr
c -------------------------------------------------------------------------
      Implicit real *8(a-h,o-z)
      Common/ULTST/A0,A1,A2,B0,B1,B2/ULTSTR/Fcu,Ft,Fcb,Ecu,Ecm,Et,Em,Ecb
      Parameter (NCORD=3)
      Dimension SIG(3),EpslnU(3),KTFAIL(3),KTcrush(3),KTAnu(3),
     *          KTstr(3,4),beta(3),KCstr(4)
c -------------------------------------------------------------------------
c *** Compute general characteristics of triaxial stress state
c
      Do 705 ik=1,NCORD
      KTFAIL(ik)=0;KTcrush(ik)=0;KTAnu(ik)=0
  705 Continue
      KCFAIL=0; KCcrush=0; KCAnu=0
c
      S1=SIG(1);S2=SIG(2);S3=SIG(3)
      SIGA=(S1+S2+S3)/3
      AR=(S1-S2)**2+(S2-S3)**2+(S3-S1)**2
      TOUA=ABS(SQRT(AR/15.0))
      SIGAB=SIGA/Fcu; TOUAB=TOUA/Fcu
      XNUM=2.0*S1-S2-S3
      XDEN=ABS(SQRT(2.0*AR))
      S=COS(XNUM/XDEN)
      Theta=ACOSD(XNUM/XDEN)
      R1=(A0+A1*SIGAB+A2*SIGAB**2)
      R2=(B0+B1*SIGAB+B2*SIGAB**2)
      R21=R2**2-R1**2
      RDEN=4.0*R21*S**2+(R2-2.0*R1)**2
      AK=SQRT(4.0*R21*S**2+5.0*R1**2-4.0*R1*R2)
      RNUM=2.0*R2*R21*S+R2*(2.0*R1-R2)*AK
      R=RNUM/RDEN
        Do 105 ig=1,NCORD
        beta(ig)=0.0
  105   beta(ig)=0.8
c
c *** Check the DOMAIN of triaxial stress state ========================
c
*       KFAIL=0  ==>inside Failure Surface
*            =1  ==>outside Failure Surface
*       ALFA=Shear Retention Factor after Ft(for tension only) Ref.: C G Cho
*       beta=Nonlinearity Index, Ref.:Chen book
c
c *** Check Domain-1 <comp-comp-comp> of Ultimate STRESS Surface
c
      If (S1.LT.0.0.AND.S2.LT.0.0.AND.S3.LT.0.0) Then
*       Write(18,*)'DOMAIN-1<C-C-C>: Checking.............'
      FUNC=TOUAB
      SURF=R
      beta1=ABS(FUNC/SURF)
      If(beta1.GT.0.8) KCAnu=1
      If(FUNC.GE.SURF) KCFAIL=1
      If(FUNC.GE.SURF)Write(18,110) kgp
  110 Format(5x,'DOMAIN-1:<C-C-C>, GP=',I2,2x,'outside Failure Surface')
c
c *** Check Domain-2 <tens-comp-comp> of Ultimate STRESS Surface
c
      Elseif (S1.GT.0.0.AND.S2.LT.0.0.AND.S3.LT.0.0) Then
*       Write(18,*)'DOMAIN-2<C-C-T>: Checking.............'
      ZETA=(S2+S3)/3.0
      R1=A0+A1*ZETA+A2*ZETA**2
      R2=B0+B1*ZETA+B2*ZETA**2
      R21=R2**2-R1**2
      XN=2.*R2*R21*S+R2*(2.*R1-R2)*SQRT(4.*R21*S**2+5.*R1**2-4.*R1*R2)
      XD=4.0*R21*S**2+(R2-2.0*R1)**2
```

A 3D Hypoelastic Model of RC Structure using lower order EAS elements.

```
      SURF=(1.0-S1/Ft)*XN/XD
      FUNC=SQRT(((S2-S3)**2+S2**2+S3**2)/15.0)/Fcu
      beta2=ABS(FUNC/SURF)
      If(beta2.GT.0.8) KCAnu=1
      If(FUNC.GE.SURF) KCFAIL=1
      If(FUNC.GE.SURF)Write(18,115) kgp
  115 Format(5x,'DOMAIN-2:<C-C-T>, GP=',I2,2x,'outside Failure Surface')
c
c *** Check Domain-3 <tens-tens-comp> of Ultimate STRESS Surface
c
      Elseif (S1.GT.0.0.AND.S2.GT.0.0.AND.S3.LT.0.0) Then
*     Write(18,*)'DOMAIN-3<T-T-C>: Checking............'
      SURF=(Ft/Fcu)*(1+S3/Fcu)
      Do 125 i=1,2
      FUNC=SIG(i)/Fcu
       beta(i)=ABS(FUNC/SURF)
       If(beta(i).GT.0.8) KTAnu(i)=1
       If(beta(i).LE.0.8) beta(i)=0.8
       If(beta(i).GE.1.0) beta(i)=1.0
       If(FUNC.GE.SURF) KTFAIL(i)=1
       If(FUNC.GE.SURF)Write(18,126) kgp,i
  126 Format(5x,'DOMAIN-3:<T-T-C>,GP=',I2,2x,'outside Failure Surface
     *for i   :::::::::::::::=',I2)
  125 Continue
c
c *** Check Domain-4 <tens-tens-tens> of Ultimate STRESS Surface
c
      Elseif (S1.GT.0.0.AND.S2.GT.0.0.AND.S3.GT.0.0) Then
*     Write(18,*)'DOMAIN-4<T-T-T>: Checking............'
      SURF=Ft/Fcu
      Do 135 i=1,3
      FUNC=SIG(i)/Fcu
       beta(i)=ABS(FUNC/SURF)
       If(beta(i).GT.0.8) KTAnu(i)=1
       If(beta(i).LE.0.8) beta(i)=0.8
       If(beta(i).GE.1.0) beta(i)=1.0
       If(FUNC.GE.SURF) KTFAIL(i)=1
       If(FUNC.GE.SURF)Write(18,136) kgp,i
  136 Format(5x,'DOMAIN-4:<T-T-T>,GP=',I2,2x,'outside Failure Surface
     *for i :::::::::::::::=',I2)
  135 Continue
      Endif
c
      If (ICASE.EQ.1) Then
      Do 710 im=1,NCORD
      If (KTFAIL(im).EQ.1) Then
      If(EpslnU(im).LE.Em) Then
      KTcrush(im)=0
      Elseif(EpslnU(im).GT.Em) Then
      KTcrush(im)=1
      Endif
      If (KTcrush(im).EQ.1) Then
      Write(18,1008) im,incs,iel
 1008 Format(5X,'++++ Reached Epsln(m) in TENSION<KTcrush(i)=1> in Dir='
     *     ,I2,/,3x,'<Load Increment No.='I2,4x,'Element no.=',I3,'>')
      Endif
      Endif
  710 Continue
*
      Do 715 idir=1,NCORD
      If (KTFAIL(idir).EQ.0) Then
      If (KTanu(idir).EQ.0) Then
      KTstr(idir,1)=1
      Elseif (KTanu(idir).EQ.1) Then
      KTstr(idir,2)=1
      Endif
```

```
        Elseif (KTFAIL(idir).EQ.1) Then
        If (KTcrush(idir).EQ.0) Then
        KTstr(idir,3)=1
        Elseif (KTanu(idir).EQ.1) Then
        KTstr(idir,4)=1
        Endif
        Endif
  715 Continue
*
      Write(18,5005) ((KTstr(idir,id),id=1,4),idir=1,NCORD)
 5005 Format(5x,'++++ Stress Level INDEX <KTstr> :',/,(10x,4(I4)))
*     Write(18,5010) Kanu,(beta(i),i=1,NCORD)
 5010 Format(3x,'Kanu=',2x,I2,3x,'beta=',3(2x,F9.1))
c
        Elseif (ICASE.EQ.0) Then
        If (KCFAIL.EQ.1) Then
        Do 720 ip=1,NCORD
        Eps=ABS(EpslnU(ip))
        If (Eps.LE.Ecm) Then
        KCcrush=0
        Elseif (Eps.GT.Ecm) Then
        KCcrush=1
        Endif
        If (KCcrush.EQ.1)Write(18,1108) ip,incs,iel
 1108 Format(5X,'++++ Reached Epsln(f) in COMPRN<KCcrush=1> in dir',I2
      *    /,3x,'<Load Increment No.=',I2,4x,'Element no.=',I3,'>')
  720 Continue
      Endif
*
      If (KCFAIL.EQ.0) Then
      If (KCAnu.EQ.0) Then
      KCstr(1)=1
      Elseif (KCAnu.EQ.1) Then
      KCstr(2)=1
      Endif
      Elseif (KCFAIL.EQ.1) Then
      If (KCcrush.EQ.0) Then
      KCstr(3)=1
      Elseif (KCcrush.EQ.1) Then
      KCstr(4)=1
      Endif
      Endif
      Write(18,1010) (KCstr(id),id=1,4)
 1010 Format(5x,'++++ Stress Level INDEX <KCstr> :',5x,4(I4))
      Endif
      Return
      End
C ********************************************************************
c
      Subroutine ARGYRIS (SIG,Rc,EpslnU,EpslnC)
c
c*** This subroutine calculates MEAN HYDROSTATIC STRESS, THETA etc. for
c    a given Principal Stress Ratio /Eqiv. Uniax Strain Ratio.
c          (*) INPUT : SIG(i) & EpslnU(i)
c          (*) OUTPUT: Rc(i) & EpslnC(i)
c -----------------------------------------------------------------
      Implicit real *8(a-h,o-z)
      Common/ULTST/A0,A1,A2,B0,B1,B2/ULTSR/EA0,EA1,EA2,EB0,EB1,EB2
      Common/ULTSTR/Fcu,Ft,Fcb,Ecu,Ecm,Et,Em,Ecb
      Parameter (NCORD=3,NDF=3,FACTO=1.01,TOLER=1.0E-03,TOLERR=1.0E-06)
      Dimension SIG(3),DEVSIG(3),Rc(3),EpslnU(3),EpslnC(3)
c -----------------------------------------------------------------
*     Write(*,*)'*-----------: E N T E R E D   ARGYRIS :------------*'
      Do 120 j=1,NCORD
      DEVSIG(j)=0.0; Rc(j)=0.0; EpslnC(j)=0.0
  120 Continue
```

```
c
c *** Compute general characteristics of triaxial stress state
c
      S1=SIG(1);S2=SIG(2);S3=SIG(3)
      SIGA=(S1+S2+S3)/3
      Do 100 j=1,NCORD
 100  DEVSIG(j)=SIG(j)-SIGA
      AR=(S1-S2)**2+(S2-S3)**2+(S3-S1)**2
      TOUA=ABS(SQRT(AR/15.0))
      SIGAB=SIGA/Fcu; TOUAB=TOUA/Fcu
      XNUM=2.0*S1-S2-S3
      XDEN=ABS(SQRT(2.0*AR))
      S=COS(XNUM/XDEN)
      Theta=ACOSD(XNUM/XDEN)
      R1=(A0+A1*SIGAB+A2*SIGAB**2)
      R2=(B0+B1*SIGAB+B2*SIGAB**2)
      R21=R2**2-R1**2
      RDEN=4.0*R21*S**2+(R2-2.0*R1)**2
      AK=SQRT(4.0*R21*S**2+5.0*R1**2-4.0*R1*R2)
      RNUM=2.0*R2*R21*S+R2*(2.0*R1-R2)*AK
      R=RNUM/RDEN
      Write (14,208)
 208  Format(/,5x,'SIG(1)',3x,'SIG(2)',3x,'SIG(3)',4x,'SIGA',3x,'TOUA',
     *3x,'TOUAB',3x,'Theta',3x,'R',/,'---------------------------------
     *----------------------')
      Write (14,209) (SIG(i),i=1,NCORD),SIGA,TOUA,TOUAB,Theta,R
 209  Format(3x,8(F8.4))
*     Write(*,*) 'A R G Y R I S   S   S.............1'
c
c *** Solve for Rc(i)/EpslnC(i) on Ultimate or Failure Surface
c
      Do 220 j=1,3
      Rc(j)=0.0
 220  Rc(j)=SIG(j)
      ITER=0
 129  Do 221 ja=1,3
 221  Rc(ja)=Rc(ja)*FACTO
      ITER=ITER+1
c
c*** Compute Corresponding SURFACE VECTOR
c
      S1=Rc(1);S2=Rc(2);S3=Rc(3)
      SIGA=(S1+S2+S3)/3
      AR=(S1-S2)**2+(S2-S3)**2+(S3-S1)**2
      TOUA=ABS(SQRT(AR/15.0))
      SIGAB=SIGA/Fcu; TOUAB=TOUA/Fcu
      XNUM=2.0*S1-S2-S3
      XDEN=ABS(SQRT(2.0*AR))
      S=COS(XNUM/XDEN)
      Theta=ACOSD(XNUM/XDEN)
      R1=(A0+A1*SIGAB+A2*SIGAB**2)
      R2=(B0+B1*SIGAB+B2*SIGAB**2)
      R21=R2**2-R1**2
      RDEN=4.0*R21*S**2+(R2-2.0*R1)**2
      AK=SQRT(4.0*R21*S**2+5.0*R1**2-4.0*R1*R2)
      RNUM=2.0*R2*R21*S+R2*(2.0*R1-R2)*AK
      RR=RNUM/RDEN
      DIFF=(RR-TOUAB)
      If (DIFF-TOLER) 128,128,129
 128  Continue
      Write (14,209) (Rc(i),i=1,NCORD),SIGA,TOUA,TOUAB,Theta,RR
c
c *** Calculate ESTRAB,EGAMAB & ETheta for Euiv. Uniaxial Strain Surface
c
      EpsU1=EpslnU(1);EpsU2=EpslnU(2);EpsU3=EpslnU(3)
      ESTRA=(EpsU1+EpsU2+EpsU3)/3.
```

```
      E1=(EpsU1-EpsU2); E2=(EpsU2-EpsU3); E3=(EpsU3-EpsU1)
      EGAMA=ABS(SQRT((E1**2+E2**2+E3**2)/15.0))
      ESTRAB=ESTRA/Ecu; EGAMAB=EGAMA/Ecu
      EXNUM=2.0*EpsU1-EpsU2-EpsU3
      EXDEN=ABS(SQRT(2*(E1**2+E2**2+E3**2)))
      ETheta=ACOSD(EXNUM/EXDEN)
      ES=COS(XNUM/XDEN)
      ER1=(EA0+EA1*ESTRAB+EA2*ESTRAB**2)
      ER2=(EB0+EB1*ESTRAB+EB2*ESTRAB**2)
      ER21=ER2**2-ER1**2
      ERDEN=4.0*ER21*ES**2+(ER2-2.0*ER1)**2
      EAK=SQRT(4.0*ER21*ES**2+5.0*ER1**2-4.0*ER1*ER2)
      ERNUM=2.0*ER2*ER21*ES+ER2*(2.0*ER1-ER2)*EAK
      ER=ERNUM/ERDEN
      Write (14,308)
  308 Format(/,3x,'EpslnU(1)',3x,'EpslnU(2)',3x,'EpslnU(3)',4x,'SIGA',3x,
     *'TOUA',5x,'Theta',5x,'R',/,'------------------------------------
     *--------------------------------')
      Write (14,309) (EpslnU(i),i=1,NCORD),ESTRA,EGAMA,ETheta,ER
  309 Format(3x,7(E10.3))
c
c *** Solve for EpslnC(i) on Equiv. Uniaxial Strain Surface
c
      Do 320 j=1,3
      EpslnC(j)=0.0
  320 EpslnC(j)=EpslnU(j)
      ITER=0
  329 Do 222 ja=1,3
  222 EpslnC(ja)=EpslnC(ja)*FACTO
      ITER=ITER+1
c
c*** Compute Corresponding SURFACE VECTOR
c
      EpsU1=EpslnC(1);EpsU2=EpslnC(2);EpsU3=EpslnC(3)
      ESTRA=(EpsU1+EpsU2+EpsU3)/3.
      E1=(EpsU1-EpsU2); E2=(EpsU2-EpsU3); E3=(EpsU3-EpsU1)
      EGAMA=ABS(SQRT((E1**2+E2**2+E3**2)/15.0))
      ESTRAB=ESTRA/Ecu; EGAMAB=EGAMA/Ecu
      EXNUM=2.0*EpsU1-EpsU2-EpsU3
      EXDEN=ABS(SQRT(2*(E1**2+E2**2+E3**2)))
      ETheta=ACOSD(EXNUM/EXDEN)
      ES=COS(XNUM/XDEN)
      ER1=(EA0+EA1*ESTRAB+EA2*ESTRAB**2)
      ER2=(EB0+EB1*ESTRAB+EB2*ESTRAB**2)
      ER21=ER2**2-ER1**2
      ERDEN=4.0*ER21*ES**2+(ER2-2.0*ER1)**2
      EAK=SQRT(4.0*ER21*ES**2+5.0*ER1**2-4.0*ER1*ER2)
      ERNUM=2.0*ER2*ER21*ES+ER2*(2.0*ER1-ER2)*EAK
      ER=ERNUM/ERDEN
      DIFF=ER-EGAMAB
      If (DIFF-TOLERR) 328,328,329
  328 Continue
c
      Write (14,309) (EpslnC(i),i=1,NCORD),ESTRA,EGAMA,ETheta,ER
*     Write(*,*)'*-------------: E X I T   ARGYRIS :--------------*'
      Return
      End
c **************************************************************************
```

List of Publications

1. **Amiya K. Samanta and Somnath Ghosh.**(2008) : 'A 3D Computational Model of RC Beam Using Lower Order Elements with Enhanced Strain Approach in the Elastic Range.', *Computers, Materials & Continua*, Vol. 8, No. 1, pp 43-52.

2. **Amiya Kr. Samanta and Somnath Ghosh.**(2008) : 'A 3D Computational Model of RC Beam Using Lower Order Elements with Enhanced Strain Approach in the Elastic Range.', *Presented in the International Conference on Computational & Experimental Engineering and Sciences* (ICCES'08), Honolulu, Hawaii, March 17-22, 2008, pp 113-113.

3. **Amiya Kr. Samanta and Somnath Ghosh**.(2008) : 'On Performance of EAS based Lower Order Element in 3D Computational Modeling of RC Beam in the Elastic Range.' *Proceedings of International Conference on Advances in Concrete and Construction* (ICACC-2008), Hyderabad, India, Feb 7-9, 2008, pp 1084-1093.

4. **Amiya Kr. Samanta and Somnath Ghosh.**(2009) : 'A 3D Hypoelastic Computational Model of Reinforced Concrete Structure.', *Icfai Journal of Structural Engineering*, 2009, Vol. II, No. 1, pp 32-53.

5. **Amiya Kr. Samanta and Somnath Ghosh.**(2009) : 'Implementation of 3D Constitutive model on RC Frame using EAS based Lower Order Element in the Elastic Range', ICCES online Journal, vol. 45, pp. 1-7.

6. **Amiya Kr. Samanta and Somnath Ghosh.**(2009) : 'Bond-slip effects on the behaviour of RC beam under monotonic loading – An Integrated 3D Computational Model using EAS Approach.', *Computers, Materials & Continua*, Vol. 12, No. 1, pp 1-38.

8.10 Reprints of some published paper :

Copyright © 2009 Tech Science Press　　　　CMC, vol.12, no.1, pp.1-37, 2009

Bond-Slip Effects on the Behaviour of RC Beam under Monotonic Loading – An Integrated 3D Computational Model using EAS Approach

Amiya K. Samanta[1] and Somnath Ghosh[2]

Abstract:　This paper presents a formulation of hypo-elasticity based RC beam model with bond-slip. Details of the constitutive model and analysis method used are provided. A procedure has been described to carry out three-dimensional analysis considering both geometrical as well as material nonlinearity for a simply supported RC beam employing finite element technique, which uses 8-noded isoparametric hexahedral element HCiS18. Enhanced assumed strain (EAS) formulation has been utilized to predict load-deformation and internal stresses both in the elastic as well as nonlinear regime. It models the composite behaviour of concrete and reinforcements in rigid /perfect bond situation and their mutual interaction in bond-slip condition considering continuous interface elements at the material level. An attempt has been made to reduce the gap significantly between the results found experimentally and numerically using the proposed model and a computer code has been developed for the purpose. The results of the analysis are presented, discussed and compared with a few benchmark experimental results.

Keywords:　Lower order elements, Finite element approach, Three-dimensional, Enhanced assumed strain (EAS), Perfect bond, Bond-slip, RC beam.

1　Introduction

1.1　The problem

There are a variety of civil engineering structures with interface discontinuities, where the assumption of rigid bond between the mating surfaces is not valid. The analysis of such domain is accompanied by sliding, separation etc., which may occur along the interfaces between the adjacent blocks. In general, this phenomenon takes place at lower level of shear than the limiting shear value. As a result, an analysis procedure of such domain, which assumes rigid bond at the interface, would

---

[1] Civil Engineering Department, NIT, Durgapur, India. aksnitd@gmail.com
[2] Civil Engineering Department, Jadavpur University, Kolkata, India

ICCES, vol.9, no.3, pp.143-149

Implementation of 3D constitutive model on RC frame using EAS based lower order element in the elastic range

Amiya Kr. Samanta[1], Somnath Ghosh[2]

Summary

This paper deals with the implementation of hypo-elasticity based 3D constitutive model on Reinforced Concrete (RC) frame employing finite element technique, which uses lower order isometric solid elements HCiS18 with enhanced assumed strain (EAS) formulation to evaluate load-deformation, internal stresses produced in the elastic regime. Due attention has been paid to model concrete and the reinforcing steel with different physical and mechanical properties, which are combined together to represent its composite behaviour accurately in perfect bond situation. An in-house FORTRAN computer code has been developed for the purpose. The results of the finite element analysis are presented, compared and discussed.

keywords: Lower order elements, Three-dimensional, Enhanced assumed strain, Perfect bond, Finite element approach, RC frame.

Introduction

3D modeling may be a potential approach in order to achieve more realistic solution in general. In many applications, the standard quadratic 20-noded solid /hexahedral element has been used, which necessitates large computational time and cost. Since comparatively lower order elements have the advantages for 3D analysis due to easy mesh generation, data interpretation and lower computational time, improvement of such type of element performance has drawn attention of the researchers. Among the lower order elements, the linear isoparametric elements are the simplest constant strain elements. Wilson, Taylor presented a method of incompatible modes in this regard to improve the performance of the standard linear quadrilateral and hexahedral elements. Simo and Rifai [9] introduced a new concept of enhanced strain method, where the strain field is enhanced with the inclusion of additional variables. These additional variables, which are introduced in the calculations of the deformed state, have got no physical significance in numerical solution as it is eliminated at the element level. In case of 2D analysis Cesar et al. [5] also contributed to eliminate the volumetric locking. Not much attention was so far attributed to improve 3D analysis using enhanced strain lower order solid elements. A remarkable progress and accuracy has been obtained in this case by the element HCiS18 introduced by Sousa et al. [10, 11], even with the coarser meshes as it improves the original strain field in an additive way. In the present case, this element has been used to model the parent material i.e. concrete of the reinforced concrete structures.

[1] Dept. of CE., NIT, Durgapur -713,209, W.B. India. ksntd@gmail.com
[2] Dept. of Civil Engg., Jadavpur University, Kolkata - 70,032, W.B. India

*Proceedings of International Conference on
Advances in Concrete and Construction, ICACC-2008
7-9 February, 2008, Hyderabad, India pp 1084-1093*

Performance of EAS based Lower Order Element in 3D Computational Modeling of RC Beam in the Elastic Range

Amiya Kr. Samanta

*Asst. professor, Department of Civil Engineering, National Institute of
Technology, Durgapur-713,209, W.B., India.
aksnital@gmail.com*

Somnath Ghosh

*Professor, Department of Civil Engineering, Jadavpur University, Kolkata –
700032, W.B., India*

Abstract

*A 3D computational model of RC beam has been presented to carry out elastic
analysis employing finite element technique, which uses lower order elements.
The proposed procedure utilizes 8-noded isometric solid element HCiS18 with
enhanced assumed strain (EAS) formulation to avoid the associated difficulties
in regard to volumetric locking as well as transverse shear locking and to
improve the performance in predicting load-deformation, internal stresses
produced in the elastic regime. Due attention has been paid to model concrete
and the reinforcing steel with different physical and mechanical properties,
which are combined together to represent its composite behaviour accurately in
perfect bond situation. The aim of this paper is to explore the potentiality of
using lower order solid elements in the 3D finite element analysis for the study
of reinforced concrete beam in the elastic range*

INTRODUCTION

Availability of high speed computing facilities as well as significant
development in finite element techniques have given a new direction to
the researchers as well as professionals to go for solution of complicated
3D problems of varieties in general. Numerous works based on two-

A 3D Hypoelastic Computational Model of Reinforced Concrete Structure

Amiya Kr Samanta* and Somnath Ghosh**

This paper deals with the formulation and application of a hypoelasticity-based Reinforced Concrete (RC) beam model. Details of the constitutive model and analysis method used are discussed and a procedure has been described to carry out three-dimensional analysis of a simply supported RC beam employing finite element technique, which uses lower order elements, 8-noded isoparametric hexahedral elements HCiS18 to predict load deformation and internal stresses in the load history. Enhanced Assumed Strain (EAS) formulation has been utilized to avoid the difficulties associated with volumetric locking as well as transverse shear locking for the lower order solid elements. It models the behavior of concrete and reinforcements with different physical and mechanical properties, which are combined together to represent its composite behavior accurately in a perfect bond situation. As the literature indicates, there is a significant gap between the results found experimentally and numerically as far the load deformation pattern is involved. An attempt has been made to reduce the gap significantly using the proposed model. The results of the finite element analysis are presented, compared and discussed. Also an in-house FORTRAN computer code has been developed for the purpose. The objective of this paper is to explore the potentiality of using such hypoelasticity based lower order solid elements in the 3D finite element analysis for the study of RC beam.

Keywords: Lower order elements, Three-dimensional, Hypoelastic, Enhanced assumed strain, Perfect bond, Finite element approach, RC beam

Introduction

The Problem

Significant development in finite element techniques as well as availability of high speed computing facilities have given a new direction to investigators as well as professionals to go for solution of complicated 3D problems of varieties in general. Numerous studies based on two-Dimensional (2D) modeling of Reinforced Concrete (RC) structure (with or without reinforcements) based on various integral methods have been reported by different authors. Attempts were mainly made to improve

* Assistant Professor, Department of Civil Engineering, NIT, Durgapur 713209, India; and the corresponding author. E-mail: aksnitd2@gmail.com

** Professor, Department of Civil Engineering, Jadavpur University, Kolkata 700032, India. E-mail: som_ghosh@yahoo.com

Lightning Source UK Ltd.
Milton Keynes UK
UKHW012352210421
382415UK00001B/20